"The Best Read Naturalist"

Under the Sign of Nature: Explorations in Ecocriticism

Editors
Michael P. Branch, SueEllen Campbell, John Tallmadge

Series Consultants
Lawrence Buell, John Elder, Scott Slovic

Series Advisory Board
Michael P. Cohen, Richard Kerridge, Gretchen Legler,
Ian Marshall, Dan Peck, Jennifer Price, Kent Ryden,
Rebecca Solnit, Anne Whiston Spirn, Hertha D. Sweet Wong

"The Best Read Naturalist"

NATURE WRITINGS OF RALPH WALDO EMERSON

Edited by Michael P. Branch
and Clinton Mohs

University of Virginia Press

Charlottesville & London

University of Virginia Press

© 2017 by the Rector and Visitors of the University of Virginia

Printed in the United States of America on acid-free paper

First published 2017

9 8 7 6 5 4 3 2 1

Library of Congress Cataloging-in-Publication Data

Names: Emerson, Ralph Waldo, 1803–1882, author. | Branch,
   Michael P., editor. | Mohs, Clinton, editor.
Title: "The best read naturalist" : nature writings of Ralph Waldo
   Emerson / edited by Michael P. Branch and Clinton Mohs.
Description: Charlottesville : University of Virginia Press,
   [2017] | Series: Under the sign of nature : explorations in
   ecocriticism | Includes bibliographical references and index.
Identifiers: LCCN 2016022155| ISBN 9780813939513 (cloth :
   acid-free paper) | ISBN 9780813939520 (pbk. :
   acid-free paper) | ISBN 9780813939537 (e-book)
Subjects: LCSH: Emerson, Ralph, 1787–1863. | Nature.
Classification: LCC PS1603 .B73 2017 | DDC 814/.3—dc23
LC record available at https://lccn.loc.gov/2016022155

Cover art: *Autumn—On the Hudson River*, Jasper Francis
Cropsey, 1860. Oil on canvas, 151.8 × 274.9 cm. (Courtesy
of the National Gallery of Art, Washington; gift of the Avalon
Foundation, 1963.9.1)

❧ *Contents*

Acknowledgments

We would like to thank the University of Nevada, Reno, College of Liberal Arts Scholarly and Creative Activities Grant and the Department of English. Without their support this book would not have been possible. For his timely advice, we extend our gratitude to Justin Race, Director of the University of Nevada Press. Many thanks to Cheryll Glotfelty for helping to make what has been a very fruitful collaboration possible. Special thanks go to Jim Bishop, Heather Krebs, Meg Kuster, Jen Westerman, and Leslie Wolcott for their early work on the project. We also appreciate the assistance we have received from Stephanie Vyce, Director of Intellectual Property at Harvard University Press; Heather Cole, Assistant Curator of Modern Books and Manuscripts at the Houghton Library at Harvard University; and Jordan Stepp, Intellectual Property Manager at the University of Georgia Press. And we'd like to extend very special thanks to David Robinson, whose superbly thorough and insightful commentary on an earlier draft of this manuscript has improved the book a great deal.

At the University of Virginia Press, our thanks go to Editor in Chief Eric Brandt, Managing Editor Ellen Satrom, and Rights and Permissions Manager Angie Hogan. And deep thanks to Boyd Zenner, who recognized the value of this book from the beginning. Boyd's superb work as editor of the flourishing University of Virginia Press book series Under the Sign of Nature: Explorations in Ecocriticism, in which this book appears, has put all scholars of environmental literature in her debt. We'd also like to thank series coeditors SueEllen Campbell and John Tallmadge, who warmly welcomed this Emerson collection into the Under the Sign of Nature series.

Mike would first like to thank the gifted Emerson scholars whose work has, over the past thirty years, profoundly influenced his thinking about this inspiring and elusive literary figure. Among these many colleagues are Ronald Bosco, Larry Buell, Kenneth Cameron, Kris Fresonke, Alfred Furguson, Len Gougeon, Richard Grusin, Will Howarth, Michael Lopez, Wesley Mott, Joel Myerson, Barbara Packer, Sherman Paul, David Robinson, Bill Rossi, Robert Spiller, Bart St. Armand, Laura Walls, Stephen Whicher, and Eric Wilson. Special thanks to the editors who invited me to work out my ideas about Emerson and natural history as a part of their larger projects: John Elder (*American Nature Writers*); Barry Tharaud (*Emerson for the Twenty-First Century: Global Perspectives on an American Icon*); and Mark Long and Sean Meehan (*Approaches to Teaching the Works of Ralph Waldo Emerson*).

I am deeply fortunate to have my family behind me in all of my projects. Thanks go to my parents, Stu and Sharon Branch. When I completed my undergraduate honors thesis on Emerson back in 1985, I doubt they imagined I'd still be working on Emerson into my fifties. Thanks always to my wife, Eryn Branch, who is not only my best editor but also a person of immense patience, generosity, and intelligence. Finally, thanks to my two young daughters for tolerating Dad's many projects. Hannah Virginia is a born writer, while Caroline Emerson, who was born about the same time I began to work on this book, is as much an Emersonian individual as the world will ever see.

Clint would like to thank Bob Mielke and Randall Fuller, under whose guidance he has found an intellectual home in the nineteenth century and the work of Emerson. Many thanks to my family, especially my parents, Pete and Candy Mohs, and my in-laws, Dave and Jené Turnure, for their unflagging belief and support from the start. And, most importantly, I would like to thank my best friend and wife, Megan, whose questions about this project have helped to clarify my thoughts on numerous occasions. Her love, support, and input are vital in all that I do.

Introduction

Rediscovering the Roots of Emerson's Philosophy of Nature

The "Sage of Concord" and Natural Science

On May 27, 1832, Ralph Waldo Emerson stepped to the pulpit of Boston's Second Church to address the nearly one hundred families that had gathered to hear his sermon that day (Richardson 89). Although only twenty-nine years old at the time, Emerson was already a respected Harvard graduate and Unitarian minister at the Second Church—a prominent Boston institution that had been in existence for nearly two centuries and could count Increase and Cotton Mather among its many distinguished ministers. Reflecting upon the science of astronomy that day, Emerson offered his listeners the surprising declaration that "since the records of the divine dealings with men claim no other origin than the author of nature, we may expect that they are to be read by the light of nature" (10). Emerson called his flock to study scripture within the larger context of nature because he believed firmly that the God of the Bible was simply a reflection of the divinity encoded in the natural world.

Emerson's homiletic style, evident in "God that Made the World," was considered unorthodox not only for its attention to the lived experience of his congregation but also for its dependence on natural imagery to convey spiritual insights. Frederic Henry Hedge, Emerson's classmate and friend from Harvard Divinity School, believed that this style "brought [Emerson] into closer *rapport* with his hearers than was commonly achieved by the pulpit" (qtd. in Cabot 150). Even so, "God that Made the World" represents an important extension of his usual preaching style. Emerson's appeal to the study of nature does not simply offer a colloquial illumination of scripture but is foundational to his evolving concept of the centrality of natural science to spiritual aims. In fact, when he later revised this sermon for delivery in Waltham, Massachusetts, on November 30, 1834, he expanded it to include a direct appeal to the congregation's shared experience of a full solar eclipse, which had occurred that very day. He described the eclipse as an "indispensable" lesson that "reminds us impressively of the powers of the human intellect" and, more importantly, that "[i]t is only the knowledge of God that unites this bright outward Creation of brute matter to the brighter inward Creation of intelligent mind" (10). Drawing on the potentially revelatory power of the eclipse to reinforce his claim for the importance of studying nature outside the confines of church, Emerson explicitly identified natural history as an effective means of exploring the vital relationship between humanity and divinity.

In spite of Emerson's clear emphasis on the importance of both nature and natural science, critics have often characterized him as a cerebral philosopher whose work is abstracted from material nature. Emerson's reputation as the "Sage of Concord," a truth seeker whose contact with the material world appears tenuous, was established largely on the basis of his published essays. Soon after Emerson's death in 1882, much of his work was collected in Houghton Mifflin's *Emerson's Complete Works* (1883–93) and the centenary edition of *The Complete Works of Ralph Waldo Emerson* (1903–4). While these volumes made all of Emerson's published essays widely available, they excluded a trove of important materials, including most of his sermons, many of his lectures and addresses, and nearly all of the manuscripts associated with his ambitious "Natural History of the Intellect" project. Because so many of these materials, including the sermon "God that Made the World," remained unedited and unpublished until relatively recently, understandings of Emerson's life and work have remained focused on the iconic "Sage of Concord"—an American philosopher who is concerned more with the metaphysical and nationalist meanings of nature than with physical encounters with the material world, or with the emergent natural science that was providing exciting and powerful new understandings of that world.

This characterization of Emerson's oeuvre is problematic because it fails to fully account for a major component of his career as a public intellectual: his work as a lecturer. Emerson's public addresses and lectures encompass his entire career, from his earliest sermons delivered as a Unitarian minister, to his many public lyceum engagements, to the later lectures upon which he labored almost until death. They served not only as a vital testing ground for Emerson's emergent philosophy but also as the foundation for many of his published essays. After first working through new ideas in the lecture format, Emerson often condensed these talks, combining them with material from his journals to form a single essay—a compositional process that helps explain his often cryptic prose style. The goal of *"The Best Read Naturalist": Nature Writings of Ralph Waldo Emerson* is to revise this view of Emerson as the "Sage of Concord" by placing his important but lesser-known natural history writings into conversation with his widely read, canonical essays. In so doing, this book reveals the profound interest Emerson had in a tangible connection with the natural world, and it elucidates the vital influence that his study of natural science had on his mature philosophy. Although scholars have discussed Emerson's relation to science, they have often failed to consider the extent to which his lifelong fascination with natural science influenced the development of his major work.[1] Because Emerson is arguably America's preeminent literary philosopher of nature, a more complete comprehension of his conception of the natural world also illuminates the importance of nineteenth-century natural science to the evolution of American ideas about the environment.

In order to trace Emerson's career-spanning interest in natural science, *"The Best Read Naturalist"* gathers for the first time widely dispersed sermons, addresses, lectures, essays, and the full text of *Nature* (1836). By including relatively unfamiliar lectures such as "The Uses of Natural History," "The Naturalist," and "The Relation of Intellect to Natural Science" alongside a widely read text like *Nature*, this book offers readers the opportunity to encounter fascinating but little-known natural history pieces and to reconsider canonical essays in their light. Organized chronologically, the contents of this book plot the trajectory of Emerson's career-long attempt to understand what he enthusiastically referred to as "all the new and astonishing facts in the book of nature" (16). Out of his sustained effort to discern the complex and often ambiguous "book of nature," a new and more environmentally connected Emerson emerges. Rather than indulging in vaporous philosophical pronouncements, this "green" Emerson is deeply concerned with the physical world, and he is fascinated by the power of scientific description and classification to reveal a correspondence between the order of nature and that of the mind.

Emerson relied heavily on the insights and methodologies of the natural history tradition and his wide reading in contemporary natural science as direct sources for his articulation of a literary natural philosophy. To evince this "green" Emerson, the remainder of this introduction highlights natural science's influence on Emerson's resignation of the ministry, and clarifies its importance to two ideas central to his philosophy: his theory of language and his conception of the heroic Poet. Although these three brief discussions serve only as representative examples of the many important ways in which Emerson's passion for natural science influenced his thinking, reading these key components of Emerson's career in the context of his natural history sermons, lectures, and essays exemplifies how *"The Best Read Naturalist"* helps us to better understand the life and work of one of America's most influential philosophers of nature.

Resigning the Ministry to Seek the Spiritual Possibilities of Natural Science

Emerson officially resigned his pastorate at Boston's Second Church in October 1832. Before leaving, he delivered his sermon "The Lord's Supper," which outlined his objections to administering the Eucharist and announced his imminent departure. Finding no scriptural evidence that Jesus intended the Last Supper to be ritualized and celebrated in perpetuity, Emerson declared that his personal discomfort with the Eucharist "is alone a sufficient objection to the ordinance. It is my own objection. This mode of commemorating Christ is not suitable to me. That is reason enough why I should abandon it" (*CS* 4:192). This bold renunciation of a foundational sacrament has come to exemplify our understanding of Emerson as a proponent of a radical form of nonconformist, self-reliant individualism. While this move away from ritualized worship does coincide with his turn toward personal forms of spiritual celebration, it is also important to understand Emerson's renunciation of the ministry in the context of his growing fascination with natural science.

Because it was the only sermon published during his lifetime, and the only one included in the centenary edition of *The Complete Works of Ralph Waldo Emerson*,[2] "The Lord's Supper" has served as primary evidence supporting the view that his resignation is attributable to an embrace of radical individualism. Within this reading, Emerson's concluding sentiment that he would continue "pursuing and exercising [the ministry's] highest functions" outside the church has been understood as part and parcel of his much-celebrated individualist ethos (*CS* 4:194). However, if "The Lord's Supper" is contextualized within Emerson's genuine engagement with natural history studies, this declaration of spiritual independence may be seen as an important precursor to "the best read naturalist" figure to whom we are introduced near the conclusion of *Nature* (105). The two sermons contained in this collection, "The Day is Thine" and "God that Made the World," elucidate how Emerson's shift away from the constraints of institutionalized religion was at the same time a move toward an exploration of the spiritual possibilities of natural science.

Emerson's sermon "The Day is Thine" centers on a call to go forth into nature. Responding to a dispiriting sense of alienation from the natural world, Emerson urged his Boston congregation to "[g]o out into a garden and examine a seed; examine the same plant in the bud and in the fruit, and you must confess the whole process a miracle, a perpetual miracle. Take it at any period, make yourself as familiar with all the facts as you can, at each period, and in each explanation, there will be some step or appearance to be referred directly to the great Creator" (4–5). While theologians of his day argued endlessly about the true nature of divine miracle, Emerson assuredly claims that the miraculous is at our fingertips and beneath our boot soles. Admonishing his parishioners to seek spiritual truth, his advice that they do so by closely observing the growth of a plant is a direct call to the study of natural history. This pastoral exhortation is clearly informed by his earnest belief in the divine order of nature. For Emerson, all organisms adhere to a grand design that, although not yet fully understood, determines their role within the larger system of nature. Emerson's contemporaries would have agreed that, through careful study, the individual can begin to understand the unique attributes of a plant. But Emerson went further, asserting that, if sufficiently developed, that power of observation and description would ultimately lead to a deeper understanding of God's design. He believed that natural science could become a means of divine revelation.

Emerson extended this emphasis on the study of natural history to include the moral nature of the individual. He concluded "The Day is Thine" by imploring his flock "to look at the fruits of the earth and the seasons of the year. Let all that we see without, only turn our attention with stricter scrutiny on all that is within us" (7). Just as a plant's design reveals its harmonious fit within the order of nature, there exists within the individual a moral nature that self-examination can help to clarify. By discovering and adhering to this moral order, each individual faithfully lives out his or her role in the divine order of the world. This sentiment, an early indication of Emerson's belief in the "Doctrine of Correspondence" (which will be taken up in the following section of this introduction), works toward a synthesis of natural science and religion by correlating scientific examination with moral introspection. In this way, studying nature is for Emerson a religious exercise wherein the "proper performance of the vegetable functions" becomes a natural means by which the individual's moral compass may be recalibrated (7).

Three years after delivering "The Day is Thine," Emerson reiterated his radical belief that "the God of nature and the God of the Bible are affirmed to be the same" in the sermon "God that Made the World" (10). Building on his previous day's journal entry, wherein he acknowledged that the science of astronomy "irresistibly modifies all theology" (*JMN* 4:26), Emerson explained to his congregation that "an important result of the study of astronomy has been to correct and exalt our views of God, and humble our view of ourselves" (12). Just as he did in his claim for the spiritual value of studying plants in "The Day is Thine," Emerson addressed the important insights that astronomy can offer to religious thought. The cosmic scope of astronomy reorients our understanding of divinity, expanding our concept of the sacred from the church to the earth, and from there to the planetary heavens in which it moves. One important result of this expansion in awareness is that Emerson's concept of God, liberated from a doctrinal adherence to human experience, is instead conceived as "an Infinite Mind" whose wisdom and power is embedded within the natural order (15).

While "The Day is Thine" is animated by an unconventional enthusiasm for the spiritual potential of natural science, "God that Made the World" is thoroughly heterodox, for in it Emerson expressed directly his growing sense that institutionalized religion was fast losing its power to illuminate the human soul. In this later sermon Emerson stressed that the primary effect astronomy has on religion "is not contradiction but correction. It is not denial but purification" (15). Whereas most nineteenth-century Americans viewed astronomy as quite separate from theology—and many theologians regarded secular science as a serious threat to spiritual health—Emerson confidently insisted on the potential of astronomy not only to drastically alter our understanding of God but also to improve our access to the divine and to "correct" errors propagated by the church.

According to Emerson, then, astronomy's reorientation of humanity's view of nature and the divine would provide a regenerative influence on religion. This declaration represents a clear evolution and extension of Emerson's thoughts on the relation between science and religion expressed in "The Day is Thine." No longer representing scripture and nature as equal partners in illuminating moral and physical nature, Emerson strikes at the roots of institutionalized religion because, unlike nature, the church depends upon "Scriptures [which] were written by human hands" (16). Instead, he believed that "God intends by giving us access to this original writing of his hand [astronomy] to correct the human errors that have crept into [the Scriptures]" (16). Emerson makes explicit not only his growing disenchantment with ritualized worship but also his embrace of science as an improved means to understanding the soul.

The ambitious claims made for the imaginative and spiritual power of science in "The Day is Thine" and "God that Made the World" help us to understand why, just a few months after delivering "God that Made the World," Emerson presented his resignation sermon, "The Lord's Supper." Within this larger context, his renunciation of his pastorate may be seen to arise from his growing interest in natural science, as well as from his embrace of the esoteric brand of radical individualism we associate with Transcendentalism. His expressed desire to continue "pursuing and exercising [the ministry's] highest functions" outside the church is simultaneously an assertion of his desire to seek divine revelation through scientific inquiry. As Emerson noted in a journal entry just days after delivering "God that Made the World," he had begun to feel that "in order to be a good minister it was necessary to leave the ministry. The profession is antiquated. In an altered age, we worship in the dead forms of our forefathers" (*JMN* 4:27). This palpable disillusionment with institutionalized religion is not only a response to forms of worship he viewed as having been reduced to static, ritualized practice; it also represents an objection to the church's resistance to the methods, insights, and influence of science. The "altered age" to which he refers is the age of natural science: the vibrant, exhilarating period of scientific advancement and discovery during which Emerson lived. His resignation from Boston's Second Church is thus emblematic of his reimagining of spirituality in light of the insights provided by natural science—a shift made evident in his stated desire to "be a naturalist" the following year in his lecture "The Uses of Natural History" (1833) (22).

Emerson's Book of Nature and the Doctrine of Correspondence

Having turned toward science after his resignation of the ministry, Emerson sought a more comprehensive means of understanding and expressing his growing sense that there exists a deep and compelling correspondence between physical and moral nature. As he observed in "The American Scholar" address, delivered to Harvard's Phi Beta Kappa Society in August 1837, "nature is the opposite of the soul, answering to it part for part. One is seal, and one is print. Its beauty is the beauty of his own mind. Its laws are the laws of his own mind" (*CW* 1:55). In this canonical and widely read address, Emerson presents a clear expression of the "Doctrine of Correspondence." This core idea, derived from the work of the Swedish scientist, philosopher, and mystic Emanuel Swedenborg, holds that the spiritual nature of humanity corresponds to and is ordered in accordance with natural systems. Consequently, an improved understanding of nature would lead directly to a more sophisticated conception of the human soul. Although a well-documented pillar of Emersonian philosophy, the "Doctrine of Correspondence" remains an abstract means of understanding the natural world—one that is compelling but difficult to demonstrate. Invoking the ancient trope of *liber naturae,* the "book of nature," Emerson turned to language to approximate the vital correspondence between physical and moral nature. While he appealed to the potential power of language to bridge the inner and outer spheres of spirit and nature, Emerson's much-studied language theory is also complex and elusive to the point of frustrating the clarity that he proclaimed language capable of. An appeal to "The Uses of Natural History," the "Language" chapter of *Nature,* and "The Relation of Intellect to Natural Science" (all of which are included in this book) substantially clarifies Emerson's provocative thoughts on these topics by delineating how his theory of language is grounded in natural science's foundational model of taxonomy.

While it was evident in work as early as his 1829 sermon "The Day is Thine," Emerson's enthusiasm for a concept of correspondence blossomed into a fascination during and after his first trip to Europe in 1833, assuming a new importance in his thinking and writing. Emerson devoted much of his time abroad to reading natural history and attending scientific lectures, and the climax of the 1833 trip was his visit to the Jardin des Plantes and the Cabinet of Natural History in Paris. He described this experience in his very first natural history lecture, "The Uses of Natural History," which he delivered just days after his return to America: "moving along these pleasant walks, you come to the botanical cabinet, an inclosed garden plot, where grows a grammar of botany—where the plants rise, each in its class, its order, and its genus. . . . If you have read [the work of the botanist] Decandolle with engravings, or with a *hortus siccus* [herbarium], conceive how much more exciting and intelligible is this natural alphabet, this green and yellow and crimson dictionary, on which the sun shines, and the winds blow" (20). What Emerson finds most striking is a profound sense of interrelationship among the plants as he encountered them arranged within French botanist Antoine-Laurent de Jussieu's orderly system of "natural classification." This innovative system—designed to correct for the perceived arbitrariness of Linnaean taxonomy—organized and exhibited plant species so as to emphasize the familial relationships among them. It is this moving realization of interrelationship that inspired Emerson's subsequent epiphany in the nearby zoological cabinet: "[w]e feel that there is an occult relation between the very worm, the crawling scorpions, and man. I am moved by strange sympathies. I say I will listen to this invitation. I will be a naturalist" (22). The botanical and zoological cabinets are evocative to Emerson because they provide a powerful ordering device that unites an overwhelming diversity of "natural facts" into an organized system by which the relationship of all things—and, importantly, the relationship of the human observer to all things—becomes strikingly clear.

In considering Emerson's moving experience in the garden, it is important to examine not only what occurs but also the way it is perceived and described. He saw there a *"grammar* of botany," a "natural *alphabet,"* a "green and yellow and crimson *dictionary"* (emphases added). Faced with a powerful taxonomy of natural order, Emerson spontaneously conceived of it in terms of *language.* An alphabet, like a taxonomy, is an organizing system by which otherwise irreducible facts—in this analogy, alphabetic letters—can be organized into meaningful units of expression such as words and sentences. Even more important to this linguistic analogy is Emerson's enduring fascination with the metaphor of cipher and key. If nature is a complex, potentially indecipherable language, then Jussieu's botanical system provides a "grammar" and a "dictionary" that allow the observer to translate the intricacies of nature's language into something that is both "exciting" and "intelligible."

Just three years after this debut natural history lecture Emerson published *Nature* (1836), a major work in which he offered an influen-

tial discussion of language—a discussion that is nevertheless tantaliz-
ingly difficult to grasp. However, by reading the "Language" chapter of
Nature in light of the linguistic analogy that is crucial to "The Uses of
Natural History," we see more clearly that this chapter is deeply concerned with the need to comprehend "analogies" between the human
and natural worlds. "[M]an is an analogist, and studies relations in all
objects," noted Emerson in *Nature*. "[A] ray of relation passes from
every other being to him. And neither can man be understood without
these objects, nor these objects without man" (85). "Ray of relation," a
key term used in "The Uses of Natural History" and repeated twice in
"Language," suggests the importance of this analogic imperative. Without the translation of nature's language by man the analogist, "[w]hole
Floras, all Linnæus' and Buffon's volumes, are but dry catalogues of
facts" (85). Significantly, Emerson's use of "Floras" here provides a
direct contrast with Jussieu's living flora, "on which the sun shines, and
the winds blow." He further suggests that the work of even the most
accomplished taxonomists, Linnaeus and Buffon, remains lifeless if
not animated by a principle of correspondence that connects them,
through a "ray of relation," to the spirit of the human observer.

This emphasis on analogy helps us to see how Emerson's theory of
language was derived from the meditations on science and taxonomy
that were so important to his early natural history lectures. Referring
to nature as a "grand cipher" in "Language," he asserted that nature's
"profusion of forms" works to "furnish man with the dictionary and
grammar of his municipal speech" (87). Nature is further described as
a "text" that, seen rightly, "shall be to us an open book" (89). The tell-
ing similarity of these passages in "Language" to earlier, less familiar
natural history writings such as "The Uses of Natural History" marks
the extent to which the concept of language Emerson articulated in
Nature depended directly on the analogical model he developed to
express his epiphany in the Jardin des Plantes. That is, he believed that
natural science might provide the "keys" (87)—the grammars and dic-
tionaries—that would allow us to translate the language of nature into
the language of the spirit, thereby revealing the "ray of relation" that
in *Nature* he called the "radical correspondence between visible things
and human thoughts" (85). By "language," then, Emerson intended

something considerably more expansive than an alphabetic system of signs; he meant, instead, the analogical "language" of correspondence that intimately connects the human and natural worlds.

So central to Emerson's thinking was this analogical language that he returned to it fifteen years later to revise his thoughts on correspondence in light of his growing sense of the limitations of language. This return to a key concept was inspired by another revelatory moment abroad. During a trip to England in 1847–48, Emerson attended the lectures of several prominent British scientists, including Richard Owen and Michael Faraday, and newly energized by this fascinating work, he turned once again to his analogical language in "The Relation of Intellect to Natural Science"—a lecture given in London during the same trip. Although continuing to emphasize the linguistic qualities of the "book of nature" and the need for "a symbol or trope" to unlock the "analogy between all the parts of nature" (174, 169), Emerson also revealed his growing awareness of the difficulties associated with transcribing these "occult sympathies." Registering this growing skepticism, Emerson identified the "[b]arriers of society" as having caused the "inadequacy of the channels of communication" (175). The problem he identified is twofold: we are separated from each other by the individuality of our experience; and, because society has distanced language from its original source in nature, it has lost much of its power to connect people. Because epiphanic moments of intuiting "occult sympathies" arise from individual encounters with nature, the possibility of sharing insights garnered from this experiential knowledge is hindered by a system of language that is often incapable of bridging the rifts between people. Extending his earlier hope that returning language to its foundation in nature would provide the "keys" from which nature "shall be to us an open book," Emerson emphasized the growing urgency of this need to renaturalize language by explaining that "[e]ach man has facts I am looking for, and, though I talk with him, I cannot get at them, for want of the clew" (175).

A return to Emerson's articulation of the "Doctrine of Correspondence" in "The American Scholar" exemplifies how the natural history writings included in this book help to clarify both his developing theory of language and its connection to natural science. Because language functions as a metaphor for the workings of natural systems and also as the means by which those systems may be interpreted and represented, it provides primary evidence for Emerson's belief in the correspondence between physical and moral nature. By improving the system of language to more accurately express the system of nature, Emerson argued that humanity will consequently experience spiritual growth. Natural science is crucial because it elucidates the complexities of natural systems while also suggesting methods for revising language to more faithfully adhere to its sources in nature. Seen in the context of the natural history writings, the "American Scholar" Emerson calls for appears to have a less mystical or nationalist connection to nature than readers of the address might suppose; rather, he works to improve language. By "sit[ting] down before each refractory fact; one after another, [he] reduces all strange constitutions, all new powers, to their class and their law" (CW 1:54). Through his careful study of the material world, Emerson's exemplary scholar orders its apparent chaos and, in so doing, perceives the analogic "ray of relation" connecting the natural world to his own soul. From this figure of the scholar renaturalizing language emerges Emerson's heroic Poet, to whom we now turn our attention.

The Refined Perception of Emerson's Poetic Naturalist

In "The Poet," the opening piece of *Essays: Second Series* (1844), Emerson expressed his oft-quoted lament that "I look in vain for the poet whom I describe" (CW 3:21). The iconic "Poet" Emerson called for "re-attaches things to nature and the Whole" (CW 3:11), because he "sees and handles that which others dream of, traverses the whole scale of experience, and is representative of man, in virtue of being the largest power to receive and to impart" (CW 3:5). The Poet enacts Emerson's theory of language by seeking to understand and express the underlying order within the material world. He labors to read the "book of nature" and to represent his subsequent insights artistically. Emerson's much-discussed call for the Poet as a redeemer has generally been understood as reflecting his desire for a culture hero whose artistic production might offer an antidote to the ills of a venal, misguided society.

However, given the importance of Emerson's philosophy of language and its essential dependence on taxonomy, the Poet's relation to natural science must also be accounted for. Rather than merely producing poetry, Emerson's Poet derives his redeeming creative power as much from the sciences as from the humanities. Emerson described the Poet as "us[ing] forms according to the life, and not according to the form. This is true science. The poet alone knows astronomy, chemistry, vegetation, and animation, for he does not stop at these facts, but employs them as signs" (*CW* 3:13). For Emerson, the Poet fulfills the highest purpose of both science and poetry by using one to illuminate the other. Through this process of renaturalizing language, significantly identified here as a "science," Emerson charged his Poet with the office of "the Namer, or Language-maker" (*CW* 3:13). He recognized this ability to make each "word . . . stand for a thing" in the literary and scientific works of Johann Wolfgang von Goethe (*JMN* 5:133). Goethe's botanical studies persuaded him that the growth of a plant is a process of development according to an organic archetype, the *urpflanz*—a concept that had a formative and enduring influence on Emerson's own thoughts on natural history. Emerson would later celebrate Goethe by including him as the emblematic writer in his essay collection *Representative Men* (1850).

While it is evident that the Poet enjoys what Emerson termed in *Nature* "an original relation to the universe" (173), it is less clear what separates this iconic figure from the culture Emerson finds to be in disrepair. Lamenting that "few adult persons can see nature," Emerson makes it clear that the figure of the Poet is the noble exception (175). Because the Poet understands the interrelationship of seemingly disparate facts, he possesses the power to "integrate all the parts" of nature into a grand unity (175). It is through this process of unification that the Poet symbolizes the potential of humans to renew themselves by discovering in nature a new sense of connection to and sympathy with a deeper "order of things" (174). While *Nature* offers no clear indication as to the source of the Poet's "original relation to the universe," an appeal to the lesser-known 1834 lecture "The Naturalist" is helpful in showing how Emerson conceived of his Poet hero.

In *Nature*, the key attribute of the Poet is his perceptive acuity—an ability that Emerson tied directly to natural science in "The Naturalist." "[P]art of the intellectual discipline of Natural Science is that it sharpens the discrimination," remarked Emerson. "It teaches the difficult art of distinguishing between the similar and the same. The whole study of Nature is perpetual division and subdivision and again new distinctions. And all these distinctions are real" (64). By heightening one's attention to detail, the study of natural science necessarily sharpens the individual's observations of the world. Unlike the debasing influence of society, which separates language from nature, natural science provides a remedy by which "the student will see a day perhaps in a light in which he never regarded it[,] . . . as an astronomical phenomenon" (65). Rather than being limited to society's artificial classifications of both world and self, natural history presents an opportunity to reconceptualize nature and the self through relation—a deeper understanding that is founded upon the recognition of the "real" distinctions that exist within nature.

While celebrating the profound benefits of natural science to how we imagine both the material world and our place within it, Emerson was quick to temper this enthusiasm in order to safeguard against a blind adherence to science. "Natural History is making with knife and scales and alembic the Theory conform to the fact," he wrote. "It is for want of this marriage that both remain unfruitful" (67). Although scientific inquiry fosters the meticulous attention to detail necessary to understand how the components of a natural system are ordered, it is the accompanying skill to make that information meaningful to the individual's experience that Emerson finds wanting. This separation of scientific theory from natural fact is most detrimental when it reduces the naturalist to being a mere "pedant," one who "los[es] sight of the end of his inquiries in the perfection of his manipulations" (67). Of greatest concern to Emerson was the propagation of a form of scientific practice that is divorced from humanity, and, therefore, detached from the spiritual imperatives he believed any quest for insight and understanding should ultimately serve.

As a response to this concern that, despite its great potential, natural science might become dehumanized and thus serve superficial ends, Emerson interjected a poetic principle into his vision for natural history. Working from this desire to link the specific with the universal, Emerson found fault with the poet who "loses himself in imaginations and for want of accuracy is a mere fabulist" (67). Whereas the natural historian can suffer from becoming too immersed in the material world, the poet who is too absorbed in producing aesthetically pleasing effects distances himself from that world. As Emerson would later observe in "The Poet," "it is not metres, but a metre-making argument, that makes a poem,—a thought so passionate and alive, that, like the spirit of a plant or an animal, it has an architecture of its own, and adorns nature with a new thing" (*CW* 3:6). Because Emerson "fully believe[d] in both, in the poetry and in the dissection" (67), he described his ideal naturalist as "a poet in his severest analysis" (69). A clear precursor to the heroic figure called for in "The Poet," this ideal poetic naturalist achieves a synthesis of scientific and artistic production by blending sophisticated perception with nuanced expression. Emerson would clarify the prophetic implications of this figure in his prescient 1836 lecture "Humanity of Science," in which he locates the poetic naturalist's emancipatory power in his ability to reveal the natural in poetry and the sacred in science. In so doing, wrote Emerson, this idealized poetic naturalist "leads us back to Truth" (64).

This figure of the prophetic naturalist reappears at the conclusion of *Nature*. While it is certainly not the case that *Nature* is driven by a protagonist in the sense that a novel might be, the text is organized around an idealized persona who embodies certain of Emerson's core ideas. Though he travels under various names, this figure has a continuous presence in *Nature*, beginning as "the poet" in the book's introduction and culminating in its final chapter, "Prospects," as two closely related and vitally important incarnations: he is both "the best read naturalist" who studies and interprets "that wonderful congruity which subsists between man and the world" and the "Orphic poet" whose prophecy ends the book, offering an apotheosis if not quite a conclusion (75, 105, 106, 108). Insights provided by "The Naturalist" help us to recognize the prophetic figure of "Prospects" as another embodiment of the poetic naturalist, an insight that is useful in several ways. First, it is helpful to imagine the chapters of *Nature* as organized around a central figure whose prosecution of the book's central inquiry—"to what end is nature?" (74)—is inspired by a desire to discern some larger pattern or order in the chaos of a refractory world. "The Naturalist" and other early natural history writings also demonstrate why Emerson felt that, in order to comprehend what the opening sentence of "Prospects" calls "the laws of the world and the frame of things," this hero would have to be both scientist and poet—an insight that helps explain the chapter's bifurcation of the redemptive hero into "the best read naturalist" and the "Orphic poet."

While "The Naturalist" identifies many of the qualities that define the poetic naturalist—and does so in ways that clarify the elusive heroic figure of *Nature*—how this poetic naturalist's skills should be developed remains vague. Not until "Country Life" (1858), a virtually unknown lecture presented more than two decades after the delivery of "The Naturalist" and the publication of *Nature,* would Emerson return to these ideas and suggest a practical, direct means of acquiring the acute perception of the poetic naturalist. It is through the focused practice of walking, he tells his Boston audience, that the sensibility of his iconic, heroic naturalist should be honed. Emerson's advocacy of walking is once again linked to his concerns about the inadequacy of language to fully express the human experience of nature. He remarked, "If you wish to know the shortcomings of poetry and language, try to reproduce the October pictures to a city company,— and see what you make of it" (199). Just as he had a decade earlier in "The Relation of Intellect to Natural Science" (1848), Emerson calls attention to the limited power of language to accurately convey an ecstatic, visceral experience of the natural landscape.

To counteract the mediation and distortion inherent in language, Emerson proposed walking as a method of becoming directly acquainted with the natural world. Although nature is capable of "develop[ing] in the cultivator the talent it requires" (186), he conceded that "[f]ew men know how to take a walk. The qualifications of a professor are endurance, plain clothes, old shoes, an eye for nature, good humor, vast curiosity, good speech, good silence, and nothing too much" (190). This walking "professor" closely resembles the poetic naturalist in his balancing of "an eye for nature" and "good speech"—in his fusion of refined perception and precise articulation. Emerson adds to this formulation the idea of "endurance," the notion that walking is "a fine art, requiring rare gifts and much experience" (201). Emerson's characterization of this enlightened professor of sauntering is suggestive of his friend Henry David Thoreau, whose "vast curiosity" and stamina as a walker have been justly celebrated. Indeed, when Emerson writes in "Country Life" that "I have sometimes thought it would be well to publish an *Art of Walking*," it is difficult not to be reminded of Thoreau's brilliant deathbed essay "Walking" (1862), which is arguably the most profound defense of walking ever written (201). While Thoreau's habitual experiential immersion in nature has often been used to contrast him with Emerson, who is frequently characterized as disconnected from the materiality of the natural world, "Country Life" makes it plain that Emerson valued walking as a practice of direct, unmediated engagement with the land.

In "Country Life" Emerson endorsed the practice of walking year-round as a practical means of developing the mode of perception he celebrated in his poetic naturalist. It is these regular, peripatetic "conversation[s] with nature" that "foster the peculiar genius of each man," he claimed (204). It is revealing that even as Emerson celebrated the "peculiar genius of each man," he explicitly identified his preferred walking companions as "an artist, or one who has an eye for beauty," and "a naturalist" who can teach "the elements of geology, of botany, of ornithology, and astronomy, by word of mouth" (201–2). Just as he did in the "Prospects" chapter of *Nature*, Emerson imagined his ideal teacher-companion as two figures, the poet and the scientist. In choosing them for his hiking partners, Emerson once again attests to the need to integrate these two ways of knowing—for their mutual benefit and, ultimately, for the potential they have to illuminate the soul. However, we learn from the insights of his natural history writings that these two figures actually make up a composite hero: they are the two halves of the long-sought redeemer whose ascension might at last reveal the grand unity of humanity and nature for which Emerson longed throughout his career.

The "Green" Emerson as "the Best Read Naturalist"

It is here, on an excursion into nature accompanied by the figures of the artist and the naturalist, that the environmental Emerson emerges most clearly. This "green" Emerson, who calls us to learn from nature by hiking in all seasons, is very different from the man readers of Emerson's canonical essays generally envision. Not at all the stuffy, cerebral "Sage of Concord," Emerson appears here much more like what is generally imagined of his protégé, Henry David Thoreau: a roving philosopher improving his relation to nature by familiarizing himself with the place he inhabits through continual walks. Just as Thoreau sought to know the natural world through immersive experiences—whether it be his adventures afloat with his brother John in *A Week on the Concord and Merrimack Rivers* (1849) or his famous life experiment recorded in *Walden* (1854)—Emerson entreated his listeners and readers to go out into the fields and forests. From the sermon "The Day is Thine" to the "Country Life" lecture almost thirty years later, Emerson espoused the importance of experiencing and observing the natural environment firsthand in order to discover that "ray of relation" connecting the individual to nature. Through these consistent appeals to the spiritual value of natural science, this "green" Emerson embraced tangible encounters with the physical world as a basis for his mature philosophy of nature.

Although this environmental Emerson celebrated the spiritual power of natural science, we must keep in mind that, despite his declaration in "The Uses of Natural History" that "I will be a naturalist," Emerson did not in fact become a scientist. In his own career he would remain a critic of both culture and science, espousing a provocative philosophy of nature from the secular pulpit of the lyceum. As a public intellectual, Emerson was able "not only to have the aids of Science but [also] to recur to Nature to guard us from the evils of Science" (64). This career embodies the unnamed third position in "Country Life," a place between his ideal companions the artist and naturalist, one that allowed him to combine the methods and insights of these two modes of engagement with nature. In this sense Emerson enacted his own version of "the best read naturalist." Widely read both in the natural sciences and in the humanities, he crossed disciplines and modes of perception in order to more fully express the spiritual implications of what he believed to be the essential correspondence between humanity and nature.

This understanding of Ralph Waldo Emerson as "the best read naturalist" offers a new way of thinking about his life's work and its connection to nature and to natural history. Rather than locating the zenith of Emerson's intellectual and literary trajectory in the *Essays* series of the 1840s, this environmental understanding of his career demonstrates a growing sophistication in his lifelong attempt to create "a kind of 'Natural History of the Intellect'" (*L* 4:51)—a phrase that Emerson first used in an 1848 letter to his wife, Lidian, and that would remain central to his work until his final lecture series of the same title in 1870. The importance of this career-spanning project is demonstrated throughout this collection, where it is visible in his return to significant moments, such as the epiphany he experienced in the Jardin des Plantes, and in his ongoing development of ideas related to analogic language and the figure of the Poet—concepts central to this "Natural History of the Intellect" project.

With the help of the little-known natural history sermons and lectures featured in this book, many of the most complex elements of Emerson's literary philosophy of nature are clarified, and some of the most perplexing passages in his canonical essays become more legible. We see plainly that Emerson revisited natural history throughout his career because he believed that its insights would lead to a richer understanding of the human spirit. Natural science was not only central to his transition into work as a public intellectual but also a key influence on his writing and lecturing, even into the final stages of his career. By tracing the long arc of this cohesive "Natural History of the Intellect" project throughout his less familiar natural history writings and lectures, *"The Best Read Naturalist": Nature Writings of Ralph Waldo Emerson* reveals an environmental component of Emerson's work not readily apparent to readers of canonical essays like "Self-Reliance" and "Experience." The "green" Emerson that appears in the pages of this book is a writer and thinker whose dynamic, lifelong engagement with nature and natural science reveals an ecstatic drive toward unrealized possibilities, a desire for a unity of nature and spirit embodied by the merging of "the best read naturalist" and "Orphic poet" figures whose inspiring prophecy concludes *Nature*.

Notes

Parts of this introduction are derived from Michael P. Branch's "Ralph Waldo Emerson" (1996) and "Paths to *Nature*" (2010).

  1. For a list of sources helpful to any consideration of Emerson's relation to natural science, see the "Further Reading" section of this book.

  2. The only other address from the pulpit that was available during Emerson's lifetime was "Right Hand of Fellowship," which he delivered at the ordination of Hersey Bradford Goodwin in February 1830 (Cabot 151). The address was published soon after the ceremony in a pamphlet that also contained James Kendall's sermon, as well as two other addresses delivered on that occasion. "Right Hand of Fellowship" would later be included in Hearst's International Library's *The Works of Ralph Waldo Emerson* (1914).

Works Cited

Branch, Michael P. "Paths to *Nature:* Emerson's Early Natural History Lectures." *Emerson for the Twenty-First Century: Global Perspectives on an American Icon.* Ed. Barry Tharaud. Newark: U of Delaware P, 2010. 219–42.

———. "Ralph Waldo Emerson." *American Nature Writers.* Ed. John Elder. Vol. 1. New York: Scribner's, 1996. 287–307.

Cabot, James Elliot. *A Memoir of Ralph Waldo Emerson.* 2 vols. Cambridge: Riverside, 1887–88.

Emerson, Ralph Waldo. *The Collected Works of Ralph Waldo Emerson.* Ed. Alfred R. Ferguson, et al. 10 vols. Cambridge: Harvard UP, 1971–2013.

———. *The Complete Works of Ralph Waldo Emerson.* Ed. Edward Waldo Emerson. 12 vols. Boston: Houghton Mifflin, 1903–4.

———. *Emerson's Complete Works.* Ed. James Elliot Cabot. 12 vols. Boston: Houghton Mifflin, 1883–93.

———. *The Journals and Miscellaneous Notebooks of Ralph Waldo Emerson.* Ed. Alfred R. Ferguson, et al. 16 vols. Cambridge: Belknap P, 1960–82.

———. *The Letters of Ralph Waldo Emerson.* Ed. Ralph L. Rusk and Eleanor M. Tilton. 10 vols. New York: Columbia UP, 1939–95.

———. "The Lord's Supper." *The Complete Sermons of Ralph Waldo Emerson.* Ed. Wesley T. Mott. Vol. 4. Columbia: U of Missouri P, 1989. 185–94.

———. "Right Hand of Fellowship." *A Sermon Delivered at the Ordination of Hersey Bradford Goodwin.* Concord, MA: Congregational Church and Society, 1830. 29–31. *Archive.org Digital Archive.*

———. *The Works of Ralph Waldo Emerson.* Ed. Chester Noyes Greenough. 5 vols. New York: Hearst's International Library Co., 1914.

Richardson, Robert D., Jr. *Emerson: The Mind on Fire.* Berkeley: U of California P, 1995.

A Note on the Text

"The Day is Thine" appears in volume 1 of *The Complete Sermons of Ralph Waldo Emerson,* edited by Albert J. von Frank and published in 1989 by the University of Missouri Press, pages 296–300. Because Emerson's sermons did not have formal titles, they are generally referenced by number and by the opening words of the scriptural passage with which they begin. "The Day is Thine" is Sermon 39 in the above volume. "God that Made the World" appears in volume 4 of *The Complete Sermons of Ralph Waldo Emerson,* edited by Wesley T. Mott and published in 1992 by the University of Missouri Press, pages 153–59. "God that Made the World" is Sermon 157 in the above volume. We gratefully acknowledge the Ralph Waldo Emerson Memorial Association and the Houghton Library of Harvard University for permission to reprint these sermons.

"The Uses of Natural History," "On the Relation of Man to the Globe," and "The Naturalist" appear in volume 1 of *The Early Lectures of Ralph Waldo Emerson,* edited by Stephen E. Whicher and Robert E. Spiller and published in 1959 by Harvard University Press, pages 5–26, 27–49, 69–83, respectively. "Humanity of Science" appears in volume 2 of *The Early Lectures of Ralph Waldo Emerson,* edited by Stephen E. Whicher, Robert E. Spiller, and Wallace E. Williams and published in 1964 by Harvard University Press, pages 22–40. In their edition of the early lectures, Whicher, Spiller, and Williams occasionally employ brackets to identify provisional readings of words not clear in the manuscript source. We have silently adopted those readings except in two instances: we have silently corrected "ceature" to read "creature" (44) and have omitted a phrase, "the stomata in [*blank*]" (*EL* 2:26), which Emerson had left unfinished in the manuscript. We gratefully acknowledge Harvard University Press for permission to reprint these lectures.

Nature and "The Method of Nature" appear in volume 1 of *The Collected Works of Ralph Waldo Emerson,* edited by Alfred R. Ferguson and published in 1971 by Harvard University Press, pages 3–45, 117–37, respectively. "Nature" appears in volume 3 of *The Collected Works of Ralph Waldo Emerson,* edited by Alfred R. Ferguson and Jean Ferguson Carr and published in 1983 by Harvard University Press, pages 97–114. "Thoreau" appears in volume 10 of *The Collected Works of Ralph Waldo Emerson,* edited by Ronald A. Bosco and Joel Myerson and published in 2013 by Harvard University Press, pages 413–31. We gratefully acknowledge Harvard University Press for permission to reprint these texts.

"The Relation of Intellect to Natural Science" appears in volume 1 of *The Later Lectures of Ralph Waldo Emerson,* edited by Ronald A. Bosco and Joel Myerson and published in 2001 by the University of Georgia Press, pages 152–72. "Country Life" and "The Natural Method of Mental Philosophy" appear in volume 2 of *The Later Lectures of Ralph Waldo Emerson,* edited by Ronald A. Bosco and Joel Myerson and published in 2001 by the University of Georgia Press, pages 49–67, 84–98, respectively. We gratefully acknowledge the Ralph Waldo Emerson Memorial Association and the Houghton Library of Harvard University for permission to reprint these lectures.

"The Best Read Naturalist"

The Day is Thine

(1829)

Emerson delivered "The Day is Thine" on June 14, 1829, to his congregation at Boston's Second Church. By that time he had been ordained the Second Church's junior pastor, a position he accepted after nearly two years of itinerant preaching throughout the Northeast. This time of so-called supply preaching allowed Emerson to continue his independent studies and hone his oratorical skills at the pulpit without the obligations of a full-time ministry. Emerson preached as part of the Unitarian movement, a gradually developing resistance to Calvinism that began among established Puritan churches in the mid-eighteenth century. Reacting against Calvinism's fatalistic conception of God and belief in the inherent depravity of humanity, Unitarianism understood life to be a proving ground for the development of one's moral charac-ter and held human nature to be inherently divine. In "The Day is Thine," Emerson looks to nature as a model to elucidate the Unitar-ian doctrine of self-culture, a belief in personal progression through moral development. For Emerson, the rhythmic cycles of seasons and plant growth exemplify how the system of nature adheres to and expresses a divine order. The perpetuation of these cycles depends on the fidelity of each plant to its role in the larger processes of nature. By drawing attention to the faithfulness of flora, Emerson calls his congregation to follow nature's example and more closely adhere to their own divine nature. This insight into the analogous correlation of nature to the soul would remain central to Emerson throughout his career. By seeing nature as a moral model and emphasizing its systemic order, "The Day is Thine" establishes a number of key ideas that Emerson would return to throughout his natural history lectures and essays. As is characteristic of his sermons, there is a general lack of reference to the scriptural reading. Rather, he uses the biblical text as a starting point for a philosophical discussion of personal religious experiences, which he connects to the natural world, which he considered a "parallel scripture."

❦

The day is thine, the night also is thine: thou hast prepared the light, and the sun. Thou hast set all the borders of the earth, thou hast made summer.
—Psalms 74:16–17

In this grateful season, the most careless eye is caught by the beauty of the external world. The most devoted of the sons of gain cannot help feeling that there is pleasure in the blowing of the southwest wind; that the green tree with its redundant foliage and its fragrant blossoms shows fairer than it did a few weeks since when its arms were naked and its trunk was sapless. The inhabitants of cities pay a high tax for their social advantages, their increased civilization, in their exclusion from the sight of the unlimited glory of the earth. Imprisoned in streets of brick and stone, in tainted air and hot and dusty corners they only get glimpses of the glorious sun, of the ever changing glory of the clouds, of the firmament, and of the face of the green pastoral earth which the great Father of all is now adorning with matchless beauty as one wide garden. Still something of the mighty process of vegetation forces itself on every human eye. The grass springs up between the pavements at our feet and the poplar and the elm send out as vigorous and as graceful branches to shade and to fan the town as in their native forest.

Those who yield themselves to these pleasant influences behold in the activity of vegetation a new expression from moment to moment of the Divine power and goodness. They know that this excellent order did not come of itself, that this organized creation of every new year indicates the presence of God.

We are confident children, confident in God's goodness. Though we all of us know that the year's subsistence to us depends on the fidelity with which rain and sun shall act on the seed, we never doubt the permanence of the Order. We do not refer our own subsistence, especially in cities, to the rain and the sun and the soil. We do not refer the loaf in our basket, or the meats that smoke on our board to the last harvest. And when we do, we fail often to derive from the changes of nature that lesson which to a pious, to a Christian, mind, they ought to convey.

My brethren, all nature is a book on which one lesson is written, and blessed are the eyes that can read it. On the glorious sky it is writ in characters of fire; on earth it is writ in the majesty of the green ocean; it is writ on the volcanoes of the south, and the icebergs of the polar sea; on the storm, in winter; in summer on every trembling leaf; on man in the motion of the limbs, and the changing expression of the face, in all his dealings, in all his language it is seen, and may be read and pondered and practised in all. This lesson is the omnipresence of God—the presence of a love that is tender and boundless. Yet man shuts his eyes to this sovereign goodness, thinks little of the evidence that comes from nature, and looks upon the great system of the world only in parcels as its order happens to affect his petty interest. In the seasons he thinks only whether a rain or sunshine will suit his convenience. In the regions of the world he thinks only of his farm or his town. Let us lift up our eyes to a more generous and thankful view of the earth and the Seasons.

Do they not come from Heaven and go like Angels round the globe scattering hope and pleasant toil and recompense and rest? Each righting the seeming disorders, supplying the defects which the former left; converting its refuse into commodity and drawing out of the ancient earth new treasures to swell the capital of human comfort. Each fulfils the errand on which it was sent. The faintness and despondence of a spring that never opened into summer; the languor of a constant summer; the satiety of an unceasing harvest; the torpor or the terror of a fourfold winter are not only prevented by the ordination of Providence, but they are not feared; and emotions of an opposite character are called forth as we hail the annual visits of these friendly changes at once too familiar to surprise and too distinct and distant to weary us.

It is in these as they come and go, that we may recognize the steps of our heavenly Father. We may accustom our minds to discern his power and benevolence in the profusion and the beauty of his common gifts, as the wheat and the vine. Nor do these seem sufficiently appreciated. We look at the works of human art—a pyramid, a stately church, and do not conceal our pleasure and surprise at the skill and force of men to lift such masses and to create such magnificent forms, which skill after all does but remove, combine, and shape the works of God. For the granite, and the marble, and the hands that hewed them from the quarry, are his work. But after they are builded, and the scaffolding is thrown down, and they stand in strength and beauty, there is more exquisite art goes to the formation of a strawberry than is in the costliest palace that human pride has ever reared. In the constitution of that small fruit is an art that eagle eyed science cannot explore, but sits down baffled. It cannot detect how the odour is formed and lodged in these minute vessels, or where the delicate life of the fruit resides.

Our patient science explores, as it can, every process, opens its microscopes upon every fibre, and hunts every globule of sap that ascends in the stem, but it never has detected the secret it seeks. It cannot restore the vegetable it has dissected and analyzed. Where should we go for an ear of corn if the earth refused her increase? With all our botany how should we transform a seed into an ear, or make from the grain of one stalk the green promise and the full harvest that covers acres with its sheaves. The frequency of occurrence makes it expected that a little kernel, properly sowed, will become at harvest time a great number of kernels. Because we have observed the same result on many trials, this multiplication is expected. But explain to me, man of learning! any part of this productiveness. There is no tale of metamorphosis in poetry, no fabulous transformation that children read in the Arabian Tales more unaccountable, none so benevolent, as this constant natural process which is going on at this moment in every garden, in every foot of vacant land in three zones of the globe.

Go out into a garden and examine a seed; examine the same plant in the bud and in the fruit, and you must confess the whole process a miracle, a perpetual miracle. Take it at any period, make yourself as familiar with all the facts as you can, at each period, and in each explanation, there will be some step or appearance to be referred directly to the great Creator; something not the effect of the sower's deposit, nor of the waterer's hope. It is not the loam, nor the gravel, it is not the furrow of the ploughshare nor the glare of the sun that calls greenness from the dust, it is the present power of Him who said 'Seedtime and harvest shall not fail.' Needs there, my brethren, any other book than this returning summer that reminds us of the first creation to suggest the presence of God? Shall we indulge our querulous temper in this earth where nature is fragrant with healthful odours and glowing with every pleasant colour? Man marks with emphatic pleasure or complaint the pleasant and the unpleasant days, as if he forgot the uses of the storm, the masses of vapour it collects and scatters over thirsty soils and the plants that were hardened or moistened by the rough weather, forgot the ships that were borne homeward by the breeze that chills him, or in short, as if he forgot that our Father is in Heaven, and the winds and the seas obey him.

We have been looking at nature as an exhibition of God's benevolence. It will be felt the more to be so when it is considered that *the same results might have been brought about without this beauty.* The earth contains abundant materials for the nourishment of the human stomach, but they do not exist there in a state proper for our use. Now the tree, the vegetable, may be properly considered as a machine by which the nutritious matter is separated from other elements, is taken up out of chalk, and clay, and manures, and prepared as by a culinary process into grateful forms and delicious flavours for the pleasure of our taste and for our sustenance. The little seed of the apple does not contain the large tree that shall spring from it; it is merely an assimilating engine which has the power to take from the ground whatever particles of water or manure it needs, and turn them to its own substance and give them its own arrangement.

For the nourishment of animal life this process goes on, and to such incomputable activity and extent, not in one spot, not in one land, but on the whole surface of the globe. Each soil is finishing its own, and each a different fruit. Not only on the hard soil of New England, the oak, the potato and the corn are swelling their fruit, but on the shores of the Red Sea the coffee tree is ripening its berries; on the hills of

France and Spain the grape is gathering sweetness. The West Indies are covered with the green canes and the East with spices—and the mulberries for the silk worm. The cotton plant is bursting its pod in the warm plantations of the south, and the orange and the fig bloom in the mediterranean islands.

But all this food might have been prepared as well without this glorious show. To what end this unmeasured magnificence? It is for the soul of man. For his eye the harvest waves, for him the landscape wears this glorious show. For to what end else can it be! Can the wheat admire its own tasselled top? or the oak in autumn its crimson foliage, or the rose and the lily their embroidery? If there were no mind in the Universe, to what purpose this profusion of design? It is adapted to give pleasure to us. I cannot behold the cheering beauty of a country landscape at this season without believing that it was intended that I should derive from it this pleasure. It is for the same reason as the rainbow is beautiful and the sun is bright.

But there is more in nature than beauty; there is more to be seen than the outward eye perceives; there is more to be heard than the pleasant rustle of the corn. There is the language of its everlasting analogies by which it seems to be the prophet and the monitor of the race of man. The Scripture is always appealing to the tree and the flower and the grass as the emblems of our mortal estate. It was the history of man in the beginning, and it is the history of man now. Man is like the flower of the field. In the morning he is like grass that groweth up; in the Evening he is cut down and withereth. There is nothing in external nature but is an emblem, a hieroglyphic of some thing in us. Youth is the Spring, and manhood the Summer, and age the Autumn, and Death the Winter of Man. My brethren, do you say these things are old and trite? that is their very value and warning; so is the harvest old— the apple that hangs on your tree, six thousand times has shown its white bloom, its green germ, and its ripening yellow since our period of the world begins. And this day, as the fruit is as fresh, so is its moral as fresh and significant to us as it was to Adam in the garden.

I have spoken of the great system of external nature as exciting in our minds the perception of the benevolence of God by the wonderful contrivance their fruits exhibit; by the food they furnish us, and by the beauty that is added to them; and now, of the admonition they seem intended to convey of our short life.

But there is yet a louder and more solemn admonition which they convey to my mind as they do from year to year their appointed work. They speak to man as a moral being, and reproach his lassitude by their brute fidelity. Here we sit waiting the growing of the grain, with an undoubting reliance. If it is blasted in one field, we are sure it will thrive in another. Yet we know that if one harvest of the earth fails, the race must perish from the face of the earth. We have an expectation always of the proper performance of the vegetable functions that would not be increased if one rose from the dead.

Well, now, whilst thus directly we depend on this process on the punctuality of the sun, on the timely action of saps and seed vessels, and rivers and rains, *are we as punctual to our orbit?* Are we as trustworthy as the weed at our feet? Yet is that a poor machine—and I, besides the animal machinery that is given me, have been entrusted with a portion of the spirit that governs the material Creation, that made and directs the machinery.—Are ye not much better than they?

Shall we to whom the light of the Almighty has been given, shall we who have been raised in the scale of the Creation to the power of self government, not govern ourselves? shall the flower of the field reprove us and make it clear that it had been better for us to have wanted than to have received intelligence?

My friends, let us accustom ourselves thus to look at the fruits of the earth and the seasons of the year. Let all that we see without, only turn our attention with stricter scrutiny on all that is within us. In the beautiful order of the world, shall man alone, the highly endowed inhabitant, present a spectacle of disorder, the misrule of the passions, and rebellion against the laws of his Maker? Let us learn also the lesson they are appointed to teach of trust in God; that he will provide for us if we do his will; remembering the words of the Lord Jesus, who said—"If God so clothe the grass of the field, which today is and tomorrow is cast into the oven, will he not much more care for you, o ye of little faith!"

God that Made the World

(1832)

"God that Made the World," often referred to as the "Astronomy" sermon, was first delivered at the Second Church in Boston on May 27, 1832. Emerson would later rewrite the introduction before delivering the sermon again in Waltham, Massachusetts, on November 30, 1834—the date of a solar eclipse. The text of the sermon that appears here includes the revised introduction. After the death of his first wife, Ellen, in February 1831, Emerson delved more fully into his independent studies, reading widely in natural science as well as theology. His journals indicate that he was also becoming increasingly engrossed in his personal encounters with the natural world at this time. These experiences instilled in him a sense of awe and inspired a desire to celebrate the wonders of nature. Drawing directly on these readings and the insights recorded in his journals, Emerson asserts that the same God animates both nature and the Bible. Because of this correspondence, he believes strongly that nature should be studied in order to more fully illuminate scripture, and vice versa. This mutually informing relationship between natural and sacred "texts" is grounded in Emerson's belief that science and religion fulfill the same spiritual function. While the natural sciences search for the universal laws that explain natural processes, religion similarly seeks a moral law that underlies spiritual development. In this move to unify the goals of science and religion, Emerson articulates his growing admiration for science and his increasing mistrust of ritualized worship and institutionalized religion. This sermon marks an important moment in Emerson's career, as he clearly expresses his movement away from orthodox religious ministry toward the spiritual possibilities of nature. It is with this sentiment that he would formally resign his pastorate in September 1832, less than five months after delivering "God that Made the World."

God that made the world and all things therein, seeing that he is Lord of heaven and earth, dwelleth not in temples made with hands; neither is worshipped with men's hands as though he needed any thing, seeing he giveth to all life and breath and all things. . . . Forasmuch, then, as we are the offspring of God we ought not to think that the Godhead is like to gold or silver or stone graven by art and man's device. And the times of this ignorance God overlooked but now commandeth all men every where to repent. Because he hath appointed a day in which he will judge the world in righteousness by that man whom he hath ordained, whereof he hath given assurance unto all men in that he hath raised him from the dead.

—Acts 17:24–25, 29–31

The remarkable spectacle we have witnessed loses nothing of its interest from the fact that it was yesterday predicted to us in every particular. What was prediction yesterday is now fact. But Nature never disappoints us. What impresses one man as grand or beautiful makes a kindred impression upon all men. And though we see the sun every day and always walk by his direct or reflected light, though every grain of wheat we eat and every drop of blood in our arteries and every bodily function is as strictly related to that distant orb as is the act of respiration to the air, this we forget in the munificent flood of his daily light, but let a shadow creep once in an age upon his southern limb and blot by degrees the light and men are seized with an instinctive dread which all foresight does not wholly remove.

It seems as if they anticipated the fatal consequence should that shadow continue to cover his face. This life, this organization, which throughout the animal and vegetable nature of our globe beats as one heart, would freeze and stop; the rejoicing nations would be still enough and the shade that covered the earth would be the pall of death to her children. Those who have seen an eclipse are likely never quite to forget how indispensable is that luminary not to beauty but to being.

This rare and striking appearance suggests many useful reflexions. Perhaps the most obvious is a feeling of joy at the fact that it was predicted. It reminds us impressively of the powers of the human intellect. What a contrast between the littleness of the observer and the magnitude and duration of the laws he observes. Compared with the great bodies in the heavens the astronomer on the earth seems a mere eye sailing in space round the circle of its small orbit. What is he to weigh the formidable masses, to measure the secular periods, to fix the faithful laws by which they all have been governed and shall be in all past and all future time!

But a better reflexion shows us no occasion for pride. This human mind is but a derived light from the source of wisdom as yonder sun is but a spark of his enkindling. It is only the knowledge of God that unites this bright outward Creation of brute matter to the brighter inward Creation of intelligent mind. The passage which I have read from the New Testament is valuable because it serves as one out of many to show that the Scriptures claim to come from the same Being that made the heavens and the earth; that the God of nature and the God of the Bible are affirmed to be the same; that the Father of Jesus Christ is the Divine Providence in whose wisdom and love all beings are embosomed.

Since this is so, since the records of the divine dealings with men claim no other origin than the author of nature, we may expect that they are to be read by the light of nature; that more knowledge of his works will enable us.

There are many considerations that associate astronomy with the history of religion. It is always at hand as the visible image of every exalted sentiment. Religion in the later ages suffering from the caprices and errors of men wanders often far from her object into strange paths and the attempt is resisted as a sort of violence which strives to reunite Religion with the love of nature. Yet the song of the morning stars was really the first hymn of praise and will be the last; the face of nature, the breath of the hills, the lights of the skies, are to a simple heart the real occasions of devout feeling more than vestries and sermon hearings, and are those natural checks that are ever exerting an insensible influence to hold us back from fanaticism and keep us within sight of the true God.

Then the aspects of the heaven cannot fail to affect all opinion, especially these speculations. These aspects are so prominent. In the beginning of society in mild climates of South Asia when as yet man had not built magnificent towns, Nature made the riches and the shows of men. What perfection and elegancy in them! Nothing else in nature has the grandeur and influence upon the mind. How delicately at sunset come out these sparks in the vault. The changes which touch us touch not them. From Time, which they measure, they suffer not. There is the light sphered in the same vessels which contained it (not in Archimedes' or Ptolemy's time) but when the first Syrian shepherd noted down with a savage's imagination the figures he saw nightly sketched in the sky, yes and for what inconceivable periods before the human race was. We are new comers into space. Our planet is gray and scarred with wrinkles of immense age, but its inhabitant is a novelty in the cheerful eternity, long ago as bright as now, into which we are born.

And hence it naturally happened that the heavenly bodies were the first objects of idolatry. Symbols of power and beauty, they were readily understood by the perverted to be power and intelligence themselves, and let the proverbial phrases still current in common speech attest how obstinate was the opinion that the stars exercised moral influence upon the lives of men.

If a large class of men are less sensible to impressions of beauty, still to them the heavens were at hand as illustration for all argument. What questions do they not suggest? Let me ask the younger members of this assembly, have you ever settled it in your mind and do you believe that space is really boundless? You cannot deny the fact without absurdity and in words you do admit it without hesitation, but I persist in asking, Do you believe it? Dwell a moment on that gigantic thought until you feel the difficulty of the question; until you discern that the first conception which this Science presents to man is a space upon whose area all the worlds of God are a mere dot, and the boldest imagination of man or angel can only enter upon its margin. All that exists is lost in the bosom of its great night.

Thus impressive and animating are the first aspects of the science.

But an important result of the study of astronomy has been to correct and exalt our views of God, and humble our view of ourselves.

In all ancient speculation men were accustomed of course to take man for the type of the highest beings, and suppose whatever is intelligent and good among God's creatures must resemble human nature. Even God himself, the infant religion of all nations has clothed in human form, and idolatry imputed to him the passions as well as the person of man. Astronomy corrects all these boastful dreams and demonstrates that whatever beings inhabit Saturn, Jupiter, Herschel, and Mercury, even in this little family of social worlds that journey like us around the sun, they must have an organization wholly different from man. The human race could not breathe in the rare atmosphere of the moon; nor the human blood circulate in the climate of Uranus; nor the strength of man suffice to raise his own foot from the ground in the dense gravity of Jupiter.

Each of the eleven globes therefore that revolve round the sun must be inhabited by a race of different structure. And to suppose that the constitution of the race of yesterday that now plants the fields of this particular planet, should be the pattern for all the orders that people the huge globes in the heaven is too improbable to be entertained.

Rather believe that the benignant Power which has assigned each creature to its own element, the fish to the sea, the bird to the air, the beast to the field, has not less nicely adjusted elsewhere his creatures to their habitation and has enriched other seats of his love with other and perhaps far more excellent endowments than he has granted to mankind.

In the next place the science of astronomy has had an irresistible effect in modifying and enlarging the doctrines of theology. It is known to all to whom I speak that until a few hundred years ago it was the settled opinion of all men that the earth was stationary in space, and that the sun and stars actually moved round it every day as they appear to do to the eye. The host of heaven were esteemed so many lanthorns to illuminate and set off the residence of man. It is only since the time of Galileo and Newton it was learned that the little ball on which we live spins upon its own axis to produce this appearance, and that it is at such a dizzy distance from the stars which were supposed thus revolving for its ornament, that it is not visible from them; and not only the earth but the whole system also to which it belongs, with the great sun in the centre, are perhaps too minute for observation from those remote luminaries.

Why need I repeat to you the swelling amount of distances and magnitudes of the stars with which calculation amazes us? They go in the pages of the Almanack into every house and shop. Every mind in the civilized world has caught the general results. Every heart responds to the pious hymn:

Yet not to earth's contracted span
Thy goodness let me bound;
Nor think thee Lord alone of man,
When thousand worlds are round.

When the solar system had been correctly explained to us we found ourselves journeying in a comparatively small opaque planet around a single star and quite too inconsiderable to be noticed amid the millions of burning suns which the telescope revealed. It was the effect of this new knowledge, to make an equal revolution in religious opinion, as in science, for it was impossible to regard the earth any longer, as the only object in the care of Providence.

It had been the belief of many generations that God from all eternity had foreseen the fall of man and had devised in his councils a method by which man might be saved.

The second being in the Universe, it was represented, undertook to save them, and in the vain imagination of man the scheme of his redemption, as it was called, occupied the attention of God and of angels as if there were nothing in being but men. 'The earth,' in the strange language of an old divine, 'was the scaffold of the divine vengeance.'

Now this system of theology was every way suited to the ancient system of the heavens. It could not but happen that the telescope should be fatal to both. I regard it as the irresistible effect of the Copernican astronomy to have made the theological *scheme of Redemption* absolutely incredible. The great geniuses who studied the mechanism of the heavens became unbelievers in the popular doctrine. Newton became a Unitarian.

In spite of the awful exhibition of wisdom and might disclosed to their eyes—the present God—in spite of the natural expectation which dictated the sentiment, The undevout astronomer is mad—the incongruity between what they beheld and the gross creeds which were called religion and Christianity by their fellow countrymen so revolted them that the profound astronomers of France rejected the hope and consolation of man and in the face of that divine mechanism which they explored denied a cause and adopted the belief of an eternal Necessity as if that very eternal necessity were any thing else than God.

In the next place, whilst the removing this veil from the creation and enabling man from the little globule in which we are embarked to send his eye so far into the surrounding infinity has at first had the very natural effect to shake down the systems of opinion which churches and doctors had built and to cast a portion of doubt upon all, this evil was balanced by an opposite beneficial tendency. The investigations of the last two hundred years have brought to light the most wonderful proofs of design—beneficent design—operating far and near, in atoms and in systems, reaching to such prodigious extent both of time and space, and so perfectly answering their end, that the mind cannot weigh them without ever-increasing surprise and delight. One inquirer ascertains that in a course of years the earth's moon has deviated from her orbit by slow increments that begin to become sensible, and alarms men by showing the future fatal consequence to the earth of these eccentric movements. A more searching observer ascertains by observation and analysis that these irregularities must from the form and relation of the two bodies be periodical, and that when, after a long course of years, they have attained their maximum, a contrary motion takes place and restores the equilibrium. It is the glory of La Grange to have demonstrated that all the irregularities which take place in our system are periodical, an error on one side being compensated by an exactly equal error on the other, and fluctuate between fixed and impassable limits, that there is no ungoverned orb, no loose pin, no lawless particle through all the heights and depths of the City of God.

Cheered by these results we come to feel that planet gravitates to planet and star attracts star, each fulfilling the last mile of its orbit as surely in the round of space as the bee which launches forth for the first time from its dark cell into light, and wandering amidst flowers all day, comes back at eve with unerring wing to the hive. It is the same invisible guide that pilots the bee and pilots the planet, that established the whole and perfected the parts, that giveth to all beauty, and order, and life, and usefulness.

And I thus say, my friends, that to the human race the discoveries of astronomy have added vast meaning to the name of God. Once God was understood to be the governor of this world. Now they perceive him to be an Infinite Mind. An awful, an adorable Being, yet as affectionate in his care as he is surpassing in Wisdom.

I proceed to say that as this enlargement of our religious views— this correction of error—and this more generous consideration of God's government comes to our minds inevitably by the progress of this science, so it cannot be doubted that it was designed. Though slow, it was the sure result of the divine faculties with which man is endowed. He who made the eye and the light and clothed the globe with its transparent atmosphere did thereby teach his creature to observe the stars and write their laws. Thereby he opened the heavens to them to reform their religion and to educate the mind. By the mild, affectionate yet thrilling voice of nature he evermore leads them to a higher truth, and rewards every exertion of their faculties by more just knowledge of Himself.

And finally what is the effect upon the doctrine of the New Testament which these contemplations produce? It is not contradiction but correction. It is not denial but purification. It proves the sublime doctrine of One God whose offspring we all are and whose care we all are. On the other hand, it throws into the shade all temporary, all indifferent, all local provisions. Here is neither tithe nor priest nor Jerusalem nor Mount Gerizim. Here is neither Jew nor Greek. Here is no mystic sacrifice, no atoning blood.

But does it take one charm from the lowly grace of Christ? does it take away any authority from his lips? It abridges what belongs to persons, to places, and to times but it does not touch *moral* truth. We are assured in any speculation we may indulge concerning the tenants of other regions in the wide commonwealth of God, that if we could carry the New Testament to the inhabitants of other worlds we might need to leave Jewish Christianity and Roman Christianity, Paul and Apollos and Cephas and Luther and Socinus, but the moral law, justice and mercy would be at home in every climate and world where life is, that we can go nowhere but wisdom will be valuable and justice venerable and humility suitable and diligence useful and truth sacred and charity divine.

The largest consideration the human mind can give to the subject, makes moral distinctions still more important, and positive distinctions less. It will not teach any expiation by Jesus; it will not teach any mysterious relations to him. It will teach great, plain, eternal truths. It will teach that he only is a mediator, as he brings us truth, and we accept it, and live by it; that he only saves us, by inducing us to save ourselves; that God now commands all men, all spirits, every where to repent, and that such principles as Jesus Christ inculcated must forevermore be the standard by which actions shall be judged.

It is, brethren, a glorious confirmation that is brought to our faith, the observation that it agrees well with all the new and astonishing facts in the book of nature. It is good to perceive that the beatitudes of the sermon on the mount will be such to all intelligent creatures.

The Scriptures were written by human hands. God intends by giving us access to this original writing of his hand to correct the human errors that have crept into them. Let us yield ourselves with a grateful heart to the instruction that comes from this source and not repine to find that God is a greater, wiser and more tender Parent than we were wont to worship.

We shall not less distinctly see Jesus to be the gracious instrument of his bounty to instruct men in the character of God and the true nature of spiritual good; the teacher, and, by his teaching, the redeemer of men. But we shall fulfil the intent of Jesus by rendering the praise to God. The hour will already have arrived in our hearts when means and instruments shall have done their office and when God shall be over all and through all and in all.

The Uses of Natural History

(1833)

E merson delivered "The Uses of Natural History,"
the first of four natural history lectures for the
lyceum, to the Boston Natural History Society on November 5, 1833.
By this time, several local lyceums had gained traction in northeastern
cities and towns with the intent of disseminating useful knowledge,
often paying particular attention to science. Emerson accepted an
invitation to give the lecture only two days after returning from his
travels in Europe, a nearly yearlong trip that followed his resignation
from the Unitarian ministry. Attending scientific lectures and visiting
museums of natural history, Emerson spent the majority of his European trip exploring his keen interest in science. The most noteworthy
of these encounters occurred during his visit to the Museum d'His-
toire Naturelle's Jardin des Plantes in Paris. Feeling himself "moved
by strange sympathies," Emerson's transformative experience at the
Jardin's cabinet of natural history greatly influenced his evolving
theory of nature, because the cabinet emphasized the interrelated
whole of nature rather than its constituent parts—an insight that is
central to "The Uses of Natural History." As the lecture's title suggests, Emerson used this occasion to discuss what he perceived to be
the primary benefits and future potential of natural history. Notably,
he reiterates his understanding of nature as adhering to a systematic
design that functions like a language. Arguing for natural history's role
in revealing and teaching that language, he marks his departure from
the church by shifting his emphasis from the designer of nature to the
design itself. Through the success of "The Uses of Natural History"
and his subsequent natural history lectures, Emerson secured his

position as a public lecturer in the lyceum, which would be his primary occupation, source of income, and theoretical testing ground for the remainder of his career.

In accepting the invitation with which the Directors of this Society have honored me to introduce the course, I have followed my inclination rather than consulted my ability. My time has been so preoccupied as to prevent any particular course of reading or collection of novel illustrations of the subjects treated, which I should gladly have proposed to myself. I shall therefore say what I think on the subject of this lecture according to such imperfect general information as I already possessed.

It seems to have been designed, if anything was, that men should be students of Natural History. Man is, by nature, a farmer, a hunter, a shepherd and a fisherman, who are all practical naturalists and by their observations the true founders of all societies for the pursuit of science. And even after society has made some progress, so that the division of labor removes men into cities, and gives rise to sedentary trades and professions, every man who is fortunate enough to be born in circumstances that require him to make any exertion to live, is compelled to pick up in his own experience, a considerable knowledge of natural philosophy,—as, an acquaintance with the properties of water, of wood, of stone, of light, of heat, and the natural history of many insects, birds and beasts.

And as if to secure this end in the constitution of all men, the eye is so fitted to the face of nature or the face of nature to the eye that the perception of beauty is continually awakened in all places and under the most ordinary circumstances. The beauty of the world is a perpetual invitation to the study of the world. Sunrise and sunset; fire; flowers; shells; the sea—in all its shades, from indigo to green and gray, by the light of day, and phosphorescent under the ship's keel at night; the airy inaccessible mountain; the sparry cavern; the glaring colours of the soil of the volcano; the forms of vegetables; and all the elegant and majestic figures of the creatures that fly, climb, or creep upon the earth—all, by their beauty, work upon our curiosity and court our attention. The earth is a museum, and the five senses a philosophical apparatus of such perfection, that the pleasure we obtain from the aids with which we arm them, is trifling, compared with their natural information.

It is frequently observed how much power, the influence of natural objects gives to the sentiment of love of country which is strongest in the most wild and picturesque regions. It deserves notice also as it is this which not only heightens but creates the charm which hunting has for many persons who would start at being thought to have any poetry in their constitution. If the running down a fox or hare were performed under cover, or in a street, it would soon lose its noble name, but great bodily exertion made along the mountain side, upon fields glittering with a million beads of dew, or in the shades of a wood—which always seem to say something, we cannot well make out what;—exhilarated by the fragrant scents, and cheered on by the trumpet of all the winds,—it is not strange that a man should learn to love these scenes, though he err in thinking he loves to kill his game.

Yielding ourselves to the same pleasant influences, let us inquire what are the advantages which may be expected to accrue from the greater cultivation of Natural Science.

They are in my judgment great and manifold, and probably more than can be now enumerated. I do not think we are yet masters of all the reasons that make this knowledge valuable to us. They will only disclose themselves by a more advanced state of science. I say this because we have all a presentiment of relations to external nature, which outruns the limits of actual science. I lately had an opportunity of visiting that celebrated repository of natural curiosities the Garden of Plants in Paris; and except perhaps to naturalists only I ought not to speak of the feelings it excited in me. There is the richest collection in the world of natural curiosities arranged for the most imposing effect. The mountain and morass and prairie and jungle, the ocean, and rivers, the mines and the atmosphere have been ransacked to furnish whatever was rich and rare; the types of each class of beings—Nature's proof impressions;—to render account of her three kingdoms to the keen insatiable eye of French science.

In spacious grounds skilfully laid out, and shaded with fine groves and shrubberies, you walk among the animals of every country, each in his own paddock with his mates, having his appropriate food before him,—his habits consulted in his accommodation. There towers the camelopard nearly twenty feet high, whose promenade and breakfast attract as much attention as the king's; the lions from Algiers and Asia; the elephants from Siam—whose bath is occasionally performed with great applause from the boys;—our own countrymen, the buffalo and the bear from New Hampshire and Labrador. All sizes and all stripes of tygers, hyenas, leopards, and jackals; a herd of monkeys; not to mention the great numbers of sheep, goats, llamas, and zebras, that sleep, browse, or ruminate in their several country fashions, (as much at ease as in their own wilds,) for the amusement of the whole world in the heart of the capital of France.

Moving along these pleasant walks, you come to the botanical cabinet, an inclosed garden plot, where grows a grammar of botany— where the plants rise, each in its class, its order, and its genus, (as nearly as their habits in reference to soils will permit,) arranged by the hand of Jussieu himself. If you have read Decandolle with engravings, or with a *hortus siccus,* conceive how much more exciting and intelligible is this natural alphabet, this green and yellow and crimson dictionary, on which the sun shines, and the winds blow.

The Cabinet of Natural History is contained in a large stone edifice in the centre of the grounds.

It is a prodigality to visit in one walk all the various halls in this great gallery of Nature. The ornithological chambers require an entire day: For who would mix and confound so fine and delicate sensations? This house of stuffed birds is a finer picture gallery than the Louvre. The whole air is flushed with the rich plumage and beautiful forms of the birds. The fancy coloured vests of those elegant beings make me as pensive as the hues and forms of a cabinet of shells have done before. They fill the mind with calm and genial thought. Some of the birds have a fabulous beauty that seems more appropriate to some sultan's garden in the Arabian Nights Entertainments than to a real tangible scientific collection. You see the favourites of nature,—creatures in whose form and coat seems to have been a design to charm the eye of cultivated taste. Observe that parrot of the parrot tribe called *Psittacus Erythropterus*. You need not write down his name for he is the beau of all birds and you will find him as you will find a Raffaelle in a gallery. Then the humming birds so little and so gay—from the least of all, the *Trochilus Niger* not so big as a beetle—to the *Trochilus Pella* with his irresistible neck of gold and silver and fire; and the *Trochilus Delalandi* from Brazil whom the French call the magnificent fly (La mouche magnifique) or glory in miniature. The birds of Paradise are singularly delicate and picturesque in their plumage. The manucode or royal Paradisaea from New Guinea, the red Paradisaea, and the Paradisaea Apoda, seem each more beautiful than the last and each, if seen alone, would be pronounced a peerless creature. I watched the different groups of people who came in to the gallery, and noticed that they picked out the same birds to point to the admiration of their companions. They all noticed the Veuve à épaulettes—the widow with epaulettes—a grotesque black fowl called Emberiza Longicanda with fine shoulder ornaments and a long mourning tail, and the Ampelis Cotinga. All admired the *Phasianus Argus*, a pheasant that appeared to have made its toilette after the pattern of the peacock, and the *Trogon pavoninus*, called also the Couroucon. But it were vain to enumerate even the conspicuous individuals in the particoloured assembly. There were black swans and white peacocks, the famous venerable ibis come hither to Paris out of Egypt,—both the sacred and the rosy; the flamingo with a neck like a snake; the toucan, rightly denominated the rhinoceros; and a vulture whom to meet in a wilderness would make the flesh creep, so truculent and executioner-like he stood.

The cabinet of birds was a single and even small part of that noble magazine of natural wonders. Not less complete, scarcely less attractive is the collection of stuffed beasts, prepared with the greatest skill to represent the forms and native attitudes of the quadrupeds. Then follow the insects, the reptiles, the fishes, the minerals. In neighboring apartments is contained the collection of comparative anatomy, a perfect series from the skeleton of the *balaena* which reminds every one of the frame of a schooner, to the upright form and highly developed skull of the Caucasian race of man.

The eye is satisfied with seeing and strange thoughts are stirred as you see more surprizing objects than were known to exist; transparent lumps of amber with gnats and flies within; radiant spars and marbles; huge blocks of quartz; native gold in all its forms of crystallization and combination, gold in threads, in plates, in crystals, in dust; and silver taken from the earth molten as from fire. You are impressed with the inexhaustible gigantic riches of nature. The limits of the possible are enlarged, and the real is stranger than the imaginary. The universe is a more amazing puzzle than ever, as you look along this bewildering series of animated forms, the hazy butterflies, the carved shells, the birds, beasts, insects, snakes, fish, and the upheaving principle of life every where incipient, in the very rock aping organized forms. Whilst I stand there I am impressed with a singular conviction that not a form so grotesque, so savage, or so beautiful, but is an expression of something in man the observer. We feel that there is an occult relation between the very worm, the crawling scorpions, and man. I am moved by strange sympathies. I say I will listen to this invitation. I will be a naturalist.

Under the influence of such thoughts, I say that I suppose many inducements to the study of Natural History will disclose themselves as its secrets are penetrated. Besides that the general progress of the science has given it a higher and higher place in the public estimation is there not every now and then some inexplicable fact or new class of relations suggested which for the time seems not so much to invite as to defy scientific solution? For example, what known laws are to classify some of the astounding facts embodied in the Report of the Committee of the French Institute in 1830 upon the subject of Animal Magnetism—a committee too, considering the persons and the circumstances, who might be regarded as a picked jury of the most competent scientific persons on earth? But not to venture upon this dangerous ground, the debateable land of the sublime and the ridiculous, let me confine my attention to the enumeration of certain specific advantages easily marked and understood which may serve as the commendation of the objects of this society.

1. It is the lowest and yet not a bad recommendation of the occupations of the Naturalist that they are serviceable to the health. The ancient Greeks had a fable of the giant Antaeus, that when he wrestled with Hercules, he was suffocated in the gripe of the hero, but every

time he touched his mother earth, his strength was renewed. The fable explains itself of the body and the mind. Man is the broken giant, and in all his weakness he is invigorated by touching his mother earth, that is, by habits of conversation with nature. It is good for the body exhausted by the bad air, and artificial life of cities, to be sent out into the fresh and fragrant fields, and there employed in exploring the laws of the creation. The study of Botany deserves the attention of those interested in Education, for this, if for no other cause. The wild rose will reflect its hues upon the cheek of the lover of nature. It is well known that the celebrated Wilson was led to the study of Ornithology for the benefit of his enfeebled health, and in his enthusiastic rambles in the wilderness his constitution was established whilst he enlarged the domain of science.

The mountain minerals will pay their searcher with active limbs and refreshed spirits. And he who wanders along the margin of the sounding sea for shellfish or marine plants, will find strength of limb and sharpness of sight and bounding blood in the same places. Dig your garden, cross your cattle, graft your trees, feed your silkworms, set your hives—in the field is the perfection of the senses to be found, and quiet restoring Sleep,—

His poppy grows among the Corn.

2. In the second place, the main advantage to be proposed from the study of natural history is that which may seem to make all further argument needless; to be itself the manifest ground on which the study stands in the favor of mankind, I mean the direct service which it renders to the cultivator and the world, the amount of useful economical information which it communicates. The proof of this assertion is the history of all discoveries, almost the history of civilization itself. It is the earth itself and its natural bodies that make the raw material out of which we construct our food, clothing, fuel, furniture, and arms. And it is the Naturalist who discovers the virtues of these bodies and the mode of converting them to use. In the most refined state of society, these are most accumulated; but these are now so numerous and the subdivision of labor has removed each process so far out of sight, that a man who by pulling a bell can command any luxury the world contains,

is in danger of forgetting that iron came out of a mine, and perfume out of a cat.

You sit in your parlor surrounded by more proofs of the cultivation of natural science than books or cabinets contain. The water that you drink was pumped up from a well by an application of the air pump. The well ventilated chimney which every mason can build, derived its hint from Franklin and Rumford. The sugar in your dish was refined by the instruction given by a modern chemist on the adjustment of temperature for the crystallization of syrup; the brasses, the silver, the iron, the gold, which enter into the construction of so many indispensable articles, and indeed the glass, the cloth, the paints and dyes, have employed the philosopher as well as the mechanic; there is scarcely any manufacture whose processes are not assisted or directed by rules and principles derived from the observations of Naturalists. Apart from the consideration that all the foreign fabrics, drugs, fruits, and condiments, which are as familiar as salt, were transported hither across the sea by the aid of that map of the stars and the record of the predicted places of the sun and the earth, which the lovers of nature from the Chaldean shepherd to Laplace and Bowditch have aided in bringing to perfection.

The history of modern times has repeatedly shown that a single man devoted to science may carry forward the mechanic arts and multiply the products of commerce more than the united population of a country can accomplish in ages wherein no particular devotion to scientific pursuits exists. This is forcibly illustrated by the historical fact of the influence produced in France by the appointment of the celebrated Duhamel to the professorship of the School of Mines. In 1822 it was stated to the Academy by its Secretary "that from the appointment of M. Duhamel to the time of his death, the products of iron in France were quadrupled; the mines of this metal opened near the Loire in the region of coal, and in the midst of combustible matter, were about to yield iron at the same price as in England. Antimony, manganese, which we formerly imported, are now exported in considerable quantities. Chrome, discovered by one of our chemists, is also the useful product of one of our mines. Zinc and tin have already been extracted from the mines on the coast of Brittany. Alum and vitriol, formerly almost unknown in France, are collected in abundance. An immense mass of rock-salt has just been discovered in Lorraine, and all promises that these new creations will not stop here. Doubtless it is not to a single man, nor to the appointment of a single professorship that all this may be attributed but it is not the less true that this one man, this one professorship has been the primary cause of these advantages."

But the advantages which science has presented to human life are in all probability the least part of her possessions. To the powers of science no limit can be assigned. All that has been is only an accumulated force to act upon the future. The prospective power, the armed hand, the learned eye are worth more than the riches they have acquired. It is a maxim in philosophy that a general truth is more valuable than all the particular facts which it has disclosed.

The natural history of water is not studied with less diligence or advantage at this moment than when Watt and Fulton made it a day laborer for mankind. It is but the other day that our country-man, Mr. Jacob Perkins, noticed the small bubbles that are formed on the sides and bottom of a vessel in which water is heated, and most rapidly on the hottest parts, and discovered that these bubbles operate as a screen between the fire and the body of water in the vessel, preventing the rise of the temperature within in any proportion to the increase of the temperature on the outside. He found especially that in the boilers of steam engines great inconvenience and danger frequently resulted from this cause because when the engineer quickened his fire it consumed the coats of the boiler more rapidly without making a proportionate expansion of the steam. This observation led to the thought that a strong circulation in the water might be caused which should continually rush against the sides of the vessel and break or remove these air bubbles. This thought he has recently executed in the machine called the Circulators and which has already been adopted in three of the locomotives on the Liverpool and Manchester Railroad with the best success and is about being introduced into all. And this may serve for a hundred examples of the benefit resulting from these observations.

3. But it is high time to enumerate a third reason for the cultivation of natural history which is the *delight which springs from the contemplation of this truth,* independent of all other considerations.

I should be ashamed to neglect this good, in too particular a showing what profit was to accrue from the knowledge of nature. The knowledge itself, is the highest benefit. He must be very young or very sordid who wishes to know what good it will do him to understand the sublime mechanism on which the stability of the solar system and the faithful return of the seasons depend. What good will it do him? Why, the good of knowing that fact. Is not that good enough?—Moreover is it not disgraceful to be served by all the arts and sciences at our tables, and in our chambers and never know who feeds us, nor understand the cunning they employ? I cannot but think it becoming that every gentleman should know why he puts on a white hat in summer, and a woolen coat in winter; and why his shoes cannot be made until the leather is tanned. Better sit still than be borne by steam, and not know how; or guided by the needle and the quadrant through thousands of miles of sea, without a mark in the horizon, and brought to a little dent in the shore on the other half the globe, as truly as if following a clew in the hand—and never ask how that feat is accomplished.

Bias was asked what good, education would do for a boy;—"When he goes there," pointing to the marble seats of the theatre, he replied, "that he might not be a stone sitting upon a stone." Every fact that is disclosed to us in natural history removes one scale more from the eye; makes the face of nature around us so much more significant. How many men have seen it snow twenty or forty winters without a thought being suggested beyond the need of stout boots, the probability of good sleighing, and the country trade; until some kind philosopher has drawn our attention to the singular beauty of that phenomenon, the formation of snow; and shown us the texture of that self weaving blanket with which the parts of the globe exposed to cold, cover themselves in pile proportioned to their exposure, at the time when the animated creation on the same side of the earth whiten and thicken their fleeces. We cannot see again without new pleasure what the Latin poet calls the thick fleece of silent waters—

densum tacitarum vellus aquarum.

You cannot go out when the snow is falling in a calm still air and catch the little hexagon upon the palm of your hand and measure the invariable angles of the radii of the star without a finer delight than ever sprang from the consideration of the convenience of the general railroad with which it covers the country for the woodcutter and the farmer. The snowstorm becomes to your eye a philosophical experiment performed in a larger laboratory and on a more magnificent scale than our chemists can command.

To the naturalist belongs all that keen gratification which arises from the observation of the singular provision for human wants that in some instances requiring ages for its completion, was begun ages before the use of it was shown.

The science of Geology which treats of the structure of the earth has ascertained that before the period when God created man upon the earth very considerable changes have taken place in the planet. It is made probable that the various rocks that are now found broken upon it, as granite, slate, chalk, etc., covered it as so many concentric crusts or coats, like the coats of the onion, one without the other. But the soils which now cover it are formed by the decomposition of these stones, so that in this position of them that mixture of them which is essential to the production of vegetable life could never have been affected. By internal volcanoes, or other means these several strata have been broken and raised and are now found lying as may be seen in mountain countries in oblique and perpendicular instead of horizontal layers so as to yield their various treasures to man and to the soil.

This is yet more striking in the case of Coal, so important to old countries, and recently to this, and has naturally attracted the particular attention of British naturalists.

It is well known how vastly the great development of the commerce of Great Britain and thence of the great civilization of that country is indebted to the boundless abundance of coal in its mines. In consequence of the abundance and accessibility of this mineral in that island, and its opportune association with beds of iron ore, and the invariable contiguity of limestone employed to flux the iron, the English have been enabled to surpass all other nations in the cheapness of machinery and thence in the extent of their manufactures.

But the discoveries of geologists have shown that the coal which is undoubtedly a vegetable formation is the relic of forests which existed at an unknown antiquity before the era of the creation of mankind, and by the overflowing of the sea and other changes of the surface had been buried below the surface at too great a depth to be reached by man. But before the creation of our race earthquakes or other convulsions of enormous force have lifted up these mineral beds into ledges so that they are found extending from 1000 feet above the level of the ocean, to unknown depths below it. And so it happens that these vast beds of fuel so essential to man's comfort and civilization, which would have been covered by the crust of the globe from his knowledge and use, are thus brought up within reach of his little hands; and a great work of Nature in an antiquity that hath no record—namely the deposit and crystallization of antediluvian forests, is made to contribute to our pleasure and prosperity at this hour.

Thus knowledge will make the face of the earth significant to us: it will make the stones speak and clothe with grace the meanest weed. Indeed it is worth considering in all animated nature what different aspect the same object presents to the ignorant and the instructed eye. It only needs to have the eye informed, to make everything we see, every plant, every spider, every moss, every patch of mould upon the bark of a tree, give us the idea of fitness, as much as the order and accommodation of the most ingeniously packed dressing box. For, every form is a history of the thing. The comparative anatomist can tell at sight whether a skeleton belonged to a carnivorous or herbivorous animal—to a climber, a jumper, a runner, a digger, a builder. The conchologist can tell at sight whether his shell were a river or a sea shell, whether it dwelt in still or in running waters, whether it were an annual or a perennial covering, and many the like particulars. And this takes away the sense of deformity from all objects; for, every thing is a monster till we know what it is for. A ship, a telescope, a surgical instrument, a box of strange tools are puzzles and painful to the eye, until we have been shown successively the use of every part, and then the thing tells its story at sight, and is beautiful. A lobster is monstrous to the eye the first time it is seen, but when we have been shown the use of the case, the color, the tentacula, and the proportion of the claws, and have seen that he has not a scale nor a bristle, nor any part, but fits exactly to some habit and condition of the creature;

he then seems as perfect and suitable to his seahouse, as a glove to a hand. A *man* in the rocks under the sea, would indeed be a monster; but a lobster is a most handy and happy fellow there. So there is not an object in nature so mean or loathsome, not a weed, not a toad, not an earwig, but a knowledge of its habits would lessen our disgust, and convert it into an object of some worth; perhaps of admiration. Nothing is indifferent to the wise. If a man should study the economy of a spire of grass—how it sucks up sap, how it imbibes light, how it resists cold, how it repels excess of moisture, it would show him a design in the form, in the color, in the smell, in the very posture of the blade as it bends before the wind.

There is an excellent story in one of our children's books called Eyes and No Eyes. A dull dumb unprofitable world is this to many a man that has all his senses in health. But bring under the same arch of day, upon the same green sod, under the shadow of the same hills Linnaeus or Buffon or Cuvier or Humboldt and the sea and the land will break forth into singing, and all the trees of the field will clap their hands. The traveller casts his eye upon a broken mountainside, and sees nothing to detain his attention a moment. Let Cuvier regard the same thing; in the rough ledges, the different shades and super-position of the strata, his eye is reading as in a book the history of the globe, the changes that were effected by fire, by water, by pressure, by friction in ages long prior to the existence of man upon the planet, he is hearkening to infallible testimony of events whereof is no chronicle but in the memory of God, and taking down minutes of the same for the guidance and confirmation of future inquirers.

It has been felt by their contemporaries as a public calamity when such an observer who knew the value of his senses has been deprived of their use. One of the most touching incidents in biography is the affliction that befel Galileo, who, after announcing in rapid succession to the world his splendid discoveries, made by the aid of the telescope, namely, the uneven surface of the moon; the spots on the sun by which the revolution of that body was proved; that Venus was horned like the moon; the satellites, and the belt of Jupiter; the ring of Saturn;—was bereaved of sight. His friend Castelli wrote to one of his correspondents, "The noblest eye is darkened that nature ever made; an eye so priveleged, and gifted with such rare qualities, that it may with truth be said to have seen more than all of those which are gone, and to have opened the eyes of all which are to come."

These men have used their senses to such good purpose, led on by the mere pleasure of observation, the high delight which they found in exploring the works of nature.

4. There is a fourth good purpose answered by the study of Natural History which deserves a distinct enumeration. I refer to its salutary effect upon the mind and character of those who cultivate it. It makes the intellect exact, quick to discriminate between the similar and the same, and greedy of truth.

Moreover I hope it will not be thought undue refinement to suppose that long habits of intimate acquaintance with nature's workmanship, which is always neat, simple, masterly, accustoms her scholars to think and work in her style. All our ideas of sublimity and beauty are got from that source. Our contrivances are good but will not bear comparison with hers.

An orrery is esteemed an ingenious and elegant machine to exhibit the relative motions of the bodies of the solar system, but compare it with nature's own orrery, as it would appear to the eye of an observer placed above the plane of the System. He should see the beautiful balls moving on self poised in empty space, no rods reaching from them to the sun—no wires fastening the moons to their planets, but all bound by firm but invisible cords, that never entangle, nor crack, nor wear, nor weigh, namely, those threads of attraction, that join every particle in creation to every other particle.

Or to take a much lower instance in an object at our feet of the simplicity of the means by which important ends are effected. Who are those that hoe and harrow the surface of the ground to keep it in a state of looseness fit for tillage, and to make the fallow land penetrable to the roots of the grasses and to the germination of forest trees? The Earthworms.

It has been observed by the entomologist that worms promote vegetation by boring, perforating, and loosening the soil, and rendering it pervious to rains, and to the fibres of plants; by drawing straws and stalks of leaves and twigs into it, and most of all by throwing up such infinite numbers of lumps of earth called worm-casts which manure the grain and grass. Without the incessant aid of these little gardeners and farmers, the earth would soon become cold, and hardbound, and void of fermentation.

Thus Nature keeps the surface of the soil open; but how does she make the soil? Who are the strong and skilful architects that build up the solid land from the bottom of the sea? A little insect, the coralline, the madrepore, almost too small for sight, possessing the power of extracting lime from the sea water, builds up the coral reefs from the bed of the ocean to the surface, and these make in the course of ages the broad floor, on which by the agency of the marine vegetation, and of the birds, and the accidents of drift timber, a coat of soil is gradually laid, and a new land opened for the accommodation of man.

There are numberless examples in the economy of bees, the celebrated discovery of Reaumur relative to the angles of the cells, the observations of Huber upon the simplicity of the means by which the hive is ventilated, that are too long and too well known to be detailed.

Can the effect be other than most beneficent upon the faculties dedicated to such observations?—upon the man given

> To reverend watching of each still report
> That Nature utters from her rural shrine.

Moreover the state of mind which nature makes indispensable to all such as inquire of her secrets is the best discipline. For she yields no answer to petulance, or dogmatism, or affectation; only to patient, docile observation. Whosoever would gain anything of her, must submit to the essential condition of all learning, must go in the spirit of a little child. The naturalist commands nature by obeying her.

And this benign influence passes from the intellect into the affections and makes not only the judgment sound but the manners simple and the whole character amiable and true.

Indeed I think that a superiority in this respect of truth and simplicity of character extends generally to people resident in the country whose manner of life so nearly resembles that of the professed naturalist. That flippancy which is apt to be so soon learned in cities is not often found in the country. Nor are men *there* all ground down to the same tame and timid mediocrity which results in cities from the fear of offending and the desire of display. But the peculiarities of original genius stand out more strongly which are the results of that framework which the hand of God has laid for each man and which it behoves every man to respect as it constitutes the only plan according to which his particular structure can ever rise to greatness. These peculiarities in the resident of the country are the effects no doubt of silence and solitude, and of constant familiarity with calm and great objects. Though this influence is often exaggerated, yet I believe none of us are quite insensible to it, as every man may prove who goes alone into a picturesque country. I apprehend that every man who goes by himself into the woods, not at the time occupied by any anxiety of mind, but free to surrender himself to the genius of the place, feels as a boy again without loss of wisdom. In the presence of nature he is a child.

One thing more under this head of the effect of these studies upon the mind and character. It generates enthusiasm, the highest quality, say rather, the highest *state* of the character. It has been the effect of these pursuits and most conspicuously upon the first class of minds to absorb their attention. What was sought at first as a secondary object, to satisfy an occasional curiosity, or amuse a rainy day, gradually won upon their interest, excluding every former occupation, until it possessed itself of the whole man.

They have felt the interest in truth as truth which was revealed to their inquiries. The story of Archimedes running as a madman, around the streets of Syracuse, after discovering the mode of determining the specific gravity of bodies, crying out as he ran, "I have found it" is familiar to children. Scarce less notorious is that trait recorded of Newton, that, when after the new measurement of a degree of the earth's surface, he renewed his comparison of the earth's attraction of the moon, to the earth's attraction of a falling apple,—and saw, in the progress of the calculation, that he was approaching the result he had formerly anticipated, he was so much agitated by the grandeur of the fact about to be disclosed, that he was unable to go on, and was obliged to call in a friend to finish the computation. As they say, the soldier who dies in hot blood never feels the wound, it is remarked of several physiologists, that they have continued their observations into the very doors of death. It is recorded of Haller, the celebrated Swiss physiologist, that he continued his observations in his last illness upon the progress of his disease with perfect calmness; taking note of the successive alterations in his system, and keeping his hand upon his own pulse,—until at last he exclaimed to his physician, "My friend, the artery ceases to beat," and expired.

And it is related of John Hunter that he retained the habit of critical observation to the last pulse, and said to a friend who sat beside him, "I wish I had power of speaking or writing that I might tell you how pleasant are the sensations of dying."

These are the heroes of science who have an instinctive preference of the value of truth, and who think that man has no nobler vocation than to watch and record the wonders that surround him.

Hence the high prophetic tone which they have sometimes assumed, speaking as with the voice of time and nature.

When Kepler had discovered the three harmonic laws that regulate the motion of the heavenly bodies, he exclaims, "At length, after the lapse of eighteen months, the first dawn of light has shone upon me; and on this remarkable day, I have perceived the pure irradiation of sublime truth. Nothing now represses me: I dare yield myself up to my holy ardor; I dare insult mankind by acknowledging, that, I have turned worldly science to advantage; that I have robbed the vessels of Egypt to erect a temple to the living God. If I am pardoned, I shall rejoice; if blamed, I shall endure it. The die is cast; I have written this book:—whether it be read by posterity or by my contemporaries, is of no consequence: it may well wait for a reader during one century since God himself during 6000 years has waited for an observer like myself."

The biography of chemists, botanists, physicians, geometers abounds with the narrative of sleepless nights, laborious days and dangerous journeyings. There is no hazard the love of science has not prompted them to brave; no wilderness they have not penetrated; no experiment suggested, which they have not tried. And with all my honour for science, so much greater is my respect for the observer Man, than for any thing he observes, that I esteem this development of character—this high unconditional devotion to their cause, this trampling under foot of every thing pitiful and selfish in the zeal of their pursuit of nature,—to be worth all the stars they have found, all the bugs or crystals or zoophytes they have described, all the laws how sublime soever, which they have deduced and divulged to mankind.

It was my intention to have added the consideration of the effect of a diffusion of a general taste in these pursuits to counteract in the community the extreme and debasing influences of party spirit, and the excessive love of gain; as we would let in the west wind blowing from the wilderness into the polluted chambers of a hospital. But I am already trespassing on your time.

5. I have spoken of some of the advantages which may flow from the culture of natural science: health; useful knowledge; delight; and the improvement of the mind and character. I should not do the subject the imperfect justice in my power if I did not add a fifth. It is in my judgment the greatest office of natural science (and one which as yet is only begun to be discharged) to explain man to himself. The knowledge of the laws of nature,—how many wild errors—political, philosophical, theological, has it not already corrected! The knowledge of all the facts of all the laws of nature will give man his true place in the system of being. But more than the correction of specific errors by the disclosure of particular facts, there yet remain questions of the highest interest which are unsolved and on which a far more profound knowledge of Nature will throw light.

The most difficult problems are those that lie nearest at hand. I suppose that every philosopher feels that the simple fact of his own existence is the most astonishing of all facts. But I suggest the question, with great humility, to the reason of every one present, whether, the most mysterious and wonderful fact, (after our own existence) with which we are acquainted, be not, the power of *expression* which belongs to external nature; or, that correspondence of the outward world to the inward world of thoughts and emotions, by which it is suited to represent what we think.

There is more beauty in the morning cloud than the prism can render account of. There is something in it which reflects the aspects of mortal life, its epochs, and its fate. Is the face of heaven and earth—this glorious scene always changing—yet always good—fading all around us into fair perspective,—overhung with the gay awning of the clouds,—floating themselves as scraps of down under the high stars, and the ever lasting vault of space,—is this nothing to us but so much oxygen, azote, and carbon of which what is visible is composed? Is there not a secret sympathy which connects man to all the animate and to all the inanimate beings around him? Where is it these fair creatures (in whom an order and series is so distinctly discernible,) find their link, their cement, their keystone, but in the Mind of Man? It is he who marries the visible to the Invisible by uniting thought to Animal Organization.

The strongest distinction of which we have an idea is that between thought and matter. The very existence of thought and speech supposes and is a new nature totally distinct from the material world; yet we find it impossible to speak of it and its laws in any other language than that borrowed from our experience in the material world. We not only speak in continual metaphors of the morn, the noon and the evening of life, of dark and bright thoughts, of sweet and bitter moments, of the healthy mind and the fading memory; but all our most literal and direct modes of speech—as right and wrong, form and substance, honest and dishonest etc., are, when hunted up to their original signification, found to be metaphors also. And this, because the whole of Nature is a metaphor or image of the human Mind. The laws of moral nature answer to those of matter as face to face in a glass. "The visible world," it has been well said, "and the relations of its parts is the dial plate of the invisible one." In the language of the poet,

> For all that meets the bodily sense I deem
> Symbolical, one mighty alphabet
> For infant minds.

It is a most curious fact that the axioms of geometry and of mechanics only translate the laws of ethics. Thus, A straight line is the shortest distance between two points; The whole is greater than its part; The smallest weight may be made to lift the greatest, the difference of force being compensated by time; Reaction is equal to action; and a thousand the like propositions which have an ethical as well as a material sense. They are true not only in geometry but in life; they have a much more extensive and universal signification as applied to human nature than when confined to technical use. And every common proverb is only one of these facts in nature used as a picture or parable of a more extensive truth; as when we say, "A bird in the hand is worth two the bush." "A rolling stone gathers no moss." "'Tis hard to carry a full cup even." "Whilst the grass grows the steed starves."—In themselves these are insignificant facts but we repeat them because they are symbolical of moral truths. These are only trivial instances designed to show the principle. But it will probably be found to hold of all the facts revealed by chemistry or astronomy that they have the same harmony with the human mind.

And this undersong, this perfect harmony does not become less with more intimate knowledge of nature's laws but the analogy is felt to be deeper and more universal for every law that Davy or Cuvier or Laplace has revealed. It almost seems as if according to the idea of Fontenelle, "We seem to recognize a truth the first time we hear it."

I look then to the progress of Natural Science as to that which is to develop new and great lessons of which good men shall understand the moral. Nature is a language and every new fact we learn is a new word; but it is not a language taken to pieces and dead in the dictionary, but the language put together into a most significant and universal sense. I wish to learn this language—not that I may know a new grammar but that I may read the great book which is written in that tongue. A man should feel that the time is not lost and the efforts not misspent that are devoted to the elucidation of these laws; for herein is writ by the Creator his own history. If the opportunity is afforded him he may study the leaves of the lightest flower that opens upon the breast of summer, in the faith that there is a meaning therein before whose truth and beauty all external grace must vanish, as it may be, all this outward universe shall one day disappear, when its whole sense hath been comprehended and engraved forever in the eternal thoughts of the human mind.

On the Relation of Man
to the Globe

(1834)

On January 6, 1834, Emerson delivered "On the Relation of Man to the Globe" as the second of his four-part natural history lecture series for the Boston lyceum. As with "The Uses of Natural History," this lecture signals another major breakthrough from his European trip. With his return to America delayed by bad weather, Emerson sketched a rough framework for *Nature* during his last days abroad. In this outline, he clearly articulated his criticism of institutionalized religion. Because of its exaltation and ritualization of the sacred text, Emerson believed religion to be too far removed from nature. This recognition of a key shortcoming in religion came on the heels of a number of generally underwhelming meetings with prominent British literary figures, such as Samuel Taylor Coleridge and William Wordsworth. These two factors led to Emerson's further disillusionment with the power of preachers or writers to adequately explain nature. Consequently, he became increasingly interested in men of science, a shift that is characteristic of his time abroad. For Emerson, science provided the means to classify and describe phenomena in order to better comprehend how they cohere as components of a natural system. His interest in this ability of science to reveal unity is evident throughout "On the Relation of Man to the Globe," in which he explores this relationship through a consideration of the interrelated adaptations of humanity to the environment, and vice versa; the potential for people's positive contributions to natural systems through active engagement with nature; and the individual's aesthetic pleasure in response to the natural world. Through these ruminations Emerson seeks to discern the role of humanity in the dynamic system of natural processes. When he concludes, "Design! It is all design. It is all beauty," Emerson indicates the enduring interest in nature's design that was evident in his sermons; however, his inquiry now seeks to understand the spiritual relationship between nature and humanity, rather than searching for evidence of a divine presence.

♣

There are many facts which from their nature cannot suddenly be known and which can only be disclosed in long periods of time. The character of a climate cannot be known by one day nor safely judged by one year. The orbit of a planet cannot be determined until it has made a full revolution which may require several of our years. The precession of the equinoxes in our own planet, requires thousands of years for its cycle. There is a fact of this sort of much nearer interest to us but which only a series of ages could fully reveal, namely the fitness which the long residence of man upon this planet has discovered between his nature and his abode. I invite your attention to some considerations of the Relation of Man to the Globe. As the subject of the last was the uses so this will be found to involve the fruits of Natural Science.

Since the middle of the last century, we have begun to study the history of organic nature by inference from certain marks left here and there about our abode; by putting together a most curious tissue of circumstantial evidence, of which Moses furnishes one fact; and the gypsum beds of Paris, another; and the mummies of Egypt, a third; and the rocks of Goat Island, a fourth; and the chance observation of some shipwrecked sailor, a fifth. We have come to look at the world in quite another light from any in which our fathers regarded it. It is not a mere farm out of which we can raise corn to eat; nor a battlefield on which the strongest arm can rob his neighbors of their property; nor a market where men set up each their various talents for sale; nor a mere abiding place which has no other interest than the action and suffering of which it is the scene; but it is found that it may serve the noblest purposes to the intellect; it is found that it is itself a monument on whose surface every age of perhaps numberless centuries has somewhere inscribed its history in gigantic letters—too deep to be obliterated—but so far apart, and without visible connexion, that only the most diligent observer—say rather—an uninterrupted succession of patient observers—can read them.

It was the opinion of a great man recently dead who long stood at the head of German literature and high in German science, "that Nature accidentally and as it were against her will became the telltale of her own secrets; that every thing was told—at least once; only not in the time and place at which we looked for or suspected it. We must collect it here and there, in all the nooks and corners in which she had let it drop. . . . That she was a book of the vastest, strangest contents from which however we might gather; that many of its leaves lay scattered around in Jupiter, Uranus and other planets."

By the study of the globe in very recent times we have become acquainted with a fact the most surprizing—I may say the most sublime, to wit, that Man who stands in the globe so proud and powerful is no upstart in the creation, but has been prophesied in nature for a thousand thousand ages before he appeared; that from times incalculably remote there has been a progressive preparation for him; an effort, (as physiologists say,) to produce him; the meaner creatures, the primeval sauri, containing the elements of his structure and pointing at it on every side, whilst the world was, at the same time, preparing to be habitable by him. He was not made sooner, because his house was not ready.

By digging into the earth anywhere it is found that the internal body of the planet is covered by successive concentric crusts lying one upon another like the coats of an onion. That envelope which now forms the surface of the land, composed of mud, sand, clay, and broken stones, is formed by the decomposition and a mixture of the several layers underneath it. Each of these several layers appears to have been at one time the external crust, until by a decomposition or mixture effected by fire or water, another was deposited over it. The lowest of all these crusts to which we have penetrated is granite, which seems to have been deposited in a state of fusion. When this formed the outer crust of the earth, there was no organic life, for no remains either of animal or vegetable fossils have ever been found in that hard rock; and how could life be supported on such a soil? By the fracture and crumbling of this stone, by a new distribution of the water or by other causes now unknown, new layers of gneiss, of slate, of clay, of limestone, were successively formed above it and then first faint traces of vegetable and animal life begin to appear, and in the lowest strata the most imperfect forms;—zoophytes, shells, and crustaceous animals; then, fishes and reptiles. There is in nature a sort of boundary where the animate and inanimate seem to strive for mastery.

It appears that the most perfect animals were at that time formed which the earth in its then condition could sustain. Granite could not feed any creature and no vegetable is found thereon. Neither could gneiss; neither could slate. But when the vegetable race which is, you know, the laboratory or kitchen in which mineral substances—earths or stones—are decomposed and *cooked* for the nourishment of animal life—had existed,—then animal life could be sustained, and animals were created. But not all animals. The earth was not fit to support the more perfect species. In the first subsiding of the waters into the hollows which they occupy from covering the whole surface, there do not appear to have been any mountains. Mountains were later formations. The surface seems to have been nearly smooth. The shells and the gigantic grasses and reeds whose impression is found in coal, show that what was not sea was a vast marshy level, unfit for human habitation. It was the abode of enormous lizards, such as the iguanodon, whose remains indicate an animal seventy feet long, and of the bulk of an elephant; but there existed an atmosphere and a soil in which man could not subsist.

There was a time when the creatures of one sort had reached that number that it became necessary to check their multiplication; or, by their habits, had wrought such changes on the surface of the globe, as to make the earth habitable for a finer and more complex creation. Then a new formation—the remains of a new and higher order—begin to appear, more nearly resembling man, and giving earnest of his approach; and, as the new race waxes, the old race retires.

At certain epochs, convulsions occur to which the changes which we witness bear no comparison. Once, it would appear, the whole globe was in a state of vapor, (such at least was the opinion of Laplace and Mitscherlich and Cuvier); afterwards of fusion; afterwards solid; then broken up; and such action of waters and fire upon it as to crumble and mix the rocks to form soils; mountain chains were raised—blown up like a blister for several thousand miles together by fire underneath. In this hemisphere, there is one chain extending along the whole western side of the continent, about 8000 miles, from Cape Horn to Behring's Strait. There is another running east and west across the whole of the old world from Cape Finisterre in Spain through Europe and Asia to Behring's Strait.

Then there is a curious fact noticed by Lord Bacon, and though the inference might seem too daring, it is yet repeated by modern geologists, that the shape of the corresponding coasts of Africa and America would induce us to infer that the two continents of Africa and America were once united, the projecting or salient part of the former fitting exactly to the Gulf of Mexico, and the bulging part of South America about Paraiba and Pernambuco being about the size and shape of the Gulf of Guinea.

In fine, the conclusion at which in general geologists have arrived, is, that there had been repeated great convulsions of nature previous to the present order of things; that we now stand in the midst of the fourth succession of terrestrial animals; that after the age of reptiles, after that of palaeotheria, after that of mammoths and mastodons, arrived the age in which the human species together with some domestic animals governs and fertilizes the earth peaceably; and that the present races are not more than five or six thousand years old.

Man is made;—the creature who seems a refinement on the form of all who went before him, and made perfect in the image of the Maker by the gift of moral nature; but his limbs are only a more exquisite organization,—say rather—the finish of the rudimental forms that have been already sweeping the sea and creeping in the mud; the brother of his hand is even now cleaving the Arctic Sea in the fin of the whale, and, innumerable ages since, was pawing the marsh in the flipper of the saurus.

Man is made; and really when you come to see the minuteness of the adaptation in him to the present earth, it suggests forcibly the familiar fact of a father setting up his children at housekeeping, building them a house, laying out the grounds, curing the chimneys, and stocking the cellar.

For, not to leave quite yet the external preparation of the house, modern chemistry has discovered some facts of striking fitness between the atmosphere and the creature who breathes it. Sir Humphrey Davy, it is well known, made experiments on many gases as to their power of supporting respiration; and placing animals in a given quantity of all those which can be breathed at all, he found that none would support life so long as the gas we breathe.

But another observation is much more singular. The common air, as you know, is made up of two gases named oxygen and azote; and the mixture is found to contain four fifths of azote, one fifth of oxygen. Now these airs can be mixed in any proportion, just as salt may be mixed in any proportion with water. They have been mixed by experimenters in different proportions, and respired, and it is found that no other mixture will support respiration so well as four parts and one part. And what makes it more strange, nobody has found out what keeps this invariable proportion in their mixture, but, wherever you procure the air you analyze, whether from the tops of mountains, or the surface of the sea, or the bottom of mines, this uniform proportion of one of oxygen and four of azote is always found, this, namely, which is best suited to the health of man.

Then the texture and the magnitude of the earth are fitted to him. If it were stone, he could not till it. If it were slime, he could not build upon it, or stand upon it. And a strict relation is found to exist between the strength of the muscles and the gravity of the globe.

Finally, a hundred tribes of animals fit for food, and many thousand species of vegetables yielding wholesome and flavored fruits, grow upon and adorn the planet; a state of things for which slow and ancient preparation has been made. In one particular this is especially remarkable.

In the case of coal there is a most singular exhibition of the relation of a long forgotten past to the present hour.

It is well known how much the great development of the commerce of Great Britain and thence of the great civilization of that country is indebted to the boundless abundance of coal in its mines. In consequence of the abundance and accessibility of this mineral in that island, and its opportune association with beds of iron ore and the invariable contiguity of limestone employed to flux the iron, the English have been enabled to surpass all other nations in the cheapness of machinery and so in the extent of their manufactures.

But the coal which geologists have shown to be a vegetable formation,—the relic of forests which existed at an unknown antiquity before the era of the creation of mankind—had been by repeated overflowings of the sea and marine and fresh water deposits and other changes of the surface, buried below the surface at too great a depth to be reached by man.

But before the creation of our race, earthquakes or other convulsions of enormous force have lifted up these mineral beds into ledges, so that they are found extending from one thousand feet above the level of the ocean to unknown depths below it. And so it happens that these vast beds of fuel so essential to man's comfort and civilization, which would have been covered by the crust of the globe forever from his knowledge and use, are thus brought up within reach of his little hands; and a great work of Nature in an antiquity that hath no record—namely the deposit and crystallization of antediluvian forests, is made to contribute to our pleasure and prosperity at this hour.

Well when the house was built and the lands were drained and the house was ventilated and the chimneys of the volcano opened as a safety valve and the cellar stocked—the creature man was formed and put into his habitation. He finds that he can breathe the air and drink the water, he finds too the temperature adjusted to his constitution. The temperature does not pass certain limits. The hottest place on earth by observation is La Guayra in Venezuela, the mean temperature being 82½°; yet at the time the observation was made, that town contained a population of eight thousand souls. The coldest temperature yet observed is about 54 degrees below zero. Yet it was found to be perfectly tolerable so long as the air was still and it is not the cold which has hindered men from reaching the pole, but the mechanical difficulties occasioned by the ice.

I have spoken of the preparation and adaptation of the abode to the inhabitant. I proceed now to the consideration of a fact not less remarkable and admitting no less variety of illustration, though—from whatever cause—it has been less frequently presented. It is this— that a proportion is faithfully kept, in all the arrangements of nature, between the powers of man and the forces with which he is to contend, for his subsistence.

This may be noticed in the animals which surround him. There are none so gigantic but man can tame or slay them. The enormous reptiles and beasts of the elder world have been destroyed before man was created. He is quite able, even in the savage state, to master all those that are alive. His traps or weapons follow every creature into his element, and the whale is not large enough, nor the lion strong enough, nor the falcon swift enough to get away from man, a tender thin skinned creature, without tusks, or claws, or horns or scales. A man cannot swim like a whale, but a man in a boat, can. A man cannot rise into the air to overtake the eagle, but a ball or an arrow can. And it is not only the New Bedford whaleman in a ship of six hundred tons, with a forge and a furnace and huge coppers on board and miles of hempen line and every equipment that American civilization can furnish, that can hunt the behemoth of the waters wherever he swims round the globe, but the poor Esquimaux also, with a harpoon pointed with bone, and inflated sealskins tied to it, contrives to worry to death that enormous and formidable swimmer.

In the first place, then, the animals on the earth are not an overmatch for man. But the fact of the proportion kept between the powers of man and the forces of nature may be observed in many more respects than this one. And in all I think we shall be struck with this fact, that man is made just strong enough to keep his place in the world; that he is not any stronger than he need to be; that the adjustment of his forces to the forces of nature from which he would be in danger, is very nice, and if it had been a little less, would have been insufficient.

And this is what I wish to illustrate.

More than three fifths of the earth's surface are covered by the ocean. Of course, it behoved the creature who was to possess the earth to find the means of crossing the sea. In Shakspeare's comedy, the fairy Puck brags that he "can put a girdle round about the earth in forty minutes." We can scarce go so fast, but the poet would not probably have thought of the thing, but that, in his own time, Sir Francis Drake had done the feat of circumnavigating the globe. It is the very language of his biographer that "his fame will last as long as the world which he for the first time surrounded."

This capital art of navigation of the deep sea deserves much attention, because it so often illustrates in the most forcible manner the smallness of the odds (if I may say so) that exist in favor of man, the nearness with which he comes to the edge of destruction and yet has powers just sufficient to bring him off in total safety. The man who has all his life been dwelling in the interior, and who comes to the coast and embarks on the sea, and finds himself for the first time in a tempest, tossed upon a roaring ocean, cannot suppress his astonishment at the daring of this enterprize. It seems to him foolhardy—a rash encounter of a most unequal and tremendous risk. But it is not. These chances are all counted and weighed and measured, and a faithful experience has begotten this confidence in the proportioned strength of spars and rigging to the ordinary forces of wind and water. This confidence being habitual constitutes the essence of the sailor's fearlessness. The danger is incessant, and the safety of the ship requires incessant attention, but that not failing, the real risk is small. Every one who has been at sea remembers probably many moments of imminent danger. Every ship has all but struck—has been within an inch of destruction fifty times. And yet how comparatively rare are fatal accidents.

A landsman at sea can scarce bring himself to rely on a reckoning scientifically kept. Much less, until he has learned the precision of a seaman's hand and eye, upon a longitude ascertained by so coarse and clumsy means as heaving the log once in two hours. But a skilful seaman seems to guess his way along with a success sometimes surprizing. About a year ago, I was a passenger on board a brig which sailed from Boston for the Mediterranean. Like most vessels of her class, she had no chronometer, and kept her reckoning by the log. At sunset, on the sixteenth day, we looked for St. Mary's, the southernmost of the Azores, but the weather was thick in the east, and we saw nothing. At nine o'clock in the evening, we descried that island,—a mere black hummock of land,—and the master's log-book being then produced, his reckoning was found to agree with our bearings within one mile.

This result astonished himself. There was in it perhaps as much chance as skill. But the chronometer and quadrant make the traveller's way over the sea as plain as in a county road. It is told of an excellent seaman of our own, who made the shortest voyage that has yet been made across the Atlantic,—accomplishing the passage from Liverpool to Boston in fourteen days,—that he had such confidence in the accuracy of his longitude, that on approaching the coast without seeing the land, he continued running in for Boston harbour though the weather was very thick. The passengers in a body intreated him to take in sail, and wait for clear weather, but in vain. Presently a man before cried "A sail!" "A sail, you simpleton," replied the Captain, "it is the lighthouse; starboard helm!" It was the lighthouse, and he ran round it, and presently came to anchor within the bay.

So narrow is the interval between perfect safety and total destruction. It is told of the same chivalrous sailor that in his voyages he rarely went below into the cabin, but slept on deck in the cable tier, for fear his mate should take in sail.

I am tempted to add yet one more instance to show how slight a circumstance may turn the balance in human favor, so nicely adjusted are our dangers to our powers. This is a very odd but very simple expedient by which a ship was saved, which is related in the Voyages of Dampier, the excellent English navigator, in his account of a dreadful storm which he encountered off the Cape de Verd islands. "The ship was scudding before wind and sea, under bare poles, when, by the inadvertence of the master, she was broached to and lay in the trough of the sea; the waves at that time running tremendously high, and threatening to overwhelm her, so that if one had struck on the deck, she must have foundered. The person who had committed this nearly fatal mistake, was in a state of distraction, and roared for any one to cut away the mizenmast to give the ship a chance of righting. All was confusion and dismay, the Captain and the officer second in command objecting to this as a certainly hazardous and probably useless attempt to save themselves. The whole crew had given themselves up for lost, when a seaman called to Dampier to ascend the foreshrouds with him; this, the man alleged, might make the ship wear, as he had seen the plan succeed before now. As he spoke, he mounted, and Dampier followed him. They went half shrouds up, spread out the flaps of their coats, and in three minutes the ship wore, though such had been the violence of the tempest, that the mainsail having got loose, as many men as could lie on it, assisted by all on deck, and though the mainyard was nearly level with the deck, were not able to furl it."

Now I say this is a striking example to show how nearly balanced are the chances of safety and destruction to man, when the ready recollection of one sailor, and so slight a circumstance as the purchase afforded to the wind by the skirts of the coats of two men, is sufficient to turn the odds in favor of man.

But these are solitary examples. Every one familiar with the sea and with histories of sea voyages will remember a multitude of similar escapes. By such simple expedients does the wit of man bring him off safe from hazards the most fearful. And so various and flexible has he contrived to make the form of his ship which in a few minutes the nimble sailors can change from the shape of a butterfly—all wing—to the shape of a log which the waves may toss and welcome; and so they go on, through all that is sublime and terrible in nature, and lose entirely the feeling of the extraordinary; the thunder may roar, the "dirty southwester" may crack his cheeks; the ship's bulwarks may be swept clean off; but the cook in his caboose never fails one morning or evening of discharging his benevolent office, and, after an incessant peril of five or six months, brings back every old trunk and cracked plate safe across half the globe.

I think the history of navigation affords the most striking instances, but by no means the only ones, of the accurate adjustment of the powers to the wants of man. The same balance is everywhere kept. A man is always in danger, and never. It is said that in battle the eye is first conquered. "Primi in proeliis oculi vincuntur." Let a man keep his presence of mind, and there is scarcely any danger so desperate from which he cannot deliver himself. For there is a very wide interval betwixt danger and destruction which men in peaceful pursuits seldom consider. A man in his parlor in this civil town, thinks that to meet a lion in the desert, or to stumble over an alligator in wading knee deep through a savannah, is certain destruction. But the Fellatahs of Africa, or the Caribee Indians think no such thing. Their habitual acquaintance with these delicate circumstances, has taught them to see a wide distance betwixt danger and death, and in that discrimination their safety lies. Mungo Park rode slowly by a red lion, expecting every moment the fatal spring. Humboldt, having left his boat on the river Orinoco, to examine some natural objects on the bank, suddenly found himself near a large jaguar, and "though extremely frightened, he retained sufficient self command to follow the advice which the Indians had so often given, and continued to walk without moving his arms, making a large circuit towards the edge of the water." The tiger did not move from the spot. An Indian girl at Urituco being seized by a crocodile—she immediately felt for his eyes and thrust her fingers into them and thus compelled the animal to let her go, though with the loss of an arm. And Dampier relates what befel one of his companions in Honduras—that wading in a meadow his knee was seized by an alligator; he quietly waited till the animal loosened its teeth to take a new and surer hold, and when it did, he snatched away his knee interposing the butt end of his gun in its stead, which the animal seized so firmly that it was snatched out of the man's hand, and carried off.

Indeed I hardly know whether we need go so far to find the proofs of this adjustment between man and external nature. Perhaps an attentive consideration of the hazards that are daily met in the prosecution of many of the outdoor trades, and even in riding or swimming, or in many games, would furnish as conclusive evidence of the uniform existence of the fact. And when we have reckoned the numberless perils, to which a very superficial knowledge of the anatomy of man shows us we are exposed in every hour of the most peaceful and sheltered life, I cannot but think that the mere existence in full possession of all their organs of sense, of *old persons*, if it were not so familiar, would be a most surprizing phenomenon.

This leads me to another consideration upon which the balance we have been considering depends, namely, the manner in which man's supreme reason is seconded by the perfect constitution of his own frame. Behold the beautiful form of the skeleton, that elegant strong and flexible box in which is packed up his nervous and sentient organization; the delicate but durable health of the system; the exquisite sensibility of a skin so acutely alive to pain that, it has been well said, it makes a better guard to him from danger, than would the hide of a rhinoceros; his ear and lungs nicely adapted to the air; his eye to the light; his palate to the flavors of vegetables; and all his powers adapted to and concentrating their action upon his hand, that unrivalled machine.

Nothing contributes more directly to human efficiency in the planet where we live, than the perfect inter-accommodation of all these senses. The eye is a miracle; the hand is another. A third is their mutual adjustment. Most of the gentlemen present, down to the very youngest, will remember the time when they studied the art of throwing a stone. I well remember my own vain endeavors to make the stone hit the mark, by all the nicety I could use in carrying the hand skilfully, until, by chance, I one day forgot to attend to the motion of my hand at all, and looking only at the mark, the stone struck it. There is a time when every boy learns this secret, that the eye and the hand are so wonderfully adjusted, that if the eye is fixed intently on the mark, the hand is sure to throw truly. I will not stop to draw the fine moral which speaks from this fact; but must not omit to mention the equal adjustment of the hand to the ear and voice in music, nay of the hand to the whole body. For you can put your hand upon any point of your body as well with your eyes shut as open.

In like manner are all the senses fitted to each other. Every one may observe the relation between the eye and the voice. It is a common rule given to young speakers, to fix the eye upon a person in the remote corner of the house, for, by so doing, the voice naturally elevates itself to such a pitch that that person can hear.

I notice these adaptations in this connexion because this minuteness of finish in the human system is the essential element of his power. It has been said, "if the hand had not been divided to fingers, man would still be wild in the forest." This symmetry of parts is his equipment for the conquest of nature.

In pursuing these observations upon the reference that exists to Man in nature, another fact which commands our attention is the manner in which man is led on by his wants to the development of his powers and so to the possession of the globe. By the geographical distribution of animals, plants, and minerals, he is forced to be a traveller and a merchant as much as by hunger he is made a hunter or a shepherd. Nature has no capital city where she accumulates her splendid treasures. She has divided her goods among all the zones. It has been said, "Every degree of latitude has its own fruit." Food is in one place, spice in another, medicine in a third, clothing in a fourth; arms in a fifth; beasts of burden in a sixth; ornaments in a seventh. And so she acquaints her children with each other, and contrives to impart whatever invention one man makes, to millions. On this great market of the world she gives opportunity to each, to ask after the family of the other, and what are the news.

May I add that there is a like equality in distributing even the decoration of the globe, as if that the shows of nature might attract so imaginative a creature from his native spot. In the south is hung the famous constellation of the Southern Cross and the Magellanic Clouds. But there is no rose in the southern hemisphere. That is one of the ornaments of the temperate zone. The equator is encumbered with magnificence of its vegetable and animal productions, and its atmospheric phenomena. But the gloom of the Pole is not without its glories,—its sublime twilights and unimaginable auroras. In the east is the baobab and the banian, and Himmaleh. In the west, Niagara. In Sumatra is the largest flower, the Rafflesia, three feet in diameter. In the islands the cocoa, in the desert the date.

Another important fact which illustrates the relation between man's condition and his powers, is found in the servitude of the lower animals. Here is a new example of the accuracy with which he is adapted not to the elements only, but to the inhabitants of the earth, and of the pliancy of his own powers and habits which permit him to live in such strict relations to them. Ages ago it was settled that man should be master. But in some respects, these creatures are wiser than he is, as they have instincts, and he has none, or none that he does not outgrow. But he has eyes and reason, and contrives to avail himself of these instincts as he would of mechanical powers. And so he "learns from the dog the physic of the field."

A species of cuckoo, called indicator, or honey-guide attracts the attention of the Hottentots by its shrill cry, and, as soon as he is observed, he flutters on to the hive of a wild bee, in hopes of sharing the honey. When the Buccaneers landed upon desert parts of South America or the West Indies, they were usually guided in their selection of unknown fruits by the birds, never eating any that were not pecked.

We have long forgotten this humble origin of our most valuable knowledge, but the debt is probably very great. Why need I recur to the conspicuous fitness of the camel to the man of the desert, the reindeer to the man of the snow, the llama to the man of the cordilleras? I prefer the picture familiar to our own eyes. See how this wary lord of the world has gone into Persia and brought thence a beautiful species of pheasant and set him down in the farmyard to strut with his tidy family of hens around the barn door. He has brought home from Southern Africa the gloved cat, to be the sentinel of his pantry. He has tamed the jackal of Syria and by domestication and improvement of the race, has made the faithful dog. He has found in Tartary or Arabia a small wild lean ragged looking animal and by cultivation of the race has formed the domestic horse, the noblest of animals and the most important auxiliary of man, who flies over the ground at the rate of a mile in a minute. He has put the boar of Europe in a sty, and the sheep in a fold. On the sunny side of his house he puts a box of wood or straw for an insect family of little distillers who suck the honey from all the flowers within a mile of his dwelling, and bring it home to him. He has tamed the goose and the duck and the turkey and lives surrounded and beloved by his slaves.

One fact seems to mark a relation yet more intimate. He has learned from the chance experience of some dairy-maids to inoculate his flesh with a disease from the udder of a cow, and by that means to defend himself from a more dangerous disease to which his own race are subject.

Let us now proceed in our observation of man's aptitude to the surrounding objects from the animate to the inanimate creation. See what a skilful and beneficent hand he has laid upon the globe. Not finding the world in its original state sufficiently commodious, he has undertaken to alter and amend it. He may be said to keep the world in repair. A German naturalist has shown that it is the tendency of every river in the course of time to elevate its bed. Two great rivers in the north of Italy, the Adige and the Po, are at this moment higher than all the land which lies between them. The territory is too valuable to be made a marsh. It is the garden of Lombardy and so the inhabitants build up their dikes above the tops of the houses of Ferrara. The whole province of Holland lies lower than the level of the sea, and a population of 820,000 souls see the waters of the Rhine and Meuse constantly suspended twenty or thirty feet above their heads. Wherever cities are built, the sea is kept out where it tends to encroach on the shore. The beds of rivers are cleared of obstructions and deepened by art to redeem the adjacent land from swamp. Bogs are drained and converted into firm land. Oaks are transplanted and a forest of fullgrown trees suddenly rises upon desolate heaths. The Swiss carries up the soil which is to form his garden, in baskets, and lays it down on the granite floor of the Alps. Downs formed by the blowing of the sand drifts from the seashore are confined by the beach grass, and the arable land saved from desolation. Climate is ameliorated by cultivation and not only the climate softened, but the air purified, and made healthful by the same cause.

> Yet nature is made better by no mean
> But nature makes that mean.

By the study of nature he improves nature, and keeps the world in repair. For, if the human race should be totally destroyed, it would take no very long time for the sea and the sand and the rivers and the bogs to make most parts of the earth uninhabitable by men.

But perhaps the most striking effect of the accurate adaptation of man to the globe is found in his love of it. The love of nature—the accord between man and the external world,—what is it but the perception how truly all our senses, and, beyond the senses, the soul, are tuned to the order of things in which we live? The constant familiarity with the objects of nature, the use of water, of fire, of the air, and sunshine, are not more necessary than they are delightful. The exercise of all the senses is an intense pleasure, as anyone will find, who recovers the use of one after being deprived of it. The effects of light and shade out of doors, the sight of an extended landscape, the wilderness of beautiful flowers by which the vegetable race is perpetuated, delight all men. Whoever has recovered from sickness, has remarked the picturesque appearance which the most common objects wore on his first ride or walk abroad. Perhaps he then found for the first time that the pigeon in the street was a handsome bird, that the trees grew in elegant forms,— and the outline of the mountains against the sky—he was never weary of gazing at.

Go into the country in the month of June or September, and stand upon a hillside in the morning, and listen to the sounds that rise from all the farms around;—the lowing of the cattle, the sound of falling water, the various cries of the domestic fowls, the notes of wild birds, and the distant voice of man,—and judge if some adjustment has not been made to fit this concert to your ear. So the scents of flowers are fitted to the sense of smell.

So with the eye. In all the variations of nature the eye is still suited. I said go into the country in June—but go in December, go at midnight, go in the mist, in the rain, in hailstorms, with thunder and lightning, at blazing noon or at daybreak and you shall find there are states of feeling in your mind which correspond to all these phenomena.

This pleasure of a conversation with nature is conspicuously exhibited in the habits of savages who cannot be won by any luxuries from the wild enjoyments of the forest.

"It is no new thing," says an old traveller in Campeachy and Honduras, "for the Indians in these woody parts of America to fly away whole towns at once, and settle themselves in the unfrequented woods to enjoy their freedom; and, if they are accidentally discovered, they will remove again, which they can easily do, their household goods being little else but their hammocks and their calabashes. They build every man his own house, and tie up their hammocks between two trees, wherein they sleep till their houses are made. The woods afford them some subsistence, such as pecaree; but they that are thus strolling or *marooning*, as the Spaniards call it, have plantain walks that no man knows but themselves, and from thence they have their food till they have raised plantation provision near their new built town. They clear no more ground than what they actually employ for their subsistence. They make no paths, but when they go far from home they break now and then a bough letting it hang down which serves as a mark to guide them in their return." Humboldt in his account of the Chayma Indians on the banks of the Colorado, attests the same fact. "Besides their cabin in the village, they usually have a smaller covered with palm or plantain leaves in some solitary place in the woods, to which they retire as often as they can; and so strong is the desire among them of enjoying the pleasures of savage life, that the children sometimes wander entire days in the forests. In fact, the towns are often almost wholly deserted."

Certainly the wild man exhibits his delight in God's world more steadily than we, but the walls of cities and their artificial modes of life have not yet tamed the savage in us. The festival of May Day finds such obstinate favor in our hearts, that even our cold winds cannot keep the young crowds at home. Every one has noticed, as well as Chaucer, that there is a season in the year when folk long to make journeys.

> Then longen folk to gon on pilgrimages,
> And palmers for to seeken strange strondes,
> To serve the holies known in sundry londes.

And the greediness with which a rose, a dahlia, a bulbous root or an Aaron's rod or some green leaf is planted in every body's sitting room attests the universal presence of the same desires.

But the most interesting and valuable form which this inextinguishable propensity in us assumes is the love of the Natural Sciences. The same organization which creates in the Chayma Indian such thirst and hunger for his boundless woods, which makes a sunny meadow spotted with flowers and visited by birds such a paradise to a child, is the cause in cultivated men of that interest in natural objects and processes which expresses itself in the sciences of botany, of zoology, of chemistry, and astronomy. The pursuit of these sciences has gradually disclosed a new and noble view of man's relation to the globe.

With the progress of the cultivation of the species the globe itself both in the mass and in its minutest part, becomes to man a school of science. For, to begin with that which is the most perfect of the sciences, to what is owing that wonderful completeness of the records in which the complex revolutions of all the bodies in the immense spaces of the universe are computed and written down, as if this planet were a living eye sailing through space to watch them? Is it not because the earth is to the astronomer a *moveable observatory*, enabling him to change his place in the universe, and get a base of two hundred millions of miles, as a surveyor would take new stations in a field to form triangles? Whilst thus the astronomer makes the earth a platform to hold his telescope and vary his observations, the geologist finds the old ball to be a register of periods of time otherwise immeasureable. Shells and fossils are the coins from which he deciphers the history of forgotten ages. Some idea of the riches of the means which the earth affords to these investigations may be formed from the fact that the savans of France have detected more than eight hundred species of shells, almost all unknown in the existing seas, in the limestone of Paris; that Cuvier has determined and classed the remains of more than one hundred and fifty mammiferous and oviparous animals, ninety of which are wholly unknown at present among living species.

Professor Buckland after having proved the identity of an antediluvian animal whose remains had been discovered, with the hyena now living in Africa, has confirmed the proof by an actual comparison of the relics of the last meal of the fossil animal—a mass of digested bone—with a similar mass that has traversed the organs of a living animal; and, it is said, an experienced eye does not readily discern the difference. And Cuvier has ascertained a disputed point—that the bird mummies which were found in the pyramids of Egypt, having a beak precisely similar to an ibis now found in the Nile not a serpent eater, *were serpent eaters,* by finding in the mummy the undigested remains of the skin and scales of serpents.

Once upon this track of scientific research, every thing invites man, aids him and unexpected disclosures start up in every corner. It is already impossible to name an object large or small existing in nature which has not been the subject of searching inquiry. The habits of microscopic insects are examined as the habits of elephants. Classification has got down to them. In the Regne Animal, I find the genus of Monades thus defined: "A genus of insects of the order infusoria. The generic character is a worm invisible to the naked eye, simple, pellucid, and resembling a point. The genus includes five species." Meantime the chemist decomposes bodies supposed to be simple, and almost anticipates the resolving all created things into a few gases, perhaps two, perhaps one. At the same time we seem to be approaching the elemental secrets of nature in finding the principle of Polarity in all the laws of matter, in light, heat, magnetism, and electricity. And how long before the laws of life will be laid open to the researches of the physiologist?

Now what is the conclusion from these hasty and to some it may appear miscellaneous sketches of the relations of man to the objects around him? I have spoken of the preparation made for man in the slow and secular changes and melioration of the surface of the planet. We have seen that as soon as he could live upon it, he was created; that the air was mixed to suit his lungs; that the temperature ranges between extremes tolerable to him; that the texture of the earth is fit; that the mineral treasures are conveniently bestowed for his use; then, that a most nicely adjusted proportion is established betwixt his powers and the forces with which he has to deal,—provided for in the excellent construction of his frame; then, that such an arrangement of the gifts of nature is made, as to invite man out to activity and commerce; then, that he forms mutually serviceable relations with his fellow creatures the brutes; then, that he improves the face of the planet itself; then, that not only a relation of use but a relation of beauty subsists between himself and nature, which leads him to Science; and, finally, that once embarked on that pursuit, all things stimulate and instruct him,—the dewdrop is a lecture, the rainbow a professor, the white Alps a specimen, the hurricane an experiment, the mine a book, and the planet in its orbit only a ship to transport the astronomer and his telescopes through the navigable heavens to more convenient stations of observation.

In the view of all these facts I conclude that other creatures reside in particular places as fishes in the sea, turtles in the mud, moles in the earth, camels in the desert, birds in the air, but the residence of man is the world. It was given him to possess it. I conclude further, that the snail is not more accurately adjusted to his shell than man to the globe he inhabits; that not only a perfect symmetry is discoverable in his limbs and senses between the head and the foot, between the hand and the eye, the heart and the lungs,—but an equal symmetry and proportion is discoverable between him and the air, the mountains, the tides, the moon, and the sun. I am not impressed by solitary marks of designing wisdom; I am thrilled with delight by the choral harmony of the whole. Design! It is all design. It is all beauty. It is all astonishment.

The Naturalist

(1834)

Emerson delivered "The Naturalist" to the Boston Natural History Society on May 7, 1834. Although speaking to the same audience that he addressed in "The Uses of Natural History," Emerson makes clear in his introduction the lecture's more formal occasion—the annual meeting of the society. Unlike the previous three natural history lectures, which were grounded in observable, scientific facts, "The Naturalist" is a philosophical reflection on the role of science in American culture. This discussion is strongly influenced by the scientific writings of Coleridge, Carlyle, and Goethe, whose work Emerson was reading at the time. While his previous lyceum lectures expressed an overwhelming enthusiasm for the possibilities of science, here Emerson tempers his praise with a prescient recognition of the potential "evils of Science." His reluctance to fully embrace science rests on a wariness about the overspecialization of a scientist's focus in a specific field and a concern for the dulling influence of technological forms of observation and measurement. Emerson worried that science might isolate the individual from the larger system of nature by focusing too closely on the minute details of that system. To safeguard against this narrowing of focus, Emerson turns to the arts. He praises the poet's efforts to express a sense of interconnectivity across apparent distinctions; however, he finds fault in the poet's imagination if it distances him or her too far from the material world. Hoping to overcome these shortcomings, Emerson identifies the work of a broad-minded naturalist as a solution. "A poet in his severest analysis," Emerson's idealized naturalist uses both the close observation of the scientist and the imagination of the poet to discern and express an understanding of humanity's relationship to nature. Emerson thus concludes his first lecture series for the lyceum by staking out a middle ground between the sciences and arts—ground he would occupy for the remainder of his career as a public intellectual.

♣

Gentlemen,

The Curators have honored me with the task of preparing an Address to the Society agreeably to the custom of its annual meetings. I shall use the occasion to consider a question which though it have not equal interest for all has great interest for many of us: What is the place of Natural History in Education? It is but a small portion of this society who have time to devote themselves exclusively to Natural History. Perhaps it is better we should not.

But the question occurs to a man mainly engaged in far different pursuits whether it is wise to embark at all in a pursuit in which it is plain he must content himself with quite superficial knowledge; whether it is no waste of time to study a new and tedious classification. I shall treat this question not for the Natural Philosopher but for the Man, and offer you some thoughts upon the intellectual influences of Natural Science.

I shall say what in my opinion is to excuse such persons as myself who without any hope of becoming masters of any department of natural science so as to attain the rank of original observers, do yet find a gratification in coming here to school, and in reading the general results of Naturalists and learning so much of the classifications of the sciences as shall enable us to understand their discoveries.

That the study of Nature should occupy some place, that it will occupy some place in education, in spite of the worst perversion or total neglect, is certain. I knew a person who sailed from Boston to Charleston, S. C. and never saw the water. But nature takes care generally that we shall see the water and the snow, the forest, the swamp, the mountain, the eclipse, the comet, the northern lights, and all her commanding phenomena.

The streets of towns cannot so completely hide the face of heaven and the face of the earth but that every generous and penetrating genius is generally found to have an interest in the works of Creation. The imagery in discourse which delights all men is that which is drawn from observation of natural processes. It is this which gives that piquancy to the conversation of a strong-minded farmer or backwoodsman which all men relish.

But it is said that Man is the only object of interest to Man. I fully believe it. I believe that the constitution of man is the centre from which all our speculations depart. But it is the wonderful charm of external nature that man stands in a central connexion with it all; not at the head, but in the midst: and not an individual in the kingdom of organized life but sends out a ray of relation to him. So that all beings seem to serve such an use as that which is sought in comparative anatomy. We study our own structure magnified or simplified in each one.

In a generous education certainly the Earth, which is the bountiful mother and nurse, the abode, the stimulus, the medicine, and the tomb of us all, will not, nor will our fellow-creatures in it, fail of our attention. These objects are the most ancient and permanent whereof we have any knowledge. If our restless curiosity lead us to unearth the buried cities and dig up the mummy pits and spell out the abraded characters on Egyptian stones, shall we see a less venerable antiquity in the clouds and the grass? An everlasting Now reigns in Nature that produces on our bushes the selfsame Rose which charmed the Roman and the Chaldaean. The grain and the vine, the ant and the moth are as long-descended. The slender violet hath preserved in the face of the sun and moon the humility of his line and the oldest work of man is an upstart by the side of the shells of the sea.

But the antiquity of these objects is merely a claim upon the feelings. They have another claim upon the Understanding, which especially concerns us in this view of intellectual influences—they are perfect creatures. It is the result of all philosophy if it is not born with us—an assured optimism. When Lagrange and Laplace found out the periodicity of the errors of the heavenly bodies and thence the stability of the

Solar System was the result unexpected by any mind? Whatever theology or philosophy we rest in, or labor after, the students of Nature have all agreed that in Nature nothing is false or unsuccessful. That which is aimed at is attained, and by means elegant and irresistible. The whole force of the Creation is concentrated upon every point. What agencies of electricity, gravity, light, affinity, combine to make every plant what it is, and in a manner so quiet that the presence of these tremendous powers is not ordinarily suspected. Woven in their loom every plant, every animal is finished and perfect as the world. A willow or an apple is a perfect being; so is a bee or a thrush. The best poem or statue or picture is not. This is the view which so much impressed the celebrated Goethe, whose life was a study of the Theory of Art, that he said "no man should be admitted into his Republic, who was not versed in Natural History."

There is deep reason for the love of nature that has characterized the highest minds. The soul and the body of things are harmonized; therefore the deeper is a man's insight into the spiritual laws the more intense will be his love of the works of nature.

"The smallest production of nature," says Goethe, "has the circle of its completeness within itself and I have only need of eyes to see with, in order to discover the relative proportions. I am perfectly sure that within this circle however narrow, an entirely genuine existence is enclosed. A work of art, on the other hand, has its completeness out of itself. The Best lies in the idea of the artist which he seldom or never reaches: all the rest lies in certain conventional rules which are indeed derived from the nature of art and of mechanical processes but still are not so easy to decipher as the laws of living nature. In works of art there is much that is traditional; the works of nature are ever a freshly uttered Word of God." Perhaps it is the province of poetry rather than of prose to describe the effect upon the mind and heart of these nameless influences. Certainly he that has formed his ideas of adaptation of beauty on these models can have nothing mean in his estimate and hence Fourier said of Laplace in his eulogy before the French Academy, "What Laplace called great, was great."

It is fit that man should look upon Nature with the eye of the Artist, to learn from the great Artist whose blood beats in our veins, whose taste is upspringing in our own perception of beauty, the laws by which our hands should work that we may build St. Peter'ses or paint Transfigurations or sing Iliads in worthy continuation of the architecture of the Andes, of the colors of the sky and the poem of life.

And as we have said in the first place these individual forms are perfect, let us speak now of the secret of their composition.

Nothing strikes me more in Nature than the effect of Composition, the contrast between the simplicity of the means and the gorgeousness of the result. Nature is particularly skilled in that rule of arithmetic called Permutation and Combination. Sometimes it is so amusing as to remind us of the French cook who could make forty dishes out of macaroni. A few elements has Nature converted into the countless variety of substances that fill the earth. Look at the grandeur of the prospect from a mountain top. It is composed of not many materials continually repeated in new unions.

Composition is more important than the elegance of individual forms. Every artist knows that beyond its own beauty the object has an additional grace from relation to surrounding objects. The most elegant shell in your cabinet does not produce such effect on the eye as the contrast and combination of a group of ordinary sea shells lying together wet upon the beach. I remember when I was a boy going upon the shore and being charmed with the colors and forms of the shells. I gathered up many and put them in my pocket. When I got home I could find nothing that I gathered, nothing but some dry, ugly mussels and snails. Thence I learned that Composition was more important than the beauty of individual forms to effect. On the shore they lay wet and social by the sea and under the sky. The smell of a field surpasses the scent of any flower and the selection of the prism is not comparable to the confusion of a sunset. A hillside expresses what has never been written down.

We are provoked by seeing how simple are the principles of her architecture. The tree is not, the botanist finds, a single structure but a vast assemblage of individuals. The difference between animal and vegetable textures is very slight at their commencement. Cellular tissue and animal fibre being similar and the vesicle and spiculum—hydrogen and oxygen deriving their original combination perhaps from their polarity—all grows up from plus and minus. How beautiful a shell is the Buccinum Harpa! but when we see that every one of these polished ridges that adorn its surface like harpstrings was in turn the outer lip the wonder is less. So many of the forms in conchology were originally determined perhaps by a mere projection. Give water in a cup a revolving motion, and it immediately assumes precisely the form most common in shells, that of the operculum of the buccinums—or helix.

"I am persuaded," said Fontenelle, "that if the majority of mankind could be made to see the order of the Universe such as it is, as they would not remark in it any virtues attached to certain numbers, nor any properties inherent in certain planets, nor fatalities in certain times and revolutions of these, they would not be able to restrain themselves on the sight of this admirable regularity and beauty from crying out with astonishment, 'What! Is this all?'"

There are specific advantages of such studies that deserve to be enumerated under the head of intellectual influences.

They restrain Imitation—Imitation, the vice of overcivilized communities. To take an example. Imitation is the vice eminently of our times, of our literature, of our manners and social action. All American manners, language, and writing are derivative. We do not write from facts, but we wish to state facts after the English manner. It is at once our strength and weakness that there is an immense floating diction from which always we draw, to which by the ear we always seek to accommodate our expression.

It is the tax we pay for the splendid inheritance of the English literature. We are exonerated by the sea and the revolution from the national debt but we pay this which is rather the worst part. Time will certainly cure us, probably through the prevalence of a bad party ignorant of all literature and of all but selfish, gross pursuits. But a better cure would be in the study of Natural History. Imitation is a servile copying of what is capricious as if it were permanent forms of Nature.

The study of things leads us back to Truth, to the great Network of organized beings made of our own flesh and blood with kindred functions and related organs and one Cause.

Another part of the intellectual discipline of Natural Science is that it sharpens the discrimination. It teaches the difficult art of distinguishing between the similar and the same. The whole study of Nature is perpetual division and subdivision and again new distinctions. And all these distinctions are real. There is no false logic in Nature. All its properties are permanent: the acids and metals never lie; their yea is yea; their nay, nay. They are newly discovered but not new. The Light yields to Dr. Brewster its unequivocal answer when he puts the dilemma but it has published the same fact to the Universe every moment since the beginning undiscerned.

Natural objects are so sharply discriminated; an oak is so unlike an orange, wax and iron so different, and any mistake in practice is so promptly exposed that it is to be desired, that so many dull understandings who make no distinctions should be set to making chemical mixtures or classifying plants. What pity, instead of that equal and identical praise which enters into all biographies and spreads poppies over all, that writers of characters cannot be forced to describe men so that they shall be known apart even if it were copied from the sharp marks of Botany, such as *dry, solitary, sour, plausible, prosing,* which were worth a graveyard of obituaries.

These are specific advantages to be sought in Education from Science.

But as we have to do now with its true place and influences there are some important distinctions to be made. We are not only to have the aids of Science but we are to recur to Nature to guard us from the evils of Science.

We are the cossets of civilization, a refinement which consists very much in multiplying comforts and luxuries, which gives us pins and caoutchouc and watches and almanacks and has the bad effect that crutches have of destroying the use of the limbs they are meant to aid. The clock and compass do us harm by hindering us from astronomy. We have made civil months until the natural signs, the solstices and the equinoxes, most men do not know. Find me a savage who does not know them. Even the farmer is losing the power to tell the hour by the sun, or of finding the compass-points by the same means, or by the pole star; and even the botanist in his skill in names is ignorant of the properties of plants. We need study to repair just that loss. In cities we are in danger of forgetting our relation to the planet and the system. There are people in Venice it is said who never leave the quarter of the city where they are born. That is one of the uses the stars render us, looking down from their far and solemn heights into every narrow and deep lane, forcibly admonishing the eye that by chance catches their beam of higher relations than he ordinarily remembers.

I cannot but think that a ramble in the country with the set purpose of observation to most persons whose duties confine them much to the city will be a useful lesson. By such excursions the student will see a day perhaps in a light in which he never regarded it. We are so enslaved by art that we always know it is about half-past four or twenty minutes of five. But go out into the woods, break your hours, carry your biscuit in your pocket, and you shall see a day as an astronomical phenomenon. You shall forget your near and petty relations to Boston and Cambridge and see nothing but the noble earth on which you was born and the great star which enlightens and warms it. The contented clouds shall be to you an image of peace. The pines glittering with their innumerable green needles in the light every breath of air will make audible. "It is Day. It is Day." That is all which Heaven saith. Then look about you and see the manifold works of which day is the occasion. At first all is solitary. You think nothing lives there. But wait a little. Hundreds of eyes and ears watched your approach. The rabbit bounded away as you entered the field. The snake glided off at the noise of your approach from the very rock on which you stand, the bee flew from the neighboring shrub, the titmouse has only taken the next pinetree, and listen a moment, and you shall hear the ground robin scratching the leaves at the side of the brook. The population of the fields is denser than that of the towns. More races here than families there.

Nature is the adroitest economist in her housekeeping and 'tis worth an especial visit to the fields to see how many creatures she contrives to tuck away in a single acre of ground without confusion or crowding.

The schoolbooks say, to illustrate the porosity of matter: Fill a tub with cannon balls, then the interstices with bullets, then the interstices with shot, and the interstices with powder. But in nature every layer of the air and of the soil hath its population and every individual its parasite. She puts the ox in the field; the bird on the bough; the insect at the flower; the scaraboeus in the rut; the turtle in the pool; woodpecker in rotten tree; the moth on the leaf; the squirrel; the hawk wheeling up to heaven; in the small interstices of the stones she hatches under a silver counterpane a spider's egg and every one of these creatures is ridden by some happy aphides and apply the microscope to the aphis and lo! the eater is eaten. Nor when you become acquainted with these centres of life will you despise them because their way of life is limited to a rood of ground. They have a life as large as yours. For their fine functions and senses stretch away into that other infinity of minute division which the microscope and the laws of polarization and chemistry have been opening to man, and there is as great an interval between a grain of sand and nothing as there is between the visible universe and the space in which it is swallowed as an atom.

As by aid of art we approach them, dust and mould quicken into races of beings, dots become genera, and, past the limit of unarmed vision, there is an infinite creation in intense activity between us and the negative Pole.

But having stated particular advantages I know that these may be met by statements of particular disadvantages and no study can be truly recommended but by showing in it an absolute Universal fitness that transcends all considerations of place, profession, age, and the like that induce us to prefer one or another liberal pursuit. Natural History seeks more directly that which all sciences, arts, and trades seek mediately—knowledge of the world we live in. Here it touches directly the highest question of philosophy, Why and How any thing is?

No reflecting man but asks these questions and however insolvable they appear would deem it brutish not to ask them of himself. We are possessed with a conviction that Nature means something, that the flower, the animals, the sea, the rock have some relation to us not understood which if known would make them more significant. As men have been fingering the characters that are carved on the Egyptian remains these thousand years, sure that they mean something if we could only find out the cipher, so for a much longer period men have been groping at the hieroglyphics of Nature to find out the cipher, assured that they mean something, assured that we shall understand ourselves better for what we shall read in the sea and the land and the sky. This their open secret is not translateable into words but is to make the face of the earth as much more to me than it is now as is a mountain chain to Humboldt than to his muleteer.

Natural History seeks directly to provide this key or dictionary by observing and recording the properties of every individual and determining its place in the Universe by its properties.

Men of extraordinary powers of a contemplative mind have in all ages pondered this secret: Pythagoras, Swedenborg, Goethe, not to mention the Brahmins. These have sought to give an explanation of Nature; of beasts, plants, minerals.

The Persian said that Oromasdes made good creatures, Ahriman the evil. Pythagoras said that the soul of man endured penance in the low forms of ferocious, gluttonous, obscene beasts. The pig was the purgatory of the glutton. A like faith had the Brahmin. Swedenborg taught that the soul creates evermore the body; that certain affections clothe themselves in certain forms as cunning in the fox, innocence in the lamb, cruelty in the laughing hyena. These opinions have failed to persuade men of their truth and yet are all valuable as the materials of truth, as proofs of an obstinate belief in the human mind that these creatures have a relation to itself.

This instinct is to be the guide, the god of inquiry or it will never come to anything. Natural History is making with knife and scales and alembic the Theory conform to the fact. It is for want of this marriage that both remain unfruitful. The poet loses himself in imaginations and for want of accuracy is a mere fabulist; his instincts unmake themselves and are tedious words. The savant on the other hand losing sight of the end of his inquiries in the perfection of his manipulations becomes an apothecary, a pedant.

I fully believe in both, in the poetry and in the dissection. I believe that we shall by and by know as The Arabian Nights tell us what the social birds say when they sit in the autumn in council chattering upon the tree, the caprices of the catbird, the affectation of the titmouse. I expect to know much of the biography of plants. Natural History is now little but a nomenclature. Nothing is known of the individuals yet who can doubt that in the history of the individuals lies all the charm as that of human history lies not in the races but in Luther, Napoleon and Webster. I should be glad to know what that delicate yellow Cistus does all the midsummer in those dry fields it inhabits. I should be glad to know what use the smilax subserves with its perennial greenness or whole wide fields of Empetrum and of brake. I should be glad to know the biographies of the extraordinary individuals. It would be even pleasanter than it is now—to see a pumpkin in Hadley meadows or to shell corn in November in the cornbarn.

See that centipede: *c'est bien chaussée.* Goethe said that Nature had cheated the snake of a body like the promise of his eyes and head and had sheathed him in a sack. Among the insects few seem to be at home in their bodies, entire and content like a bird, but rather as efforts, foreshadowings. Here and there comes a very decided form like that odd Brentus Anchorago which suggests something very different from man, but in general man is the type by which we measure the insect.

I do not, whilst I lay stress on this point, undervalue the ordinary aids of science. The necessity of nomenclature, of minute physiological research, of the retort, the scalpel, and the scales, is incontestable. But there is no danger of its being underestimated. We only wish to insist upon their being considered as *Means.* We only wish to give equal and habitual prominence to the Love and Faith from which these should flow. This passion, the enthusiasm for nature, the love of the Whole, has burned in the breasts of the Fathers of Science. It was the ever present aim of Newton, of Linnaeus, of Davy, of Cuvier, to ascend from nomenclature to classification; from arbitrary to natural classes; from natural classes, to primary laws; from these, in an ever narrowing circle, to approach the elemental law, the *causa causans,* the supernatural force.

And the necessity of guarding this original taste, of keeping the mind of the student in a healthful state belongs especially to the consideration of the intellectual influences of science. When a reasoning man looks upon the Creation around him, he feels that it is most fit as a part of the study of himself that he should inquire into the nature of these related beings. He sees that the same laws that govern their structure govern his own; that his very superiority is yet in strict harmony with their natures. He wishes to comprehend their nature, to have such knowledge as shall place him as it were at the heart of the Creation that he may see its tribes and races unfolding themselves in order (as the orbs of our system are seen from the sun) that he may have a Theory of animated nature, understand its Law, so that his eye may predict the functions and habits of the individual before yet they show themselves.

Now this is to be attained only by those who resolutely keep their reason in its seat, who guard themselves against their own habits, who persist in seeking the Idea in the particulars, the Type in the manifold forms. It seems the duty of the Naturalist to study in faith and in love, never to lose sight of the simplest questions, "Why?" and "Whence?" and "What of that?", to be a poet in his severest analysis; rather, I should say, to make the Naturalist subordinate to the Man. He only can derive all the advantage from intimate knowledge who forces the magnified objects back into their true perspective, who after he has searched the proximate atoms integrates them again as in nature they are integrated and keeps his mind open to their beauty and to the moral impressions which it is their highest office to convey. To him they suggest a feeling as grand as the knowledge is accurate.

To this end of furnishing us with hints, intimations of the inward Law of Nature, a cabinet is useful. It would seem as if there were better means of expressing these thoughts than words. 'Tis said that the idea which always haunted John Hunter, that Life was independent of organization, protecting and continually recreating the parts and wonderfully varying its means of action, he never succeeded in expressing but in his Museum. So no intelligent person can come into a well arranged cabinet of natural productions without being excited to unusual reveries, without being conscious by instinctive perception of relations which he can only feel without being able to comprehend or define.

The later discoveries of naturalists seem to point more and more steadily at Method, at a Theory. The more superficial their observations the more unconnected and remote do the objects seem: the sticking of iron to the loadstone seems to have no connexion with the rainbow or the lightning or chemical changes but when the observation is more searching and profound the most remote objects are made to approach and seen to be various effects of one law: the spherules and spicula which the physiologist finds at the foundation both of vegetable and animal organization, these oxygenous, those hydrogenous; the little flower which makes lime and metals out of the elements of elements, and so promises to give us a course of chemical lessons worth knowing, and strip the little Proteus, Hydrogen, of his last coat, and the whole philosophy of their colours, the redundancy of oxygen in the red and yellow leaves in the autumn woods, the equilibrium of hydrogen and oxygen in the green leaf of midsummer; the application of polarized light as a chemical test; the new laws of crystalline architecture which the autophyllite in polarized light has suggested; Dr. Jenner's derivation of the migration of birds and of fishes from a single organic change; Hatchett's analysis of the egg and its analogies in the intestinal secretions: these seem to be most important steps and the most superficial reader cannot learn them without feeling himself in the precincts of that primary area whence the few great powers of Nature depart to produce by endless combinations their various and innumerable works.

I have great confidence, Gentlemen, that the spirit which has led you to such conspicuous efforts in the cause of Natural History, is founded in so true and deep a love of the laws of the Creation, in so simple a desire to explore and publish to others their precious secrets, as promises to our society the benefits without the pedantry of knowledge. The benefit to the community, amid the harsh and depraving strife of political parties, of these pure pursuits is inestimable.

We are born in an age which to its immense inheritance of natural knowledge has added great discoveries of its own. We should not be citizens of our own time, not faithful to our trust, if we neglected to avail ourselves of their light. The eternal beauty which led the early

Greeks to call the globe κόσμος or Beauty pleads ever with us, shines from the stars, glows in the flower, moves in the animal, crystallizes in the stone. No truth can be more self evident than that the highest state of man, physical, intellectual, and moral, can only coexist with a perfect Theory of Animated Nature.

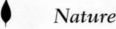

Nature

(1836)

Nature represents the culmination of Emerson's extensive reading, journal writing, and lecturing over the previous decade. Although he would not begin writing *Nature* until the spring of 1835, Emerson first mentioned a book about nature as early as his return trip from Europe in 1833. He initially conceived of the project as two distinct works: one focusing on the material world and another, tentatively titled "Spirit," exploring the internal processes of perception and observation. He would later combine the two texts, publishing them anonymously as *Nature* on September 9, 1836. While he was not named as the book's author, it was widely known that Emerson had written the work. The day before *Nature*'s publication, a group of Concord intellectuals, including Emerson, founded the Transcendental Club. The club's members were organized around a general dissatisfaction with the current state of American philosophy, religion, and art. These two events in September of 1836 ushered in the Transcendentalist movement. Emerson's authorship of *Nature* and his extensive involvement with the Transcendental Club—both as a founder and frequent host of gatherings—established his role as one of the preeminent figures of this cultural movement. As was typical of his writing process, Emerson revised and expanded material from his exhaustive journals, sermons, and lectures in order to produce *Nature*. This concentration and synthesis of myriad sources into a single work help explain the often cryptically succinct prose of Emerson's essays. His method of condensation and compression may be seen at the outset of *Nature*, where he asks, "[T]o what end is nature?"—a clear echo of the inchoate questions initially raised in his natural history sermons and lectures. Emerson attempts to articulate a comprehensive theory of nature by answering this question throughout the remainder of the essay. After he has established a working definition of nature, each subsequent chapter is an exploration of nature's proper purpose in terms of economics ("Commodity"), aesthetics ("Beauty"), symbolism ("Language"), education ("Discipline"), philosophy ("Idealism"), spirituality ("Spirit"), and prophecy ("Prospects"). *Nature* would become the most influential document in American Transcendentalism and, along with his already established reputation as a lecturer, would thrust Emerson to the fore of American literature and culture for the next three decades.

❧

A subtle chain of countless rings
The next unto the farthest brings;
The eye reads omens where it goes,
And speaks all languages the rose;
And, striving to be man, the worm
Mounts through all the spires of form.

Introduction

Our age is retrospective. It builds the sepulchres of the fathers. It writes biographies, histories, and criticism. The foregoing generations beheld God and nature face to face; we, through their eyes. Why should not we also enjoy an original relation to the universe? Why should not we have a poetry and philosophy of insight and not of tradition, and a religion by revelation to us, and not the history of theirs? Embosomed for a season in nature, whose floods of life stream around and through us, and invite us by the powers they supply, to action proportioned to nature, why should we grope among the dry bones of the past, or put the living generation into masquerade out of its faded wardrobe? The sun shines to-day also. There is more wool and flax in the fields. There are new lands, new men, new thoughts. Let us demand our own works and laws and worship.

Undoubtedly we have no questions to ask which are unanswerable.

We must trust the perfection of the creation so far, as to believe that whatever curiosity the order of things has awakened in our minds, the order of things can satisfy. Every man's condition is a solution in hieroglyphic to those inquiries he would put. He acts it as life, before he apprehends it as truth. In like manner, nature is already, in its forms and tendencies, describing its own design. Let us interrogate the great apparition, that shines so peacefully around us. Let us inquire, to what end is nature?

All science has one aim, namely, to find a theory of nature. We have theories of races and of functions, but scarcely yet a remote approach to an idea of creation. We are now so far from the road to truth, that religious teachers dispute and hate each other, and speculative men are esteemed unsound and frivolous. But to a sound judgment, the most abstract truth is the most practical. Whenever a true theory appears, it will be its own evidence. Its test is, that it will explain all phenomena. Now many are thought not only unexplained but inexplicable; as language, sleep, madness, dreams, beasts, sex.

Philosophically considered, the universe is composed of Nature and the Soul. Strictly speaking, therefore, all that is separate from us, all which Philosophy distinguishes as the NOT ME, that is, both nature and art, all other men and my own body, must be ranked under this name, NATURE. In enumerating the values of nature and casting up their sum, I shall use the word in both senses;—in its common and in its philosophical import. In inquiries so general as our present one, the inaccuracy is not material; no confusion of thought will occur. *Nature*, in the common sense, refers to essences unchanged by man; space, the air, the river, the leaf. *Art* is applied to the mixture of his will with the same things, as in a house, a canal, a statue, a picture. But his operations taken together are so insignificant, a little chipping, baking, patching, and washing, that in an impression so grand as that of the world on the human mind, they do not vary the result.

Chapter I. Nature

To go into solitude, a man needs to retire as much from his chamber as from society. I am not solitary whilst I read and write, though nobody is with me. But if a man would be alone, let him look at the stars. The rays that come from those heavenly worlds, will separate between him and vulgar things. One might think the atmosphere was made transparent with this design, to give man, in the heavenly bodies, the perpetual presence of the sublime. Seen in the streets of cities, how great they are! If the stars should appear one night in a thousand years, how would men believe and adore; and preserve for many generations the remembrance of the city of God which had been shown! But every night come out these envoys of beauty, and light the universe with their admonishing smile.

The stars awaken a certain reverence, because though always present, they are always inaccessible; but all natural objects make a kindred impression, when the mind is open to their influence. Nature never wears a mean appearance. Neither does the wisest man extort all her secret, and lose his curiosity by finding out all her perfection. Nature never became a toy to a wise spirit. The flowers, the animals, the mountains, reflected all the wisdom of his best hour, as much as they had delighted the simplicity of his childhood.

When we speak of nature in this manner, we have a distinct but most poetical sense in the mind. We mean the integrity of impression made by manifold natural objects. It is this which distinguishes the stick of timber of the wood-cutter, from the tree of the poet. The charming landscape which I saw this morning, is indubitably made up of some twenty or thirty farms. Miller owns this field, Locke that, and Manning the woodland beyond. But none of them owns the landscape. There is a property in the horizon which no man has but he whose eye can integrate all the parts, that is, the poet. This is the best part of these men's farms, yet to this their warranty-deeds give no title.

To speak truly, few adult persons can see nature. Most persons do not see the sun. At least they have a very superficial seeing. The sun illuminates only the eye of the man, but shines into the eye and the heart of the child. The lover of nature is he whose inward and outward senses are still truly adjusted to each other; who has retained the spirit of infancy even into the era of manhood. His intercourse with heaven and earth, becomes part of his daily food. In the presence of nature, a wild delight runs through the man, in spite of real sorrows. Nature says,—he is my creature, and maugre all his impertinent griefs, he shall be glad with me. Not the sun or the summer alone, but every hour and season yields its tribute of delight; for every hour and change corresponds to and authorizes a different state of the mind, from breathless noon to grimmest midnight. Nature is a setting that fits equally well a comic or a mourning piece. In good health, the air is a cordial of incredible virtue. Crossing a bare common, in snow puddles, at twilight, under a clouded sky, without having in my thoughts any occurrence of special good fortune, I have enjoyed a perfect exhilaration. Almost I fear to think how glad I am. In the woods too, a man casts off his years, as the snake his slough, and at what period soever of life, is always a child. In the woods, is perpetual youth. Within these plantations of God, a decorum and sanctity reign, a perennial festival is dressed, and the guest sees not how he should tire of them in a thousand years. In the woods, we return to reason and faith. There I feel that nothing can befal me in life,—no disgrace, no calamity, (leaving me my eyes,) which nature cannot repair. Standing on the bare ground,—my head bathed by the blithe air, and uplifted into infinite space,—all mean egotism vanishes. I become a transparent eye-ball. I am nothing. I see all. The currents of the Universal Being circulate through me; I am part or particle of God. The name of the nearest friend sounds then foreign and accidental. To be brothers, to be acquaintances,—master or servant, is then a trifle and a disturbance. I am the lover of uncontained and immortal beauty. In the wilderness, I find something more dear and connate than in streets or villages. In the tranquil landscape, and especially in the distant line of the horizon, man beholds somewhat as beautiful as his own nature.

The greatest delight which the fields and woods minister, is the suggestion of an occult relation between man and the vegetable. I am not alone and unacknowledged. They nod to me and I to them. The waving of the boughs in the storm, is new to me and old. It takes me by surprise, and yet is not unknown. Its effect is like that of a higher thought or a better emotion coming over me, when I deemed I was thinking justly or doing right.

Yet it is certain that the power to produce this delight, does not reside in nature, but in man, or in a harmony of both. It is necessary to use these pleasures with great temperance. For, nature is not always tricked in holiday attire, but the same scene which yesterday breathed perfume and glittered as for the frolic of the nymphs, is overspread with melancholy today. Nature always wears the colors of the spirit. To a man laboring under calamity, the heat of his own fire hath sadness in it. Then, there is a kind of contempt of the landscape felt by him who has just lost by death a dear friend. The sky is less grand as it shuts down over less worth in the population.

Chapter II. Commodity

Whoever considers the final cause of the world, will discern a multitude of uses that enter as parts into that result. They all admit of being thrown into one of the following classes: Commodity; Beauty; Language; and Discipline.

Under the general name of Commodity, I rank all those advantages which our senses owe to nature. This, of course, is a benefit which is temporary and mediate, not ultimate, like its service to the soul. Yet although low, it is perfect in its kind, and is the only use of nature which all men apprehend. The misery of man appears like childish petulance, when we explore the steady and prodigal provision that has been made for his support and delight on this green ball which floats him through the heavens. What angels invented these splendid ornaments, these rich conveniences, this ocean of air above, this ocean of water beneath, this firmament of earth between? this zodiac of lights, this tent of dropping clouds, this striped coat of climates, this fourfold year? Beasts, fire, water, stones, and corn serve him. The field is at once his floor, his work-yard, his play-ground, his garden, and his bed.

> "More servants wait on man
> Than he'll take notice of."—

Nature, in its ministry to man, is not only the material, but is also the process and the result. All the parts incessantly work into each other's hands for the profit of man. The wind sows the seed; the sun evaporates the sea; the wind blows the vapor to the field; the ice, on the other side of the planet, condenses rain on this; the rain feeds the plant; the plant feeds the animal; and thus the endless circulations of the divine charity nourish man.

The useful arts are but reproductions or new combinations by the wit of man, of the same natural benefactors. He no longer waits for favoring gales, but by means of steam, he realizes the fable of Æolus's bag, and carries the two and thirty winds in the boiler of his boat. To diminish friction, he paves the road with iron bars, and, mounting a coach with a ship-load of men, animals, and merchandise behind him, he darts through the country, from town to town, like an eagle or a swallow through the air. By the aggregate of these aids, how is the face of the world changed, from the era of Noah to that of Napoleon! The private poor man hath cities, ships, canals, bridges, built for him. He goes to the post-office, and the human race run on his errands; to the book-shop, and the human race read and write of all that happens, for him; to the court-house, and nations repair his wrongs. He sets his house upon the road, and the human race go forth every morning, and shovel out the snow, and cut a path for him.

But there is no need of specifying particulars in this class of uses. The catalogue is endless, and the examples so obvious, that I shall leave them to the reader's reflection, with the general remark, that this mercenary benefit is one which has respect to a farther good. A man is fed, not that he may be fed, but that he may work.

Chapter III. Beauty

A nobler want of man is served by nature, namely, the love of Beauty.

The ancient Greeks called the world κόσμος, beauty. Such is the constitution of all things, or such the plastic power of the human eye, that the primary forms, as the sky, the mountain, the tree, the animal, give us a delight *in and for themselves;* a pleasure arising from out-line, color, motion, and grouping. This seems partly owing to the eye itself. The eye is the best of artists. By the mutual action of its structure and of the laws of light, perspective is produced, which integrates every mass of objects, of what character soever, into a well colored and shaded globe, so that where the particular objects are the mean and unaffecting, the landscape which they compose, is round and symmet-

rical. And as the eye is the best composer, so light is the first of painters. There is no object so foul that intense light will not make beautiful.
And the stimulus it affords to the sense, and a sort of infinitude which
it hath, like space and time, make all matter gay. Even the corpse hath
its own beauty. But beside this general grace diffused over nature,
almost all the individual forms are agreeable to the eye, as is proved
by our endless imitations of some of them, as the acorn, the grape, the
pine-cone, the wheat-ear, the egg, the wings and forms of most birds,
the lion's claw, the serpent, the butterfly, sea-shells, flames, clouds,
buds, leaves, and the forms of many trees, as the palm.

For better consideration, we may distribute the aspects of Beauty
in a threefold manner.

1. First, the simple perception of natural forms is a delight. The
influence of the forms and actions in nature, is so needful to man,
that, in its lowest functions, it seems to lie on the confines of commodity and beauty. To the body and mind which have been cramped
by noxious work or company, nature is medicinal and restores their
tone. The tradesman, the attorney comes out of the din and craft of
the street, and sees the sky and the woods, and is a man again. In their
eternal calm, he finds himself. The health of the eye seems to demand
a horizon. We are never tired, so long as we can see far enough.

But in other hours, Nature satisfies the soul purely by its loveliness,
and without any mixture of corporeal benefit. I have seen the spectacle
of morning from the hill-top over against my house, from day-break to
sun-rise, with emotions which an angel might share. The long slender
bars of cloud float like fishes in the sea of crimson light. From the
earth, as a shore, I look out into that silent sea. I seem to partake its
rapid transformations: the active enchantment reaches my dust, and I
dilate and conspire with the morning wind. How does Nature deify us
with a few and cheap elements! Give me health and a day, and I will
make the pomp of emperors ridiculous. The dawn is my Assyria; the
sun-set and moon-rise my Paphos, and unimaginable realms of faerie;
broad noon shall be my England of the senses and the understanding;
the night shall be my Germany of mystic philosophy and dreams.

Not less excellent, except for our less susceptibility in the after-
noon, was the charm, last evening, of a January sunset. The western

clouds divided and subdivided themselves into pink flakes modulated with tints of unspeakable softness; and the air had so much life and sweetness, that it was a pain to come within doors. What was it that nature would say? Was there no meaning in the live repose of the valley behind the mill, and which Homer or Shakspeare could not re-form for me in words? The leafless trees become spires of flame in the sunset, with the blue east for their background, and the stars of the dead calices of flowers, and every withered stem and stubble rimed with frost, contribute something to the mute music.

The inhabitants of cities suppose that the country landscape is pleasant only half the year. I please myself with observing the graces of the winter scenery, and believe that we are as much touched by it as by the genial influences of summer. To the attentive eye, each moment of the year has its own beauty, and in the same field, it beholds, every hour, a picture which was never seen before, and which shall never be seen again. The heavens change every moment, and reflect their glory or gloom on the plains beneath. The state of the crop in the surrounding farms alters the expression of the earth from week to week. The succession of native plants in the pastures and road-sides, which make the silent clock by which time tells the summer hours, will make even the divisions of the day sensible to a keen observer. The tribes of birds and insects, like the plants punctual to their time, follow each other, and the year has room for all. By water-courses, the variety is greater. In July, the blue pontederia or pickerel-weed blooms in large beds in the shallow parts of our pleasant river, and swarms with yellow butterflies in continual motion. Art cannot rival this pomp of purple and gold. Indeed the river is a perpetual gala, and boasts each month a new ornament.

But this beauty of Nature which is seen and felt as beauty, is the least part. The shows of day, the dewy morning, the rainbow, mountains, orchards in blossom, stars, moonlight, shadows in still water, and the like, if too eagerly hunted, become shows merely, and mock us with their unreality. Go out of the house to see the moon, and 't is mere tinsel; it will not please as when its light shines upon your necessary journey. The beauty that shimmers in the yellow afternoons of October, who ever could clutch it? Go forth to find it, and it is gone: 't is only a mirage as you look from the windows of diligence.

2. The presence of a higher, namely, of the spiritual element is essential to its perfection. The high and divine beauty which can be loved without effeminacy, is that which is found in combination with the human will, and never separate. Beauty is the mark God sets upon virtue. Every natural action is graceful. Every heroic act is also decent, and causes the place and the bystanders to shine. We are taught by great actions that the universe is the property of every individual in it. Every rational creature has all nature for his dowry and estate. It is his, if he will. He may divest himself of it; he may creep into a corner, and abdicate his kingdom, as most men do, but he is entitled to the world by his constitution. In proportion to the energy of his thought and will, he takes up the world into himself. "All those things for which men plough, build, or sail, obey virtue;" said an ancient historian. "The winds and waves," said Gibbon, "are always on the side of the ablest navigators." So are the sun and moon and all the stars of heaven. When a noble act is done,—perchance in a scene of great natural beauty; when Leonidas and his three hundred martyrs consume one day in dying, and the sun and moon come each and look at them once in the steep defile of Thermopylæ; when Arnold Winkelried, in the high Alps, under the shadow of the avalanche, gathers in his side a sheaf of Austrian spears to break the line for his comrades; are not these heroes entitled to add the beauty of the scene to the beauty of the deed? When the bark of Columbus nears the shore of America;—before it, the beach lined with savages, fleeing out of all their huts of cane; the sea behind; and the purple mountains of the Indian Archipelago around, can we separate the man from the living picture? Does not the New World clothe his form with her palm-groves and savannahs as fit drapery? Ever does natural beauty steal in like air, and envelope great actions. When Sir Harry Vane was dragged up the Tower-hill, sitting on a sled, to suffer death, as the champion of the English laws, one of the multitude cried out to him, "You never sate on so glorious a seat." Charles II., to intimidate the citizens of London, caused the patriot Lord Russell to be drawn in an open coach, through the principal streets of the city, on his way to the scaffold. "But," to use the simple narrative of his biographer, "the multitude imagined they saw liberty and virtue sitting by his side." In private places, among sordid

objects, an act of truth or heroism seems at once to draw to itself the sky as its temple, the sun as its candle. Nature stretcheth out her arms to embrace man, only let his thoughts be of equal greatness. Willingly does she follow his steps with the rose and the violet, and bend her lines of grandeur and grace to the decoration of her darling child. Only let his thoughts be of equal scope, and the frame will suit the picture. A virtuous man is in unison with her works, and makes the central figure of the visible sphere. Homer, Pindar, Socrates, Phocion, associate themselves fitly in our memory with the whole geography and climate of Greece. The visible heavens and earth sympathize with Jesus. And in common life, whosoever has seen a person of powerful character and happy genius, will have remarked how easily he took all things along with him,—the persons, the opinions, and the day, and nature became ancillary to a man.

3. There is still another aspect under which the beauty of the world may be viewed, namely, as it becomes an object of the intellect. Beside the relation of things to virtue, they have a relation to thought. The intellect searches out the absolute order of things as they stand in the mind of God, and without the colors of affection. The intellectual and the active powers seem to succeed each other in man, and the exclusive activity of the one, generates the exclusive activity of the other. There is something unfriendly in each to the other, but they are like the alternate periods of feeding and working in animals; each prepares and certainly will be followed by the other. Therefore does beauty, which, in relation to actions, as we have seen, comes unsought, and comes because it is unsought, remain for the apprehension and pursuit of the intellect; and then again, in its turn, of the active power. Nothing divine dies. All good is eternally reproductive. The beauty of nature reforms itself in the mind, and not for barren contemplation, but for new creation.

All men are in some degree impressed by the face of the world; some men even to delight. This love of beauty is Taste. Others have the same love in such excess, that, not content with admiring, they seek to embody it in new forms. The creation of beauty is Art.

The production of a work of art throws a light upon the mystery of humanity. A work of art is an abstract or epitome of the world. It is the result or expression of nature, in miniature. For although the works of nature are innumerable and all different, the result or the expression of them all is similar and single. Nature is a sea of forms radically alike and even unique. A leaf, a sun-beam, a landscape, the ocean, make an analogous impression on the mind. What is common to them all,—that perfectness and harmony, is beauty. Therefore the standard of beauty is the entire circuit of natural forms,—the totality of nature; which the Italians expressed by defining beauty "il piu nell' uno." Nothing is quite beautiful alone: nothing but is beautiful in the whole. A single object is only so far beautiful as it suggests this universal grace. The poet, the painter, the sculptor, the musician, the architect, seek each to concentrate this radiance of the world on one point, and each in his several work to satisfy the love of beauty which stimulates him to produce. Thus is Art, a nature passed through the alembic of man. Thus in art, does nature work through the will of a man filled with the beauty of her first works.

The world thus exists to the soul to satisfy the desire of beauty. Extend this element to the uttermost, and I call it an ultimate end. No reason can be asked or given why the soul seeks beauty. Beauty, in its largest and profoundest sense, is one expression for the universe. God is the all-fair. Truth, and goodness, and beauty, are but different faces of the same All. But beauty in nature is not ultimate. It is the herald of inward and eternal beauty, and is not alone a solid and satisfactory good. It must therefore stand as a part and not as yet the last or highest expression of the final cause of Nature.

Chapter IV. Language

A third use which Nature subserves to man is that of Language. Nature is the vehicle of thought, and in a simple, double, and threefold degree.

1. Words are signs of natural facts.
2. Particular natural facts are symbols of particular spiritual facts.
3. Nature is the symbol of spirit.

1. Words are signs of natural facts. The use of natural history is to give us aid in supernatural history. The use of the outer creation is to

give us language for the beings and changes of the inward creation. Every word which is used to express a moral or intellectual fact, if traced to its root, is found to be borrowed from some material appearance. *Right* originally means *straight; wrong* means *twisted. Spirit* primarily means *wind; transgression,* the crossing of a *line; supercilious,* the *raising of the eye-brow.* We say the *heart* to express emotion, the *head* to denote thought; and *thought* and *emotion* are, in their turn, words borrowed from sensible things, and now appropriated to spiritual nature. Most of the process by which this transformation is made, is hidden from us in the remote time when language was framed; but the same tendency may be daily observed in children. Children and savages use only nouns or names of things, which they continually convert into verbs, and apply to analogous mental acts.

2. But this origin of all words that convey a spiritual import,—so conspicuous a fact in the history of language,—is our least debt to nature. It is not words only that are emblematic; it is things which are emblematic. Every natural fact is a symbol of some spiritual fact. Every appearance in nature corresponds to some state of the mind, and that state of the mind can only be described by presenting that natural appearance as its picture. An enraged man is a lion, a cunning man is a fox, a firm man is a rock, a learned man is a torch. A lamb is innocence; a snake is subtle spite; flowers express to us the delicate affections. Light and darkness are our familiar expression for knowledge and ignorance; and heat for love. Visible distance behind and before us, is respectively our image of memory and hope.

Who looks upon a river in a meditative hour, and is not reminded of the flux of all things? Throw a stone into the stream, and the circles that propagate themselves are the beautiful type of all influence. Man is conscious of a universal soul within or behind his individual life, wherein, as in a firmament, the natures of Justice, Truth, Love, Freedom, arise and shine. This universal soul, he calls Reason: it is not mine or thine or his, but we are its; we are its property and men. And the blue sky in which the private earth is buried, the sky with its eternal calm, and full of everlasting orbs, is the type of Reason. That which, intellectually considered, we call Reason, considered in relation to nature, we call Spirit. Spirit is the Creator. Spirit hath life in itself.

And man in all ages and countries, embodies it in his language, as the FATHER.

It is easily seen that there is nothing lucky or capricious in these analogies, but that they are constant, and pervade nature. These are not the dreams of a few poets, here and there, but man is an analogist, and studies relations in all objects. He is placed in the centre of beings, and a ray of relation passes from every other being to him. And neither can man be understood without these objects, nor these objects without man. All the facts in natural history taken by themselves, have no value, but are barren like a single sex. But marry it to human history, and it is full of life. Whole Floras, all Linnæus' and Buffon's volumes, are but dry catalogues of facts; but the most trivial of these facts, the habit of a plant, the organs, or work, or noise of an insect, applied to the illustration of a fact in intellectual philosophy, or, in any way associated to human nature, affects us in the most lively and agreeable manner. The seed of a plant,—to what affecting analogies in the nature of man, is that little fruit made use of, in all discourse, up to the voice of Paul, who calls the human corpse a seed,—"It is sown a natural body; it is raised a spiritual body." The motion of the earth round its axis, and round the sun, makes the day, and the year. These are certain amounts of brute light and heat. But is there no intent of an analogy between man's life and the seasons? And do the seasons gain no grandeur or pathos from that analogy? The instincts of the ant are very unimportant considered as the ant's; but the moment a ray of relation is seen to extend from it to man, and the little drudge is seen to be a monitor, a little body with a mighty heart, then all its habits, even that said to be recently observed, that it never sleeps, become sublime.

Because of this radical correspondence between visible things and human thoughts, savages, who have only what is necessary, converse in figures. As we go back in history, language becomes more picturesque, until its infancy, when it is all poetry; or, all spiritual facts are represented by natural symbols. The same symbols are found to make the original elements of all languages. It has moreover been observed, that the idioms of all languages approach each other in passages of the greatest eloquence and power. And as this is the first language, so is it the last. This immediate dependence of language upon nature, this conversion of an outward phenomenon into a type of somewhat in human life, never loses its power to affect us. It is this which gives that piquancy to the conversation of a strong-natured farmer or back-woodsman, which all men relish.

Thus is nature an interpreter, by whose means man converses with his fellow men. A man's power to connect his thought with its proper symbol, and so to utter it, depends on the simplicity of his character, that is, upon his love of truth and his desire to communicate it without loss. The corruption of man is followed by the corruption of language. When simplicity of character and the sovereignty of ideas is broken up by the prevalence of secondary desires, the desire of riches, the desire of pleasure, the desire of power, the desire of praise,—and duplicity and falsehood take place of simplicity and truth, the power over nature as an interpreter of the will, is in a degree lost; new imagery ceases to be created, and old words are perverted to stand for things which are not; a paper currency is employed when there is no bullion in the vaults. In due time, the fraud is manifest, and words lose all power to stimulate the understanding or the affections. Hundreds of writers may be found in every long-civilized nation, who for a short time believe, and make others believe, that they see and utter truths, who do not of themselves clothe one thought in its natural garment, but who feed unconsciously upon the language created by the primary writers of the country, those, namely, who hold primarily on nature.

But wise men pierce this rotten diction and fasten words again to visible things; so that picturesque language is at once a commanding certificate that he who employs it, is a man in alliance with truth and God. The moment our discourse rises above the ground line of familiar facts, and is inflamed with passion or exalted by thought, it clothes itself in images. A man conversing in earnest, if he watch his intellectual processes, will find that always a material image, more or less luminous, arises in his mind, cotemporaneous with every thought, which furnishes the vestment of the thought. Hence, good writing and brilliant discourse are perpetual allegories. This imagery is spontaneous. It is the blending of experience with the present action of the mind. It is proper creation. It is the working of the Original Cause through the instruments he has already made.

These facts may suggest the advantage which the country-life possesses for a powerful mind, over the artificial and curtailed life of cities. We know more from nature than we can at will communicate. Its light flows into the mind evermore, and we forget its presence. The poet, the orator, bred in the woods, whose senses have been nourished by their fair and appeasing changes, year after year, without design and without heed,—shall not lose their lesson altogether, in the roar of cities or the broil of politics. Long hereafter, amidst agitation and terror in national councils,—in the hour of revolution,—these solemn images shall reappear in their morning lustre, as fit symbols and words of the thoughts which the passing events shall awaken. At the call of a noble sentiment, again the woods wave, the pines murmur, the river rolls and shines, and the cattle low upon the mountains, as he saw and heard them in his infancy. And with these forms, the spells of persuasion, the keys of power are put into his hands.

3. We are thus assisted by natural objects in the expression of particular meanings. But how great a language to convey such pepper-corn informations! Did it need such noble races of creatures, this profusion of forms, this host of orbs in heaven, to furnish man with the dictionary and grammar of his municipal speech? Whilst we use this grand cipher to expedite the affairs of our pot and kettle, we feel that we have not yet put it to its use, neither are able. We are like travellers using the cinders of a volcano to roast their eggs. Whilst we see that it always stands ready to clothe what we would say, we cannot avoid the question, whether the characters are not significant of themselves. Have mountains, and waves, and skies, no significance but what we consciously give them, when we employ them as emblems of our thoughts? The world is emblematic. Parts of speech are metaphors because the whole of nature is a metaphor of the human mind. The laws of moral nature answer to those of matter as face to face in a glass. "The visible world and the relation of its parts, is the dial plate of the invisible." The axioms of physics translate the laws of ethics. Thus, "the whole is greater than its part;" "reaction is equal to action;" "the smallest weight may be made to lift the greatest, the difference of weight being compensated by time;" and many the like propositions, which have an ethical as well as physical sense. These propositions have a

much more extensive and universal sense when applied to human life, than when confined to technical use.

In like manner, the memorable words of history, and the proverbs of nations, consist usually of a natural fact, selected as a picture or parable of a moral truth. Thus; A rolling stone gathers no moss; A bird in the hand is worth two in the bush; A cripple in the right way, will beat a racer in the wrong; Make hay whilst the sun shines; 'T is hard to carry a full cup even; Vinegar is the son of wine; The last ounce broke the camel's back; Long-lived trees make roots first;—and the like. In their primary sense these are trivial facts, but we repeat them for the value of their analogical import. What is true of proverbs, is true of all fables, parables, and allegories.

This relation between the mind and matter is not fancied by some poet, but stands in the will of God, and so is free to be known by all men. It appears to men, or it does not appear. When in fortunate hours we ponder this miracle, the wise man doubts, if, at all other times, he is not blind and deaf;

> —"Can these things be,
> And overcome us like a summer's cloud,
> Without our special wonder?"

for the universe becomes transparent, and the light of higher laws than its own, shines through it. It is the standing problem which has exercised the wonder and the study of every fine genius since the world began; from the era of the Egyptians and the Brahmins, to that of Pythagoras, of Plato, of Bacon, of Leibnitz, of Swedenborg. There sits the Sphinx at the road-side, and from age to age, as each prophet comes by, he tries his fortune at reading her riddle. There seems to be a necessity in spirit to manifest itself in material forms; and day and night, river and storm, beast and bird, acid and alkali, preëxist in necessary Ideas in the mind of God, and are what they are by virtue of preceding affections, in the world of spirit. A Fact is the end or last issue of spirit. The visible creation is the terminus or the circumference of the invisible world. "Material objects," said a French philosopher, "are necessarily kinds of *scoriæ* of the substantial thoughts of the Creator, which must always preserve an exact relation to their first origin; in other words, visible nature must have a spiritual and moral side."

This doctrine is abstruse, and though the images of "garment," "scoriæ," "mirror," &c., may stimulate the fancy, we must summon the aid of subtler and more vital expositors to make it plain. "Every scripture is to be interpreted by the same spirit which gave it forth,"—is the fundamental law of criticism. A life in harmony with nature, the love of truth and of virtue, will purge the eyes to understand her text. By degrees we may come to know the primitive sense of the permanent objects of nature, so that the world shall be to us an open book, and every form significant of its hidden life and final cause.

A new interest surprises us, whilst, under the view now suggested, we contemplate the fearful extent and multitude of objects; since "every object rightly seen, unlocks a new faculty of the soul." That which was unconscious truth, becomes, when interpreted and defined in an object, a part of the domain of knowledge,—a new weapon in the magazine of power.

Chapter V. Discipline

In view of this significance of nature, we arrive at once at a new fact, that nature is a discipline. This use of the world includes the preceding uses, as parts of itself.

Space, time, society, labor, climate, food, locomotion, the animals, the mechanical forces, give us sincerest lessons, day by day, whose meaning is unlimited. They educate both the Understanding and the Reason. Every property of matter is a school for the understanding,— its solidity or resistance, its inertia, its extension, its figure, its divisibility. The understanding adds, divides, combines, measures, and finds everlasting nutriment and room for its activity in this worthy scene. Meantime, Reason transfers all these lessons into its own world of thought, by perceiving the analogy that marries Matter and Mind.

1. Nature is a discipline of the understanding in intellectual truths. Our dealing with sensible objects is a constant exercise in the necessary lessons of difference, of likeness, of order, of being and seem-

ing, of progressive arrangement; of ascent from particular to general; of combination to one end of manifold forces. Proportioned to the importance of the organ to be formed, is the extreme care with which its tuition is provided,—a care pretermitted in no single case. What tedious training, day after day, year after year, never ending, to form the common sense; what continual reproduction of annoyances, inconveniences, dilemmas; what rejoicing over us of little men; what disputing of prices, what reckonings of interest,—and all to form the Hand of the mind;—to instruct us that "good thoughts are no better than good dreams, unless they be executed!"

The same good office is performed by Property and its filial systems of debt and credit. Debt, grinding debt, whose iron face the widow, the orphan, and the sons of genius fear and hate;—debt, which consumes so much time, which so cripples and disheartens a great spirit with cares that seem so base, is a preceptor whose lessons cannot be foregone, and is needed most by those who suffer from it most. Moreover, property, which has been well compared to snow,—"if it fall level to-day, it will be blown into drifts to-morrow,"—is merely the surface action of internal machinery, like the index on the face of a clock. Whilst now it is the gymnastics of the understanding, it is hiving in the foresight of the spirit, experience in profounder laws.

The whole character and fortune of the individual are affected by the least inequalities in the culture of the understanding; for example, in the perception of differences. Therefore is Space, and therefore Time, that man may know that things are not huddled and lumped, but sundered and individual. A bell and a plough have each their use, and neither can do the office of the other. Water is good to drink, coal to burn, wool to wear; but wool cannot be drunk, nor water spun, nor coal eaten. The wise man shows his wisdom in separation, in gradation, and his scale of creatures and of merits, is as wide as nature. The foolish have no range in their scale, but suppose every man is as every other man. What is not good they call the worst, and what is not hateful, they call the best.

In like manner, what good heed, nature forms in us! She pardons no mistakes. Her yea is yea, and her nay, nay.

The first steps in Agriculture, Astronomy, Zoölogy, (those first steps which the farmer, the hunter, and the sailor take,) teach that nature's dice are always loaded; that in her heaps and rubbish are concealed sure and useful results.

How calmly and genially the mind apprehends one after another the laws of physics! What noble emotions dilate the mortal as he enters into the counsels of the creation, and feels by knowledge the privilege to BE! His insight refines him. The beauty of nature shines in his own breast. Man is greater that he can see this, and the universe less, because Time and Space relations vanish as laws are known.

Here again we are impressed and even daunted by the immense Universe to be explored. 'What we know, is a point to what we do not know.' Open any recent journal of science, and weigh the problems suggested concerning Light, Heat, Electricity, Magnetism, Physiology, Geology, and judge whether the interest of natural science is likely to be soon exhausted.

Passing by many particulars of the discipline of nature we must not omit to specify two.

The exercise of the Will or the lesson of power is taught in every event. From the child's successive possession of his several senses up to the hour when he saith, "thy will be done!" he is learning the secret, that he can reduce under his will, not only particular events, but great classes, nay the whole series of events, and so conform all facts to his character. Nature is thoroughly mediate. It is made to serve. It receives the dominion of man as meekly as the ass on which the Saviour rode. It offers all its kingdoms to man as the raw material which he may mould into what is useful. Man is never weary of working it up. He forges the subtile and delicate air into wise and melodious words, and gives them wing as angels of persuasion and command. More and more, with every thought, does his kingdom stretch over things, until the world becomes, at last, only a realized will,—the double of the man.

2. Sensible objects conform to the premonitions of Reason and reflect the conscience. All things are moral; and in their boundless changes have an unceasing reference to spiritual nature. Therefore is nature glorious with form, color, and motion, that every globe in the remotest heaven; every chemical change from the rudest crystal up to the laws of life; every change of vegetation from the first principle of

growth in the eye of a leaf, to the tropical forest and antediluvian coal-mine; every animal function from the sponge up to Hercules, shall hint or thunder to man the laws of right and wrong, and echo the Ten Commandments. Therefore is nature ever the ally of Religion: lends all her pomp and riches to the religious sentiment. Prophet and priest, David, Isaiah, Jesus, have drawn deeply from this source.

This ethical character so penetrates the bone and marrow of nature, as to seem the end for which it was made. Whatever private purpose is answered by any member or part, this is its public and universal function, and is never omitted. Nothing in nature is exhausted in its first use. When a thing has served an end to the uttermost, it is wholly new for an ulterior service. In God, every end is converted into a new means. Thus the use of Commodity, regarded by itself, is mean and squalid. But it is to the mind an education in the great doctrine of Use, namely, that a thing is good only so far as it serves; that a conspiring of parts and efforts to the production of an end, is essential to any being. The first and gross manifestation of this truth, is our inevitable and hated training in values and wants, in corn and meat.

It has already been illustrated, in treating of the significance of material things, that every natural process is but a version of a moral sentence. The moral law lies at the centre of nature and radiates to the circumference. It is the pith and marrow of every substance, every relation, and every process. All things with which we deal, preach to us. What is a farm but a mute gospel? The chaff and the wheat, weeds and plants, blight, rain, insects, sun,—it is a sacred emblem from the first furrow of spring to the last stack which the snow of winter overtakes in the fields. But the sailor, the shepherd, the miner, the merchant, in their several resorts, have each an experience precisely parallel and leading to the same conclusion: because all organizations are radically alike. Nor can it be doubted that this moral sentiment which thus scents the air, and grows in the grain, and impregnates the waters of the world, is caught by man and sinks into his soul. The moral influence of nature upon every individual is that amount of truth which it illustrates to him. Who can estimate this? Who can guess how much firmness the sea-beaten rock has taught the fisherman? how much tranquillity has been reflected to man from the azure sky, over whose unspotted deeps the winds forevermore drive flocks of stormy clouds, and leave no wrinkle or stain? how much industry and providence and affection we have caught from the pantomime of brutes? What a searching preacher of self-command is the varying phenomenon of Health!

Herein is especially apprehended the Unity of Nature,—the Unity in Variety,—which meets us everywhere. All the endless variety of things make a unique, an identical impression. Xenophanes complained in his old age, that, look where he would, all things hastened back to Unity. He was weary of seeing the same entity in the tedious variety of forms. The fable of Proteus has a cordial truth. Every particular in nature, a leaf, a drop, a crystal, a moment of time is related to the whole, and partakes of the perfection of the whole. Each particle is a microcosm, and faithfully renders the likeness of the world.

Not only resemblances exist in things whose analogy is obvious, as when we detect the type of the human hand in the flipper of the fossil saurus, but also in objects wherein there is great superficial unlikeness. Thus architecture is called "frozen music," by De Stael and Goethe. Vitruvius thought an architect should be a musician. "A Gothic church," said Coleridge, "is a petrified religion." Michael Angelo maintained, that, to an architect, a knowledge of anatomy is essential. In Haydn's oratorios, the notes present to the imagination not only motions, as, of the snake, the stag, and the elephant, but colors also; as the green grass. The law of harmonic sounds reappears in the harmonic colors. The granite is differenced in its laws only by the more or less of heat, from the river that wears it away. The river, as it flows, resembles the air that flows over it; the air resembles the light which traverses it with more subtle currents; the light resembles the heat which rides with it through Space. Each creature is only a modification of the other; the likeness in them is more than the difference, and their radical law is one and the same. Hence it is, that a rule of one art, or a law of one organization, holds true throughout nature. So intimate is this Unity, that, it is easily seen, it lies under the undermost garment of nature, and betrays its source in universal Spirit. For, it pervades Thought also. Every universal truth which we express in words, implies or supposes every other truth. *Omne verum vero consonat.* It is like a great circle on a sphere, comprising all possible circles; which, however, may be drawn, and comprise it, in like manner. Every such truth is the absolute Ens seen from one side. But it has innumerable sides.

The same central Unity is still more conspicuous in actions. Words are finite organs of the infinite mind. They cannot cover the dimensions of what is in truth. They break, chop, and impoverish it. An action is the perfection and publication of thought. A right action seems to fill the eye, and to be related to all nature. "The wise man, in doing one thing, does all; or, in the one thing he does rightly, he sees the likeness of all which is done rightly."

Words and actions are not the attributes of mute and brute nature. They introduce us to the human form, of which all other organizations appear to be degradations. When this organization appears among so many that surround it, the spirit prefers it to all others. It says, 'From such as this, have I drawn joy and knowledge. In such as this, have I found and beheld myself. I will speak to it. It can speak again. It can yield me thought already formed and alive.' In fact, the eye,— the mind,—is always accompanied by these forms, male and female; and these are incomparably the richest informations of the power and order that lie at the heart of things. Unfortunately, every one of them bears the marks as of some injury; is marred and superficially defective. Nevertheless, far different from the deaf and dumb nature around them, these all rest like fountain-pipes on the unfathomed sea of thought and virtue whereto they alone, of all organizations, are the entrances.

It were a pleasant inquiry to follow into detail their ministry to our education, but where would it stop? We are associated in adolescent and adult life with some friends, who, like skies and waters, are coextensive with our idea; who, answering each to a certain affection of the soul, satisfy our desire on that side; whom we lack power to put at such focal distance from us, that we can mend or even analyze them. We cannot chuse but love them. When much intercourse with a friend has supplied us with a standard of excellence, and has increased our respect for the resources of God who thus sends a real person to outgo our ideal; when he has, moreover, become an object of thought, and, whilst his character retains all its unconscious effect, is converted in the mind into solid and sweet wisdom,—it is a sign to us that his office is closing, and he is commonly withdrawn from our sight in a short time.

Chapter VI. Idealism

Thus is the unspeakable but intelligible and practicable meaning of the world conveyed to man, the immortal pupil, in every object of sense. To this one end of Discipline, all parts of nature conspire.

A noble doubt perpetually suggests itself, whether this end be not the Final Cause of the Universe; and whether nature outwardly exists. It is a sufficient account of that Appearance we call the World, that God will teach a human mind, and so makes it the receiver of a certain number of congruent sensations, which we call sun and moon, man and woman, house and trade. In my utter impotence to test the authenticity of the report of my senses, to know whether the impressions they make on me correspond with outlying objects, what difference does it make, whether Orion is up there in heaven, or some god paints the image in the firmament of the soul? The relations of parts and the end of the whole remaining the same, what is the difference, whether land and sea interact, and worlds revolve and intermingle without number or end,—deep yawning under deep, and galaxy balancing galaxy, throughout absolute space, or, whether, without relations of time and space, the same appearances are inscribed in the constant faith of man? Whether nature enjoy a substantial existence without, or is only in the apocalypse of the mind, it is alike useful and alike venerable to me. Be it what it may, it is ideal to me, so long as I cannot try the accuracy of my senses.

The frivolous make themselves merry with the Ideal theory, as if its consequences were burlesque; as if it affected the stability of nature. It surely does not. God never jests with us, and will not compromise the end of nature, by permitting any inconsequence in its procession. Any distrust of the permanence of laws, would paralyze the faculties of man. Their permanence is sacredly respected, and his faith therein is perfect. The wheels and springs of man are all set to the hypothesis of the permanence of nature. We are not built a like a ship to be tossed, but like a house to stand. It is a natural consequence of this structure, that, so long as the active powers predominate over the reflective, we resist with indignation any hint that nature is more short-lived or mutable than spirit. The broker, the wheelwright, the carpenter, the toll-man, are much displeased at the intimation.

But whilst we acquiesce entirely in the permanence of natural laws, the question of the absolute existence of nature, still remains open. It is the uniform effect of culture on the human mind, not to shake our faith in the stability of particular phenomena, as of heat, water, azote; but to lead us to regard nature as a phenomenon, not a substance; to attribute necessary existence to spirit; to esteem nature as an accident and an effect.

To the senses and the unrenewed understanding, belongs a sort of instinctive belief in the absolute existence of nature. In their view, man and nature are indissolubly joined. Things are ultimates, and they never look beyond their sphere. The presence of Reason mars this faith. The first effort of thought tends to relax this despotism of the senses, which binds us to nature as if we were a part of it, and shows us nature aloof, and, as it were, afloat. Until this higher agency intervened, the animal eye sees, with wonderful accuracy, sharp outlines and colored surfaces. When the eye of Reason opens, to outline and surface are at once added, grace and expression. These proceed from imagination and affection, and abate somewhat of the angular distinctness of objects. If the Reason be stimulated to more earnest vision, outlines and surfaces become transparent, and are no longer seen; causes and spirits are seen through them. The best, the happiest moments of life, are these delicious awakenings of the higher powers, and the reverential withdrawing of nature before its God.

Let us proceed to indicate the effects of culture. 1. Our first institution in the Ideal philosophy is a hint from nature herself.

Nature is made to conspire with spirit to emancipate us. Certain mechanical changes, a small alteration in our local position apprizes us of a dualism. We are strangely affected by seeing the shore from a moving ship, from a balloon, or through the tints of an unusual sky. The least change in our point of view, gives the whole world a pictorial air. A man who seldom rides, needs only to get into a coach and traverse his own town, to turn the street into a puppet show. The men, the women,—talking, running, bartering, fighting,—the earnest mechanic, the lounger, the beggar, the boys, the dogs, are unrealized at once, or, at least, wholly detached from all relation to the observer, and seen as apparent, not substantial beings. What new thoughts are suggested by seeing a face of country quite familiar, in the rapid movement of the rail-road car! Nay, the most wonted objects, (make a very slight change in the point of vision,) please us most. In a camera obscura, the butcher's cart, and the figure of one of our own family amuse us. So a portrait of a well-known face gratifies us. Turn the eyes upside down, by looking at the landscape through your legs, and how agreeable is the picture, though you have seen it any time these twenty years!

In these cases, by mechanical means, is suggested the difference between the observer and the spectacle,—between man and nature. Hence arises a pleasure mixed with awe; I may say, a low degree of the sublime is felt from the fact, probably, that man is hereby apprized, that, whilst the world is a spectacle, something in himself is stable.

2. In a higher manner, the poet communicates the same pleasure. By a few strokes he delineates, as on air, the sun, the mountain, the camp, the city, the hero, the maiden, not different from what we know them, but only lifted from the ground and afloat before the eye. He unfixes the land and the sea, makes them revolve around the axis of his primary thought, and disposes them anew. Possessed himself by a heroic passion, he uses matter as symbols of it. The sensual man conforms thoughts to things; the poet conforms things to his thoughts. The one esteems nature as rooted and fast; the other, as fluid, and impresses his being thereon. To him, the refractory world is ductile and flexible; he invests dust and stones with humanity, and makes them the words of the Reason. The imagination may be defined to be, the use which the Reason makes of the material world. Shakspeare possesses the power of subordinating nature for the purposes of expression, beyond all poets. His imperial muse tosses the creation like a bauble from hand to hand, and uses it to embody any capricious shade of thought that is uppermost in his mind. The remotest spaces of nature are visited, and the farthest sundered things are brought together, by a subtile spiritual connexion. We are made aware that magnitude of

material things is merely relative, and all objects shrink and expand to serve the passion of the poet. Thus, in his sonnets, the lays of birds, the scents and dyes of flowers, he finds to be the *shadow* of his beloved; time, which keeps her from him, is his *chest;* the suspicion she has awakened, is her *ornament;*

> The ornament of beauty is Suspect,
> A crow which flies in heaven's sweetest air.

His passion is not the fruit of chance; it swells, as he speaks, to a city, or a state.

> No, it was builded far from accident;
> It suffers not in smiling pomp, nor falls
> Under the brow of thralling discontent;
> It fears not policy, that heretic,
> That works on leases of short numbered hours,
> But all alone stands hugely politic.

In the strength of his constancy, the Pyramids seem to him recent and transitory. And the freshness of youth and love dazzles him with its resemblance to morning.

> Take those lips away
> Which so sweetly were forsworn;
> And those eyes,—the break of day,
> Lights that do mislead the morn.

The wild beauty of this hyperbole, I may say, in passing, it would not be easy to match in literature.

This transfiguration which all material objects undergo through the passion of the poet,—this power which he exerts, at any moment, to magnify the small, to micrify the great,—might be illustrated by a thousand examples from his Plays. I have before me the Tempest, and will cite only these few lines.

> ARIEL. The strong based promontory
> Have I made shake, and by the spurs plucked up
> The pine and cedar.

Prospero calls for music to sooth the frantic Alonzo, and his companions;

A solemn air, and the best comforter
To an unsettled fancy, cure thy brains
Now useless, boiled within thy skull.

Again;

The charm dissolves apace
And, as the morning steals upon the night,
Melting the darkness, so their rising senses
Begin to chase the ignorant fumes that mantle
Their clearer reason.
Their understanding
Begins to swell: and the approaching tide
Will shortly fill the reasonable shores
That now lie foul and muddy.

The perception of real affinities between events, (that is to say, of
ideal affinities, for those only are real,) enables the poet thus to make
free with the most imposing forms and phenomena of the world, and
to assert the predominance of the soul.

3. Whilst thus the poet delights us by animating nature like a creator, with his own thoughts, he differs from the philosopher only
herein, that the one proposes Beauty as his main end; the other Truth.
But, the philosopher, not less than the poet, postpones the apparent
order and relations of things to the empire of thought. "The problem
of philosophy," according to Plato, "is, for all that exists conditionally,
to find a ground unconditioned and absolute." It proceeds on the faith
that a law determines all phenomena, which being known, the phenomena can be predicted. That law, when in the mind, is an idea. Its
beauty is infinite. The true philosopher and the true poet are one,
and a beauty, which is truth, and a truth, which is beauty, is the aim
of both. Is not the charm of one of Plato's or Aristotle's definitions,
strictly like that of the Antigone of Sophocles? It is, in both cases, that
a spiritual life has been imparted to nature; that the solid seeming

block of matter has been pervaded and dissolved by a thought; that this feeble human being has penetrated the vast masses of nature with an informing soul, and recognised itself in their harmony, that is, seized their law. In physics, when this is attained, the memory disburthens itself of its cumbrous catalogues of particulars, and carries centuries of observation in a single formula.

Thus even in physics, the material is ever degraded before the spiritual. The astronomer, the geometer, rely on their irrefragable analysis, and disdain the results of observation. The sublime remark of Euler on his law of arches, "This will be found contrary to all experience, yet is true;" had already transferred nature into the mind, and left matter like an outcast corpse.

4. Intellectual science has been observed to beget invariably a doubt of the existence of matter. Turgot said, "He that has never doubted the existence of matter, may be assured he has no aptitude for metaphysical inquiries." It fastens the attention upon immortal the necessary uncreated natures, that is, upon Ideas; and in their beautiful and majestic presence, we feel that our outward being is a dream and a shade. Whilst we wait in this Olympus of gods, we think of nature as an appendix to the soul. We ascend into their region, and know that these are the thoughts of the Supreme Being. "These are they who were set up from everlasting, from the beginning, or ever the earth was. When he prepared the heavens, they were there; when he established the clouds above, when he strengthened the fountains of the deep. Then they were by him, as one brought up with him. Of them took he counsel."

Their influence is proportionate. As objects of science, they are accessible to few men. Yet all men are capable of being raised by piety or by passion, into their region. And no man touches these divine natures, without becoming, in some degree, himself divine. Like a new soul, they renew the body. We become physically nimble and lightsome; we tread on air; life is no longer irksome, and we think it will never be so. No man fears age or misfortune or death, in their serene company, for he is transported out of the district of change. Whilst we behold unveiled the nature of Justice and Truth, we learn the difference between the absolute and the conditional or relative. We apprehend the absolute. As it were, for the first time, *we exist*. We become immortal, for we learn that time and space are relations of matter; that, with a perception of truth, or a virtuous will, they have no affinity.

5. Finally, religion and ethics, which may be fitly called,—the practice of ideas, or the introduction of ideas into life,—have an analogous effect with all lower culture, in degrading nature and suggesting its dependence on spirit. Ethics and religion differ herein; that the one is the system of human duties commencing from man; the other, from God. Religion includes the personality of God; Ethics does not. They are one to our present design. They both put nature under foot. The first and last lesson of religion is, "The things that are seen, are temporal; the things that are unseen are eternal." It puts an affront upon nature. It does that for the unschooled, which philosophy does for Berkeley and Viasa. The uniform language that may be heard in the churches of the most ignorant sects, is,—'Contemn the unsubstantial shows of the world; they are vanities, dreams, shadows, unrealities; seek the realities of religion.' The devotee flouts nature. Some theosophists have arrived at a certain hostility and indignation towards matter, as the Manichean and Plotinus. They distrusted in themselves any looking back to these flesh-pots of Egypt. Plotinus was ashamed of his body. In short, they might all better say of matter, what Michael Angelo said of external beauty, "it is the frail and weary weed, in which God dresses the soul, which he has called into time."

It appears that motion, poetry, physical and intellectual science, and religion, all tend to affect our convictions of the reality of the external world. But I own there is something ungrateful in expanding too curiously the particulars of the general proposition, that all culture tends to imbue us with idealism. I have no hostility to nature, but a child's love to it. I expand and live in the warm day like corn and melons. Let us speak her fair. I do not wish to fling stones at my beautiful mother, nor soil my gentle nest. I only wish to indicate the true position of nature in regard to man, wherein to establish man, all right education tends; as the ground which to attain is the object of human life, that is, of man's connexion with nature. Culture inverts the vulgar views of nature, and brings the mind to call that apparent, which it uses to call real, and that real, which it uses to call visionary. Children, it is true, believe in the external world. The belief that it appears only, is an afterthought, but with culture, this faith will as surely arise on the mind as did the first.

The advantage of the ideal theory over the popular faith, is this, that it presents the world in precisely that view which is most desirable to the mind. It is, in fact, the view which Reason, both speculative and practical, that is, philosophy and virtue, take. For, seen in the light of thought, the world always is phenomenal; and virtue subordinates it to the mind. Idealism sees the world in God. It beholds the whole circle of persons and things, of actions and events, of country and religion, not as painfully accumulated, atom after atom, act after act, in an aged creeping Past, but as one vast picture, which God paints on the instant eternity, for the contemplation of the soul. Therefore the soul holds itself off from a too trivial and microscopic study of the universal tablet. It respects the end too much, to immerse itself in the means. It sees something more important in Christianity, than the scandals of ecclesiastical history or the niceties of criticism; and, very incurious concerning persons or miracles, and not at all disturbed by chasms of historical evidence, it accepts from God the phenomenon, as it finds it, as the pure and awful form of religion in the world. It is not hot and passionate at the appearance of what it calls its own good or bad fortune, at the union or opposition of other persons. No man is its enemy. It accepts whatsoever befals, as part of its lesson. It is a watcher more than a doer, and it is a doer, only that it may the better watch.

Chapter VII. Spirit

It is essential to a true theory of nature and of man, that it should contain somewhat progressive. Uses that are exhausted or that may be, and facts that end in the statement, cannot be all that is true of this brave lodging wherein man is harbored, and wherein all his faculties find appropriate and endless exercise. And all the uses of nature admit of being summed in one, which yields the activity of man an infinite scope. Through all its kingdoms, to the suburbs and outskirts of things, it is faithful to the cause whence it had its origin. It always speaks of Spirit. It suggests the absolute. It is a perpetual effect. It is a great shadow pointing always to the sun behind us.

The aspect of nature is devout. Like the figure of Jesus, she stands with bended head, and hands folded upon the breast. The happiest man is he who learns from nature the lesson of worship.

Of that ineffable essence which we call Spirit, he that thinks most, will say least. We can foresee God in the course and, as it were, distant phenomena of matter; but when we try to define and describe himself, both language and thought desert us, and we are as helpless as fools and savages. That essence refuses to be recorded in propositions, but when man has worshipped him intellectually, the noblest ministry of nature is to stand as the apparition of God. It is the great organ through which the universal spirit speaks to the individual, and strives to lead back the individual to it.

When we consider Spirit, we see that the views already presented do not include the whole circumference of man. We must add some related thoughts.

Three problems are put by nature to the mind; What is matter? Whence is it? and Whereto? The first of these questions only, the ideal theory answers. Idealism saith: matter is a phenomenon, not a *perceivable* substance. Idealism acquaints us with the total disparity between the evidence of our own being, *divest* and the evidence of the world's being. The one is perfect; the other, incapable of any assurance; the mind is a part of the nature of things; the world is a divine dream, from which we may presently awake to the glories and certainties of day. Idealism is a hypothesis to account for nature by other principles than those of carpentry and chemistry. Yet, if it only deny the existence of matter, it does not satisfy the demands of the spirit. It leaves God out of me. It leaves me in the splendid labyrinth of my perceptions, to wander without end. Then the heart resists it, because it baulks the affections in denying substantive being to men and women. Nature is so pervaded with human life, that there is something of humanity in all, and in every particular. But this theory makes nature foreign to me, and does not account for that consanguinity which we acknowledge to it.

Let it stand then, in the present state of our knowledge, merely as a useful introductory hypothesis, serving to apprize us of the eternal distinction between the soul and the world.

But when, following the invisible steps of thought, we come to

What is in us that is also in nature?

inquire, Whence is matter? and Whereto? many truths arise to us out of the recesses of consciousness. We learn that the highest is present to the soul of man, that the dread universal essence, which is not wisdom, or love, or beauty, or power, but all in one, and each entirely, is that for which all things exist, and that by which they are; that spirit creates; that behind nature, throughout nature, spirit is present; that spirit is one and not compound; that spirit does not act upon us from without, that is, in space and time, but spiritually, or through ourselves. Therefore, that spirit, that is, the Supreme Being, does not build up nature around us, but puts it forth through us, as the life of the tree puts forth new branches and leaves through the pores of the old. As a plant upon the earth, so a man rests upon the bosom of God; he is nourished by unfailing fountains, and draws, at his is need, inexhaustible power. Who can set bounds to the possibilities of man? Once inhale the upper air, being admitted to behold the absolute natures of justice and truth, and we learn that man has access to the entire mind of the Creator, is himself the creator in the finite. This view, which admonishes me where the sources of wisdom and power lie, and points to virtue as to

"The golden key
Which opes the palace of eternity,"

God, Nature and man all the same, but we are as much Aliens from Nature as we are from God

carries upon its face the highest certificate of truth, because it animates me to create my own world through the purification of my soul.

The world proceeds from the same spirit as the body of man. It is a remoter and inferior incarnation of God, a projection of God in the unconscious. But it differs from the body in one important respect. It is not, like that, now subjected to the human will. Its serene order is inviolable by us. It is therefore, to us, the present expositor of the divine mind. It is a fixed point whereby we may measure our departure. As we degenerate, the contrast between us and our house is more evident. We are as much strangers in nature, as we are aliens from God. We do not understand the notes of birds. The fox and the deer run away from us; the bear and tiger rend us. We do not know the uses of more than a few plants, as corn and the apple, the potato and the vine. Is not the landscape, every glimpse of which hath a grandeur, a face of him? Yet this may show us what discord is between man and nature, for you cannot freely admire a noble landscape, if laborers are digging in the field hard by. The poet finds something ridiculous in his delight, until he is out of the sight of men.

Chapter VIII. Prospects

In inquiries respecting the laws of the world and the frame of things, the highest reason is always the truest. That which seems faintly possible—it is so refined, is often faint and dim because it is deepest seated in the mind among the eternal verities. Empirical science is apt to cloud the sight, and, by the very knowledge of functions and processes, to bereave the student of the manly contemplation of the whole. The savant becomes unpoetic. But the best read naturalist who lends an entire and devout attention to truth, will see that there remains much to learn of his relation to the world, and that it is not to be learned by any addition or subtraction or other comparison of known quantities, but is arrived at by untaught sallies of the spirit, by a continual self-recovery, and by entire humility. He will perceive that there are far more excellent qualities in the student than preciseness and infallibility; that a guess is often more fruitful than an indisputable affirmation, and that a dream may let us deeper into the secret of nature than a hundred concerted experiments.

Intuition

For, the problems to be solved are precisely those which the physiologist and the naturalist omit to state. It is not so pertinent to man to know all the individuals of the animal kingdom, as it is to know whence and whereto is this tyrannizing unity in his constitution, which evermore separates and classifies things, endeavoring to reduce the most diverse to one form. When I behold a rich landscape, it is less to my purpose to recite correctly the order and superposition of the strata, than to know why all thought of multitude is lost in a tranquil sense of unity. I cannot greatly honor minuteness in details, so long as there is no hint to explain the relation between things and thoughts, no ray upon the *metaphysics* of conchology, of botany, of the arts, to show the relation of the forms of flowers, shells, animals, architecture, to the mind, and build science upon ideas. In a cabinet of natural history, we become sensible of a certain occult recognition and sympathy in regard

display cabinet of species / Plants

to the most unwieldy and eccentric forms of beast, fish, and insect. The American who has been confined, in his own country, to the sight of buildings designed after foreign models, is surprised on entering York Minster or St. Peter's at Rome, by the feeling that these structures are imitations also,—faint copies of an invisible archetype. Nor has science sufficient humanity, so long as the naturalist overlooks that wonderful congruity which subsists between man and the world; of which he is lord, not because he is the most subtile inhabitant, but because he is its head and heart, and finds something of himself in every great and small thing, in every mountain stratum, in every new law of color, fact of astronomy, or atmospheric influence which observation or analysis lay open. A perception of this mystery inspires the muse of George Herbert, the beautiful psalmist of the seventeenth century. The following lines are part of his little poem on Man.

"Man is all symmetry,
Full of proportions, one limb to another,
And to all the world besides.
Each part may call the farthest, brother;
For head with foot hath private amity,
And both with moons and tides.

"Nothing hath got so far
But man hath caught and kept it as his prey;
His eyes dismount the highest star;
He is in little all the sphere.
Herbs gladly cure our flesh, because that they
Find their acquaintance there.

"For us, the winds do blow,
The earth doth rest, heaven move, and fountains flow;
Nothing we see, but means our good,
As our delight, or as our treasure;
The whole is either our cupboard of food,
Or cabinet of pleasure.

"The stars have us to bed:
Night draws the curtain; which the sun withdraws.

Music and light attend our head.
All things unto our flesh are kind,
In their descent and being; to our mind,
In their ascent and cause.

"More servants wait on man
Than he'll take notice of.
In every path,
He treads down that which doth befriend him
When sickness makes him pale and wan.
Oh mighty love! Man is one world, and hath
Another to attend him."

The perception of this class of truths makes the eternal attraction which draws men to science, but the end is lost sight of in attention to the means. In view of this half-sight of science, we accept the sentence of Plato, that, "poetry comes nearer to vital truth than history." Every surmise and vaticination of the mind is entitled to a certain respect, and we learn to prefer imperfect theories, and sentences, which contain glimpses of truth, to digested systems which have no one valuable suggestion. A wise writer will feel that the ends of study and composition are best answered by announcing undiscovered regions of thought, and so communicating, through hope, new activity to the torpid spirit.

I shall therefore conclude this essay with some traditions of man and nature, which a certain poet sang to me; and which, as they have always been in the world, and perhaps reappear to every bard, may be both history and prophecy.

'The foundations of man are not in matter, but in spirit. But the element of spirit is eternity. To it, therefore, the longest series of events, the oldest chronologies are young and recent. In the cycle of the universal man, from whom the known individuals proceed, centuries are points, and all history is but the epoch of one degradation.

'We distrust and deny inwardly our sympathy with nature. We own and disown our relation to it, by turns. We are, like Nebuchadnezzar, dethroned, bereft of reason, and eating grass like an ox. But who can set limits to the remedial force of spirit?

'A man is a god in ruins. When men are innocent, life shall be longer, and shall pass into the immortal, as gently as we awake from dreams. Now, the world would be insane and rabid, if these disorganizations should last for hundreds of years. It is kept in check by death and infancy. Infancy is the perpetual Messiah, which comes into the arms of fallen men, and pleads with them to return to paradise.

'Man is the dwarf of himself. Once he was permeated and dissolved by spirit. He filled nature with his overflowing currents. Out from him sprang the sun and moon; from man, the sun; from woman, the moon. The laws of his mind, the periods of his actions externized themselves into day and night, into the year and the seasons. But, having made for himself this huge shell, his waters retired; he no longer fills the veins and veinlets; he is shrunk to a drop. He sees, that the structure still fits him, but fits him colossally. Say, rather, once it fitted him, now it corresponds to him from far and on high. He adores timidly his own work. Now is man the follower of the sun, and woman the follower of the moon. Yet sometimes he starts in his slumber, and wonders at himself and his house, and muses strangely at the resemblance betwixt him and it. He perceives that if his law is still paramount, if still he have elemental power, "if his word is sterling yet in nature," it is not conscious power, it is not inferior but superior to his will. It is Instinct.' Thus my Orphic poet sang.

At present, man applies to nature but half his force. He works on the world with his understanding alone. He lives in it, and masters it by a penny-wisdom; and he that works most in it, is but a half-man, and whilst his arms are strong and his digestion good, his mind is imbruted and he is a selfish savage. His relation to nature, his power over it, is through the understanding; as by manure; the economic use of fire, wind, water, and the mariner's needle; steam, coal, chemical agriculture; the repairs of the human body by the dentist and the surgeon. This is such a resumption of power, as if a banished king should buy his territories inch by inch, instead of vaulting at once into his throne. [Meantime, in the thick darkness, there are not wanting gleams of a better light,—occasional examples of the action of man upon nature with his entire force,—with reason as well as understanding. Such examples are; the traditions of miracles in the earliest antiquity of all nations; the history of Jesus Christ; the achievements of a principle, as in religious

↑
Envisions Unbridled
Power of Man

and political revolutions, and in the abolition of the Slave-trade; the miracles of enthusiasm, as those reported of Swedenborg, Hohenlohe, and the Shakers; many obscure and yet contested facts, now arranged under the name of Animal Magnetism; prayer; eloquence; self-healing; and the wisdom of children. These are examples of Reason's momentary grasp of the sceptre; the exertions of a power which exists not in time or space, but an instantaneous in-streaming causing power. The difference between the actual and the ideal force of man is happily figured by the schoolmen, in saying, that the knowledge of man is an evening knowledge, *vespertina cognitio*, but that of God is a morning knowledge, *matutina cognitio*.

The problem of restoring to the world original and eternal beauty, is solved by the redemption of the soul. The ruin or the blank, that we see when we look at nature, is in our own eye. The axis of vision is not coincident with the axis of things, and so they appear not transparent but opake. The reason why the world lacks unity, and lies broken and in heaps, is, because man is disunited with himself. He cannot be a naturalist, until he satisfies all the demands of the spirit. Love is as much its demand, as perception. Indeed, neither can be perfect without the other. In the uttermost meaning of the words, thought is devout, and devotion is thought. Deep calls unto deep. But in actual life, the marriage is not celebrated. There are innocent men who worship God after the tradition of their fathers, but their sense of duty has not yet extended to the use of all their faculties. And there are patient naturalists, but they freeze their subject under the wintry light of the understanding. Is not prayer also a study of truth,—a sally of the soul into the unfound infinite? No man ever prayed heartily, without learning something. But when a faithful thinker, resolute to detach every object from personal relations, and see it in the light of thought, shall, at the same time, kindle science with the fire of the holiest affections, then will God go forth anew into the creation.

It will not need, when the mind is prepared for study, to search for objects. The invariable mark of wisdom is to see the miraculous in the common. What is a day? What is a year? What is summer? What is woman? What is a child? What is sleep? To our blindness, these things seem unaffecting. We make fables to hide the baldness of the fact and

Self-reliance = trusting intuition

conform it, as we say, to the higher law of the mind. But when the fact is seen under the light of an idea, the gaudy fable fades and shrivels. We behold the real higher law. To the wise, therefore, a fact is true poetry, and the most beautiful of fables. These wonders are brought to our own door. You also are a man. Man and woman, and their social life, poverty, labor, sleep, fear, fortune, are known to you. Learn that none of these things is superficial, but that each phenomenon hath its roots in the faculties and affections of the mind. Whilst the abstract question occupies your intellect, nature brings it in the concrete to be solved by your hands. It were a wise inquiry for the closet, to compare, point by point, especially at remarkable crises in life, our daily history, with the rise and progress of ideas in the mind.

So shall we come to look at the world with new eyes. It shall answer the endless inquiry of the intellect,—What is truth? and of the affections,—What is good? by yielding itself passive to the educated Will. Then shall come to pass what my poet said; 'Nature is not fixed but fluid. Spirit alters, moulds, makes it. The immobility or bruteness of nature, is the absence of spirit; to pure spirit, it is fluid, it is volatile, it is obedient. Every spirit builds itself a house; and beyond its house, a world; and beyond its world, a heaven. Know then, that the world exists for you. For you is the phenomenon perfect. What we are, that only can we see. All that Adam had, all that Cæsar could, you have and can do. Adam called his house, heaven and earth; Cæsar called his house, Rome; you perhaps call yours, a cobler's trade; a hundred acres of ploughed land; or a scholar's garret. Yet line for line and point for point, your dominion is as great as theirs, though without fine names. Build, therefore, your own world. As fast as you conform your life to the pure idea in your mind, that will unfold its great proportions. A correspondent revolution in things will attend the influx of the spirit. So fast will disagreeable appearances, swine, spiders, snakes, pests, mad-houses, prisons, enemies, vanish; they are temporary and shall be no more seen. The sordor and filths of nature, the sun shall dry up, and the wind exhale. As when the summer comes from the south, the snow-banks melt, and the face of the earth becomes green before it, so shall the advancing spirit create its ornaments along its path, and carry with it the beauty it visits, and the song which enchants it; it shall draw beautiful faces, and warm hearts, and wise discourse, and heroic acts, around its way, until evil is no more seen. The kingdom of man over nature, which cometh not with observation,—a dominion such as now is beyond his dream of God,—he shall enter without more wonder than the blind man feels who is gradually restored to perfect sight.'

Humanity of Science

(1836)

Emerson delivered "Humanity of Science" on
December 22, 1836, at the Masonic Temple in
Boston as part of The Philosophy of History lecture series. A sign of
Emerson's growing stature, these lectures made up his first inde-
pendently managed series. This new freedom provided the forum for
his prodigious creativity in the autumn of 1836 through the spring of
1837—a remarkably productive period that included the publication
of *Nature,* the establishment of the Transcendental Club, and the
birth of his first son, Waldo. In The Philosophy of History lectures,
Emerson attempted to identify the few immutable laws that under-
lie all natural phenomena—what he referred to as the "nature of
things"—through a study of art, science, literature, and history. The
second lecture of the series, "Humanity of Science," presents what
Emerson sees as the primary benefit of science to humanity: the
mapping of relationships in the natural world. Emerson identifies this
effort to classify what is new or unfamiliar as a primary instinct. He
postulates that this natural tendency is reinforced by the feelings of
delight inspired by a discovery of interrelation. For Emerson, these
moments of perceiving connections are possible because nature
adheres to a grand unity, which is inherent in each natural object
and can be understood only through an examination of relation. The
ability to discern this connection is evidence of the correspondence
between the order of nature and that of the mind, an idea central to
Emerson's philosophy. Often referred to as the "Doctrine of Correspondence," this idea—derived from the work of the Swedish
scientist and mystic Emanuel Swedenborg—holds that everything

in nature has a counterpart in the human mind. Although it is never wholly knowable, a greater understanding of this unity is the primary mission of Emerson's poetic naturalist.

♣

It is the perpetual effort of the mind to seek relations between the multitude of facts under its eye, by means of which it can reduce them to some order. The mind busies itself in a perpetual comparison of objects to find resemblances by which those resembling may be set apart as a class. Of those resembling it seeks to abstract the common property; which it compares again with another common property of another resembling class, to derive from these two, a still higher common property. This is method, classification.

The child puts his playthings in a circle or in a row; he builds his blocks into a spire or a house; he aims still at some intelligible arrangement. A man puts his tools in one place; his food in another; his clothes in a third, his ornaments in a fourth. Woman is an angel of system. Her love of order is a proverbial blessing. A house is her classification. The art of bookkeeping is a striking example of the pleasure and the power of arbitrary classification. A state, an army, a shop, a school, a post-office are others.

The first process of thought in examining a new object is to compare it with known objects and refer it to a class. The mind is reluctant to make many classes or to suppose many causes. This reduction to a few laws, to one law, is not a choice of the individual. It is the tyrannical instinct of the mind.

This act of classifying is attended with pleasure, as it is a sort of unlocking the spiritual sight. I am shown a violet, the heartsease, for example. If I have never seen a plant of the sort I fasten my attention on the stem, leaves, and petals, of this; and I do not easily believe in the existence of any other sort of violet, than that I see. But another is shown me, the white; then the round-leaved; then the yellow. I see each with a livelier pleasure, and begin to see that there exists a violet family, after which type all these particular varieties are made. I experience the like delight in being shown each of the tribes in the natural system of Botany, as the liliaceous, the papilionaceous, the mosses, or the grasses.

There is great difference between men in this habit or power of classifying. Some men unite things by their superficial resemblances, as if you should arrange a company by the color of their dress, or by their size, or complexion. Others by occult resemblances, which is the habit of wit; others by intrinsic likeness, which is science. The great moments of scientific history, have been the perception of these relations.

Newton sees an apple fall, and cries—"the motion of the moon is but an apple-fall; the motion of the earth is but a larger apple-fall. I see the law of all nature"—and slow observation makes good this bold word. It happened in our time that a German poet beholding a plant and seeing, as we may see in a pond-lily, a petal in transition from a leaf, exclaimed, And why is not every part of a plant a transformed leaf? a petal is a leaf, a fruit is a leaf, a seed is a leaf, metamorphosed, and slow-paced experiment has made good this prophetic vision, that is, it may be demonstrated that a flower is analogous in its structure to a branch covered with leaves,—is a branch of metamorphosed leaves. This is shown by proving a bract to be a modification of a leaf; a sepal of a bract; a petal of a sepal; a stamen of a petal; the carpel of a leaf; the ovule of a leaf-bud, a view now accepted by the English and French botanists.

The same gifted man walking in the Jews' burying ground in the city of Venice saw a sheep's skull on the ground and was struck with the gradation by which the vertebrae passed into the bones of the head. Instantly he said to himself, the vertebra of the spine is the unit of anatomy; all other parts are merely metamorphoses, degradations, abortions, or enlargements of this. The head was only the uppermost vertebra transformed. "The plant goes from knot to knot, closing at last with the flower and the seed. So the tapeworm, the caterpillar, goes from knot to knot, and closes with the head. Man and the higher animals are built up through the vertebrae, the powers being concentrated in the head." He is the author of a beautiful theory of colors beginning to be studied in which the prismatic hues are reckoned simply mixtures of darkness and light.

The system of Lamarck aims to find a monad of organic life which shall be common to every animal, and which becomes an animalcule, a poplar-worm, a mastiff, or a man, according to circumstances. It says to the caterpillar, "How dost thou, Brother! Please God, you shall yet be a philosopher." In the like spirit of audacious system another physiologist concludes that the monad becomes animal or plant only according to the element of darkness or light in which it unfolds. These are extreme examples of the impatience of the human mind in the presence of a multitude of facts, and the energy with which it aims to find some mark on them according to which they can all be set in some order.

Classification is one of the main actions of the intellect. A man of great sagacity divides, distributes, with every word he speaks. And we are always at the mercy of a better classifier than ourselves.

Every system of faith, every theory of science, every argument of a barrister, is a classification, and gives the mind the sense of power in proportion to the truth or centrality of the traits by which it arranges. Calvinism, Romanism, and the Church of Swedenborg, are three striking examples of coherent systems which each organize the best-known facts of the world's history, and the qualities of character into an order that reacts directly on the will of the individual. The success of Phrenology is a lively proof of the pleasure which a classification of the most interesting phenomena gives to the unscientific.

Whilst we consider this appetite of the mind to arrange its phenomena, there is another fact which makes this useful.

There is in nature a parallel unity, which corresponds to this unity in the mind, and makes it available. This methodizing mind meets no resistance in its attempts. The scattered blocks with which it strives to form a symmetrical structure, fit. This design following after, finds with joy that like design went before. Not only man puts things in a row, but things belong in a row. The immense variety of objects is really composed of a few elements. The world is the fulfilment of a few laws.

Hence, the possibility of Science. When one considers the feeble physical nature of man, how disproportionate to the natures which he investigates, he may well ask, How to such an animal, of seventy inches, walking and in the earth, is the solar system measurable and the nature of matter universally? Because a straw shows how the stream runs, and the wind blows; because as falls the apple, so falls the moon; because as grows one inch of one vegetable in a flowerpot, so grow all the forests; and as one animal of one species is formed, so are formed all animals of all species; because in short the wide universe is made up of a few elements and a few laws; perhaps of one element and one law.

Nature works unique through many forms. All agents the most diverse are pervaded by radical analogies, so that music, optics, mechanics, galvanism, electricity, magnetism are only versions of one law. The study of one natural object is like the study of a book in a foreign language. When he has mastered that one book, the learner finds with joy that he can read with equal facility in ten thousand books. A half inch of vegetable tissue will tell all that can be known on the subject from all the forests; and one skeleton or a fragment of animal fibre intimately known is a zoological cabinet.

But whilst the laws of the world coexist in each particle, they cannot be learned by the exclusive study of one creature. A man shall not say, I will dedicate my life to the study of this moss, and through that I will achieve nature. Nature hates cripples and monomaniacs. All her secrets are locked in one plant; but she does not unlock them in any one. She shows one function in a tree, and another function in a seaweed. If the spiral vessels are exposed in a hyacinth, the vesicles are seen in a chara; the pila in a mullein; and chromule in sage; and to a show all the parts of one plant, she leads you round the whole garden. She writes every obscure and minute fact in colossal characters somewhere. Our microscopes are not necessary. They are a pretty toy for chamber philosophers, but nature has brought every fact within reach of the unarmed eye somewhere. It is difficult in the most level country or on the highest mountain to appreciate the outline of the earth, but on the seashore the dark blue sea line reveals at once the true curve of the globe. The question was once vexed whether mineral coal was of vegetable origin. Playfair found the bough of a tree which was perfect wood at one end, and passed through imperceptible gradations to perfect mineral coal at the other.

In the old fossil fishes, the earliest creation, the vertebrae of the back are not divided; but an unbroken cord or bone runs from the head to the tail. Modern science has discovered one or two fishes yet existing, in which the vertebral column is still undivided; thus bringing to the eye of the anatomist the reality of this antique and fabulous structure, and connecting it with the living races. Again; the utmost attention has been given by modern physiologists to microscopic observations of the changes of the egg, especially in fishes and reptiles. It is now found that the order of changes in the egg determines the order of the strata containing remains. Each of the temporary states through which the young animal passes in the egg, is the type of a great class of animals which existed in that form on the earth for thousands of years, and when doubt existed as to the priority of two strata, it has been determined by reference to the living egg.

A peat bog may show us how the coal mines were formed. A shower of rain in the mountains may explain the diluvial and alluvial formations: the frost shooting on the windowpane, the process of crystallization; the deposit of sediment in a boiling pot, is a small Vesuvius; as Vesuvius is a small Himalaya.

Science is the arrangement of the phenomena of the world after their essential relations. It is the reconstruction of nature in the mind. This is at once its ideal and its historical aspect.

The most striking trait of modern science is its approximation towards central truths. On all sides it is simplifying its laws and finding one cause for many effects. Unexpected resemblances in the most distant objects betray a common origin. It has been observed in earthquakes that remote countries were shaken at the same hour, showing that the explosion was far within the globe, and the vibrations communicated through vast hollows radiating from a deep centre to equidistant points on the surface, but points very distant from each other. In like manner, from a common law at the foundation of terrestrial natures may spring a great variety of surface actions. This is the theory of comparative anatomy. One grand idea hovers over a wide variety of forms. Look at the skeleton of man, with legs and arms. Then look at the horse or the ox, and you see the same skeleton with some variations. Occasionally, the type comes out conspicuously, when five fingers are severed, usually bound up in a hoof. In a bird, you see the same radical skeleton, but whilst the legs remain of the same use, the arm is deprived of the hand, is covered with feathers and made a wing. In the whale the forearm is a flipper to swim the sea. By insensible gradations, this one type may be detected in fishes and insects. It is so conspicuous, that Camper, the physiologist, was wont to draw on his blackboard the man, and by a few strokes transform him into a horse, then into an ox, into a bird, into a fish.

In like manner see how the type of a leaf is present and creative in all leaves. It was once supposed that the various forms of leaves required each a new theory for its form. A leaf was a body originally undivided which owing to some unintelligible action became cut into segments in different ways so as to acquire at last a lobed form. But more accurate botanists showed that at a certain distance from the stem the stalk of the leaf follows the analogy of the tree and begins to branch; each branch carrying with it its green coat of parenchyma. If these branches remain distinct we have the simplest form of leaf with many threadlike claws, such as occurs in some species of the ranunculus. If these claws should grow together at their edges, a more entire leaf is formed; if still more, a leaf more perfect like the wild geranium; then a fivefinger like the passion flower; and when the green web quite joins the claws, a round leaf like the plane tree or lime tree is at last produced.

The phenomena of sound and of light were observed to be strikingly similar. Both observed the same law of reflection, of radiation, of interference and harmony. Both were subject to the same law of interference. That is, two rays of light meeting, cause darkness; two beats of sound meeting, cause silence. Whenever the eye is affected by one prevailing color, it sees at the same time the accidental color; and in music, the ear is sensible at the same time to the fundamental note and its harmonic sounds.

It was then observed that the same laws might be translated into the laws of Heat; that all the principal phenomena of heat might be illustrated by a comparison with those of sound. The analogy is followed out, and Light, Heat, Sound, and the Waves of fluids are found to have the same laws of reflection, and are explained as undulations of an elastic medium.

This analogy is followed by others of deeper origin. Light and Heat are analogous in their law to Electricity and Magnetism. Magnetism and Electricity are shown to be identical,—the spark has been drawn from the magnet and polarity communicated to the needle by electricity. Then Davy thought that the primary cause of electrical effects and of chemical effects is one and the same,—the one acting on masses, the other on particles. The phenomena of crystallization resemble electric laws. The famous experiment of Chladni demonstrates a relation between harmonic sounds and proportioned forms. Finally the sublime conjecture sanctioned by the minds of Newton, Hooke, Boscovich, and now of Davy, that the forms of natural bodies depend upon different arrangements of the same particles of matter; that possibly the world shall be found to be composed of oxygen and hydrogen; and that even these two elements are but one matter in different states of electricity;—all these, whether they are premature generalizations or not, indicate the central unity, the common law that pervades nature from the deep centre to the unknown circumference.

In a just history, what is the face of science? What lesson does it teach? What wisdom will a philosopher draw from its recent progress?

A lesson which science teaches, unanimous in all her discoveries, is the omnipresence of spirit. Life, creation, and final causes meet us everywhere. The world is saturated with law. Beautifully shines a spirit through all the bruteness and toughness of matter. Alone omnipotent it converts all things to its own end. The adamant streams into softest but precise form before it. The same ponderable matter which lay yesterday in a clod of earth, today takes the form of a grain of wheat, and tomorrow, in fine nourishment, enters the stomach of man, replenishes the waste of the day, and sparkles in the humors of the eye, or grasps, pulls, or pushes, in the fingers of the hand. Life refuses to be analysed. The best studies of modern naturalists have developed the doctrines of Life and of Presence, of Life conceived as a sort of guardian genius of each animal and vegetable form which overpowers chemical laws, and of Presence whereby in chemistry atoms have a certain restraining atmospheric influence where they do not chemically act. Behind all the processes which the lens can detect, there is a *Life* in a seed, which predominates over all brute matter, and which irresistibly forces carbon, hydrogen, and water, to take shape in a shaft, in leaves, in colors of a lily, which they could never take themselves. More wonderful is it in animal nature. Above every being, over every organ, floats this predetermining law, whose inscrutable secret defies the microscope and the alembic. The naturalist must presuppose it, or his results are foolish and offensive. As the proverb says, "he counts without his host who leaves God out of his reckoning," so science is bankrupt which attempts to cut the knot which always spirit must untie.

In monsters there is never a new thing, but merely the joining of two normal forms that do not belong together; one being developed, the other not yet developed, as part fish, part man: it is right things out of place. "This we learn if from nothing else from malformations and monsters. If we never saw anything but what followed a known law, we should think there was a necessity for this thing; it could not be otherwise. But deviations, degradations, monsters, teach us that the law is not only firm and eternal, but is also alive; that the creature can turn itself, not indeed out of itself into somewhat else, but, within its own limits, into deformity; always however being holden back as with bit and bridle by the inexorable masterdom of the law."

This spiritual presence which awes us in the phenomena of life is not inactive elsewhere; for every step of Science is to find measures, checks, adaptations. There is no outlaw, no forgotten or useless matter in the globe. Nowhere is death, deformity, immoveableness; but as the ivy creeps over the ruined tower, and grass over the new-made grave, so, over the spoils of a mountain chain, shivered, abraded, and pulverized by frost, rain, and gravity, and brought down in ruins into the sea, a new architecture is commenced and perfected in darkness. Under the ooze of the Atlantic, she builds her basalts and pours melted granite like warm wax into fissures of clay and lime and when the deposits of a thousand rivers have strewn the bed of the ocean with every year a new floor of spoils, she blows her furnaces with a gas and lifts the bed of the ocean above the water and man enters from a boat, kindles a fire in the new world, and worships God thereon, plants a field and builds a school.

The ameliorating presence of spirit, using to great ends what is base and cheap, teaches in a very impressive manner. The order of the world has been wisely called "an open secret." And it is true that Nature's mode of concealing a law is in its very simplicity; she hides facts by putting them next us. Where is that power not present? Where are the crypts in which Nature has deposited her secret and notched every day of her thousand millenniums? In facts that stare at us all day; in the slab of the pavement, the stone of the wall, the side of the hill, the gravel of the brook. In these pages every strong agent has written his name, the whirlpool, the lake, the volcano, and the wind. The facts are capable of but one interpretation; as the rings on the tree or on the cow's horn record every year of their age. No leaps, no magic, eternal, tranquil procession of old familiar laws, the wildest convulsion never overstepping the calculable powers of the agents; the earthquake and boiling geyser as accurate results of known laws as the rosebud and the hatching of a robin's egg. The irresistible destroyers of the old are all the time strong builders of the new—the irresistible destroyers who have rent and shivered the planet being now as near and potent as ever, nay the beautiful companions and lights of man's daily walk, mountain and stream, cloud and frost, sun and moon. "In the economy of the world," said Hutton, "I can find no traces of a beginning, no prospect of an end."

The permanence and at the same time endless variety of spiritual nature finds its fit symbol in the durable world, which never preserves the same face for two moments. All things change; moon and star stand still never a moment. Heaven, earth, sea, air, and man are in a perpetual flux, yet is all motion circular, so that, whilst all parts move the All is still.

The two sciences of astronomy and geology have been explored with wonderful diligence in these times, and have bestowed splendid gifts on men. Astronomy, which seems to be geometry exemplified in the glorious diagrams of the sidereal heavens, is the most appeasing influence to the agitations of human life and is our symbol of material grandeur exhausting in its realities the straining conception of possible power, size, and duration.

But in all this extent our little globe and its friendly globes or globules that attend it, farther or nearer, are a sufficient guide and index.

Far as we rove in observation or induction, we never come into new laws. We can go nowhere into a foreign country, though we run along the vast diameters of the sidereal spaces.

In Geology, again, we have a book of Genesis, wherein we read when and how the worlds were made, and are introduced to periods as portentous as the distances of the sky. But here too, we are never strangers; it is the same functions, slower performed; the wheel of the clock which now revolves in the life of our species, once took the duration of many races of animals on the planet to complete its circle. The world was newer; the blood was colder; life had not yet so fierce a glow; or rather, the vast chart of being which lay in outline already, was to be prospectively and symmetrically consummated; an immense unity of plan we infer from these old medals of deluges and conflagrations, which has never been departed from, and can never: a plan successively realized and the now existing types were in view at the beginning.

Yet in all the multitude and range of spawning life, there is no unrelated creature, and the laws so firm and so apprehensible, that Cuvier not long since from a fragment of a fossil bone succeeded in restoring correctly the true skeleton and outline of a saurian; and Agassiz, in these very days, from a single scale of one fossil fish, undertook to determine the form of the perfect fish, and when, soon after, a specimen of the fish was found in the strata, it did not differ materially from the professor's drawing.

The presence and the antecedence of Spirit are impressively taught by modern science. Step by step with these facts, we are apprised of another, namely, the Humanity of that Spirit; or, that nature proceeds from a mind analogous to our own.

Nature proceeds from a mind congenial with ours. Nature is overflowed and saturated with humanity. All things solicit us to know them by obscure attractions which we call the beauty of nature. We explore them and learn their law; straightway we find the discovery an exalting influence. So that I may say, we more fully possess ourselves for our new possession. A certain enthusiasm, as all know, has attended the great naturalists. As we learn more, we see that it is natural to know. Each discovery takes away some deformity from things, and gives them beauty; or takes away a less beauty, which hid a greater. There is nothing in nature disagreeable, which science does not bereave of its offence. Anatomy and Chemistry awake an absorbing interest in processes and sights the most tedious and revolting to the ignorant, so that it is observed at universities that of all the liberal professions it is only students of medicine who work out of study hours.

As we advance in knowledge we learn that all wears this great countenance of wisdom. Nothing is mean. It speaks to the noblest faculties. It conspires with piety: it conspires with poetry. It is the work of a perfect mind but of one which he can follow and evermore become. The reason which in us is so dim a ray, is a conflagration of light in Nature. Man sees that it is the measure of his attainments, for so much of nature as he is ignorant of, just so much of his own mind does he not yet possess.

Reason finds itself at home in nature and everything fits man and is intelligible to him. My mind is not only an inlet into the human mind but into the inferior intelligences that surround us in the field and stall. To this point let me quote a passage from the works of an acute observer, the eminent historian of the Anglo-Saxons.

"If I could transfer my own mind divested of all the human knowledge it has acquired, but with its natural faculties unimpaired into the body of any fowl, and could give it the ideas and memory which their organs and habits have acquired—should I in the exercise of my judgment on such sensations as theirs act otherwise than they do? When I have put the question to myself I have not been able to discern that I should. They seem to do all the things they ought, and to act with what may be called a steady common sense in their respective situations. I have never seen a bird do a foolish thing for a creature of its powers, frame, and organs. Each acts with a uniform propriety, nothing fantastic, absurd, inconsistent, maniacal, or contradictory appears in their simple habits or daily conduct. They seem to have mental faculties and feelings like mine up to a certain extent, but to that they are limited. They have not the universality, the diversifying capacity, nor the improvability of the human intellect."

Whilst this analogy exists in the animated creation the inanimate is so far pervaded by a homogeneous design that the human reason is its interpreter and its prophet; for in how many instances has the sagacity of men of science anticipated a late discovery.

A very curious and sublime subject of speculation is the identity of nature's mind, and man's. We always confide that there is a reason for every fact in the order of nature, which, whenever we hit upon it, will justify the arrangement to our judgment also. I have seen certain fishes found in the waters of the Mammoth Cave of Kentucky, which have no eyes, nor any rudiments of eyes; for they are born in darkness, and live in the dark. It is an example of the eternal relation betwixt power and use, and such as we should expect beforehand. Indeed, man may well be of the same mind as nature, for he too is a part of nature, and is inundated with the same genius or spirit. He lives by some pulsations of her life.

Man's wit is secondary to nature's wit. He applies himself to nature to copy her method, to imbibe her wisdom. The art of the surgeon limits itself to relieving the dislocated parts from their false position, putting them free;—they fly into place by action of their own muscles. The art of medicine is in removing and withholding causes of irritation. On this art of nature, all our arts rely. The correction of the refraction of glass, was borrowed from the use of two humours in the eye.

For nature is made better by no mean
But nature makes that mean.

One can feel that we are brothers of the oak and of the grass, that the vegetable principle pervades human nature also. The old Norsemen represented the power of life by the tree Ygdrasil, which groweth out of Mimir's spring, where knowledge and wit are hidden.

It grows when we sleep. It is observed that our mental processes go forward, even when they seem suspended. Scholars say, that, if they return to the study of a new language, after some interruption, the intelligence of it seems to have grown in their mind. A subject of thought to which we return from month to month, from year to year, has always some ripeness, of which we can give no account. Hence we say, the book grew in the author's mind.

And we are very conscious that this identity extends far wider than we know,—that it has no limits, or none that we can ascertain;

as appears in the language men use in regard to men of extraordinary genius. For the signal performances of great men seem only the same art of nature applied to toys or puppets. Thus in Laplace and Napoleon, is the old planetary arithmetic now walking in a man; in the builder of Egyptian or in the designer of Gothic piles a reduction of nature's great aspects in caverns or forests to a scale of human convenience. And there is a conviction in the mind that some such impulse is constant, that if the Solar System is good art and architecture, the same achievement is in our brain also, if only we can be kept in height of health, and hindered from any interference with our great instincts. The current knows the way to be realized in some distant future. Something like this is the root of all the great arts; of picture, music, sculpture, architecture, poetry. And the history of the highest genius will warrant the conclusion, that, in proportion as a man's life comes into union with nature, his thoughts run parallel with the creative law.

The history of science in the last and the present age teems with this truth. The multitude of problems; the stimulated curiosity with which they have been pondered and solved, the formation of societies, the expeditions of discovery and the surveys, the gifts which science has made to the domestic arts are signs that the human race is in sympathy with this omnipresent spirit and in a perception of its rights and duties in regard to external nature.

Hence arises a corollary which every page of modern history repeats; that is, that science should be humanly studied. It will publish all its plan to a spirit akin to that which framed it. When science shall be studied with piety; when in a soul alive with moral sentiments, the antecedence of spirit is presupposed; then humanity advances, step by step with the opening of the intellect and its command over nature. Shall the problems never be assayed in a feeling of their beauty? Is not the poetic side of science entitled to be felt and presented by its investigators? Is it quite impossible to unite severe science with a poetic vision? Nature's laws are as charming to Taste and as pregnant with moral meaning as they are geometrically exact. Why then must the student freeze his sensibilities and cease to be a man that he may be a chemist and a physiologist? I know the cry which always arises from the learned at this expectation. It is like Bonaparte who charged Lafayette and every lover of freedom with being an ideologist. They tax us directly with enthusiasm and being dreamers.

It is certainly true that the tendency of imaginative men is to rash generalization and to the confounding of intuitive perception, with conjecture. Conscious of good-meaning the poet leaps to a conclusion which is false. Whilst he is thus swift, Nature is not; she holds by herself; and he must be brought back from his error by a faithful comparison of the facts with his premature anticipation. On the other hand not less dangerous is the tendency of men of detail to distrust final causes, and the generous sovereign glances of the soul over things, and to cling to the cadaverous fact until Science becomes a dead catalogue, and arbitrary classification. Then, when facts are allowed to usurp the throne of the mind, and the naturalist works as the slave of nature, and loses sight of its origin in spirit connate, yea identical with his own, then is wrong done to human nature, science is unhallowed, and baneful; as happened signally in philosophic France; and has often befallen individuals.

And just so far as the fear of theory and the idolatry of facts characterises science, just so far must it lack the sympathy of humanity. The great men, the heroes of science, are persons who added to their accuracy of study a sympathy with men, a strong common sense; and an earnest nature susceptible of religion, as Kepler, Galileo, Newton, Linnaeus, and in our days Davy, Cuvier, Humboldt. For it certainly must be, that not those parts of science which here and there a virtuoso may love, as the reckoning of logarithms or minute and merely curious chemical compositions, are the most attractive to the great naturalist, but those which catch the eye and fire the curiosity of all men, the discovery of a new planetary system, the discovery of a new analogy uniting great classes of hitherto sundered facts, the decomposition of diamond and the earths.

It is a characteristic of the present day that public education has advanced so far as to create a great number of books, lectures, and experiments having for their object to acquaint the people with the elements of the sciences. This was at first ridiculed, and undoubtedly a large deduction is to be made from the apparent result. What did it all signify? The Mechanics' Institutes had acquainted a few laboring men with the order of oolitic series or the habits of the kangaroo. But here is the benefit. It will be the effect of the popularization of science to keep the eye of scientific men on that human side of nature wherein lie grandest truths. The poet, the priest must not only receive an inspiration, but they must bring the oracle low down to men in the marketplace. And why not Newton and Laplace? The education of the people forces the savant to show the people something of his lore which they can comprehend. It lets in good sense upon it, which is to laboratories and telescopes what the air of heaven is to dungeons or the hot chamber of the sick.

Any reader of history will see this clearly in comparing the science of antiquity with that of the present day, that the modern science is pervaded with good sense. In antiquity a great man was allowed to give currency to a silly opinion; as we read in Plutarch's *Placita Philosophorum* the grave nonsense of Empedocles and Anaxagoras about astronomy and physics. It could not happen otherwise; it was the influence of genius when science was confined to a few. But now the effect of national education and of the press is that great numbers of men are directly or indirectly parties to the experiment of the philosopher and judges of it; so that the great instincts of mankind, and indeed the verdict of the Universal mind has an irresistible check upon the whims and spirit of system of the individual. But it is only the morning of the day. The philosopher and the philanthropist may forebode the time when an interest like that which now is felt in scientific circles in the wonders opened by Faraday, Ampère, Ørsted, in Magnetism and Electricity; a finger-pointing at laws and powers of unrivalled simplicity and extent,—shall take the place in the general mind of contemptible questions concerning persons and interests which now divide men into parties and embitter and degrade the mind of millions.

The highest moral of science is the transference of that trust which is felt in nature's admired arrangements, light, heat, gravity,—to the social and moral order. The first effect of science is to stablish the mind, to disclose beneficent arrangements, to remove groundless terrors. Once we thought the errors of Jupiter's moons were alarming; it was then shown that they were periodic. More recently mankind have been frighted with news of a resisting medium in the celestial spaces which threatens to throw all things into a lump. Men of science conversant with these unerring agents, with stars, with acids, with plants, with light, heat, gravity are observed to grow calm and simple in their manners and tastes, the calm and security of the order of nature steals into their lives, and the contrast between them and the irritability of poetic genius appears to all and one may easily believe that a man of lifelong habit of observation of nature in the laboratory or the observatory who should come into politics, or into courts of justice, or into trade, and see the meanness and the falsehood which are so busy in these places, would conceive an impatience and disgust at this lawless and confused living. Let Newton or Cuvier or Laplace, peaceful with beholding the order of planets and of strata, come into senates or bureaus, and see some pert boy with some conceited proposition which he wishes to impose as a civil law on the millions of subjects of an empire: and indeed the whole history of states has been the uncalled-for interference of foolish, selfish persons with the course of events. They might well wish to fly,—as the old hermits, to their desart and cell;—so these to their alembic and thermometer. Indeed, if they could entertain the belief that these rash hands really possessed any power to change the course of events, men would wish to rush by suicide out of the door of this staggering Temple.

But the survey of nature irresistibly suggests that the world is not a tinderbox left at the mercy of incendiaries. No outlaw, no anomaly, no violation, no impulse of absolute freedom is permitted to exist; that the circles of Law round in every exception and resistance, provide for every exigency, balance every excess. The self-equality in the birth of the sexes is constant; so is the relation of the animal to his food; so is the composition of the air in all places. The same symmetry and security is universal; and the inference is inevitable that the same Law extends into the kingdom of human life, and balances these refractory parties one against the other, and from age to age carries forward by war as well as by peace, by selfishness and ignorance and cheating, as well as by honour and love, the general prosperity and education of souls.

The Method of Nature

(1841)

The early 1840s were a busy and productive time for Emerson. In addition to the publication of *Essays: First Series* in March 1841, he was being asked to commit more time and energy to the advancement of the Transcendentalist movement. Margaret Fuller implored him to carry on his editorial duties at *The Dial*—a magazine devoted to Transcendentalist ideology that had been founded in 1840—while George Ripley unsuccessfully sought his participation in his communal social experiment at Brook Farm. In response to these growing pressures, Emerson took a brief holiday in July 1841 at Nantasket, a then-uninhabited beach on the south shore of Massachusetts Bay. During this trip, he wrote "The Method of Nature" as the commencement address for the Erosophian Adelphi undergraduate literary society at Waterville College in Maine. This talk is particularly significant for Emerson's explanation of his emerging sense that nature is a constantly evolving force. While he had discussed nature's dynamism in the sermon "God that Made the World" and the lecture "The Uses of Natural History," it was in "The Method of Nature" that Emerson connected this concept of nature as a fluid system to a state of continuing creation. Using this model of nature as dynamically productive, he levels a critique at social definitions of genius. Emerson laments that individuals have stopped listening to their inner spirit, which continually points the intellect toward a vital connection of the self to nature. He calls for a forward-looking scholar who, like nature itself, constantly invents and evolves, as opposed to the intellectual who merely reflects on past achievement.

This metaphor of nature as metamorphosis would remain Emerson's predominant trope throughout this prolific era of his career.

An Oration
Delivered Before the Society of the Adelphi, in
Waterville College, in Maine, August 11, 1841

Gentlemen:

Let us exchange congratulations on the enjoyments and the promises of this day and this hour. A literary anniversary is a celebration of the intellect, and so the inlet of a great force into the assembly of the learned, and through them into the world. The land we live in has no interest so dear, if it knew its want, as the fit consecration of days of reason and thought. Where there is no vision, the people perish. The scholars are the priests of that thought which establishes the foundations of the earth. No matter what is their special work or profession, they stand for the spiritual interest of the world, and it is a common calamity if they neglect their post in a country where the material interest is so predominant as it is in America. We hear something too much of the results of machinery, commerce, and the useful arts. We are a puny and a fickle folk. Avarice, hesitation, and following, are our diseases. The rapid wealth which hundreds in the community acquire in trade, or by the incessant expansions of our population and arts, enchants the eyes of all the rest; the luck of one is the hope of thousands, and the proximity of the bribe acts like the neighborhood of a gold mine to impoverish the farm, the school, the church, the house, and the very body and feature of man.

I do not wish to look with sour aspect at the industrious manufacturing village, or the mart of commerce. I love the music of the water-wheel; I value the railway; I feel the pride which the sight of a ship inspires; I look on trade and every mechanical craft as education also. But let me discriminate what is precious herein. There is in each of these works one act of invention, one intellectual step, or short series of steps taken; that act or step is the spiritual act: all the rest is mere repetition of the same a thousand times. And I will not be deceived into admiring the routine of handicrafts and mechanics, how splendid soever the result, any more than I admire the routine of the scholars or clerical class. That splendid results ensue from the labors of stupid men, is the fruit of higher laws than their will, and the routine is not to be praised for it. I would not have the laborer sacrificed to the splendid result,—I would not have the laborer sacrificed to my convenience and pride, nor to that of a great class of such as me. Let there be worse cotton and better men. The weaver should not be bereaved of that nobility which comes from the superiority to his work, and the knowledge that the product or the skill is a momentary end of no value, except so far as it embodies his spiritual prerogatives. If I see nothing to admire in the unit, shall I admire a million units? Men stand in awe of the city, but do not I honor any individual citizen; and are continually yielding to this dazzling result of numbers, that which they would never yield to the solitary example of any one.

Whilst, therefore, the multitude of men live to degrade each other, and give currency to desponding doctrines, the scholar must be a bringer of hope, and must reinforce man against himself. I sometimes believe that our literary anniversaries will presently assume a greater importance, as the eyes of men open to their capabilities. Here, a new set of distinctions, a new order of ideas, prevail. Here, we set a bound to the respectability of wealth, and a bound to the pretensions of the law and the church. The bigot must cease to be a bigot to-day. Into our charmed circle, power cannot enter; and the sturdiest defender of existing institutions feels the terrific inflammability of this air which condenses heat in every corner that may restore to the elements the fabrics of ages. Nothing solid is secure; everything tilts and rocks. Even the scholar is not safe; he too is searched and revised. Is his learning dead? Is he living in his memory? The power of mind is not mortification, but life. But come forth, thou curious child! hither, thou loving, all-hoping poet! hither, thou tender, doubting heart, who hast not yet found any place in the world's market fit for thee; any wares which thou couldst buy or sell,—so large is thy love and ambition,—thine and not theirs is the hour. Smooth thy brow, and hope and love on, for the kind heaven justifies thee, and the whole world feels that thou only art in the right.

We ought to celebrate this hour by expressions of manly joy. Not thanks, not prayer seem quite the highest or truest name for our communication with the infinite,—but glad and conspiring reception,— reception that becomes giving in its turn, as the receiver is only the All-Giver in part and in infancy. I cannot,—nor can any man,—speak precisely of things so sublime, but it seems to me, the wit of man, his strength, his grace, his tendency, his art, is the grace and the presence of God. It is beyond explanation. When all is said and done, the rapt saint is found the only logician. Not exhortation, not argument becomes our lips, but pæans of joy and praise. But not of adulation: we are too nearly related in the deep of the mind to that we honor. It is God in us which checks the language of petition by a grander thought. In the bottom of the heart, it is said; 'I am, and by me, O child! this fair body and world of thine stands and grows. I am: all things are mine: and all mine are thine.'

The festival of the intellect, and the return to its source, cast a strong light on the always interesting topics of Man and Nature. We are forcibly reminded of the old want. There is no man; there hath never been. The Intellect still asks that a man may be born. The flame of life flickers feebly in human breasts. We demand of men a richness and universality we do not find. Great men do not content us. It is their solitude, not their force, that makes them conspicuous. There is somewhat indigent and tedious about them. They are poorly tied to one thought. If they are prophets, they are egotists; if polite and various, they are shallow. How tardily men arrive at any thought! how tardily they pass from it to another thought! The crystal sphere of thought is as concentrical as the geological structure of the globe. As all our soils and rocks lie in strata, concentric strata, so do all men's thinkings run laterally, never vertically. Here comes by a great inquisitor with auger and plumb-line, and will bore an Artesian well through all our conventions and theories, and pierce to the core of things. But as soon as he probes one crust, behold gimlet, plumb-line, and philosopher, all take a lateral direction, in spite of all resistance, as if some strong wind took everything off its feet, and if you come month after month to see what progress our reformer has made,—not an inch has he pierced,—you still find him with new words in the old place, floating about in new parts of the same old vein or crust. The new book says, 'I will give you the key to nature,' and we expect to go like a thunderbolt to the centre. But the thunder is a surface phenomenon, makes a skin-deep cut, and so does the sage. The wedge turns out to be a rocket. Thus a man lasts but a very little while, for his monomania becomes insupportably tedious in a few months. It is so with every book and person: and yet— and yet—we do not take up a new book, or meet a new man without a pulse-beat of expectation. And this discontent with the poor and pinched result, this invincible hope of a more adequate interpreter, is the sure prediction of his advent.

In the absence of man we turn to nature, which stands next. In the divine order, intellect is primary: nature, secondary: it is the memory of the mind. That which once existed in intellect as pure law, has now taken body as Nature. It existed already in the mind in solution: now, it has been precipitated, and the bright sediment is the world. We can never be quite strangers or inferiors in nature. We are parties to its existence; it is flesh of our flesh, and bone of our bone. But we no longer hold it by the hand: we have lost our miraculous power: our arm is no more as strong as the frost; nor our will equivalent to gravity and the elective attractions. Yet we can use nature as a convenient standard, and the meter of our rise and fall. It has this advantage as a witness,—it will not lie, it cannot be debauched. When man curses, nature still testifies to truth and love. We may, therefore, safely study the mind in nature, because we cannot steadily gaze on it in mind; as we explore the face of the sun in a pool, when our eyes cannot brook his direct splendors.

It seems to me, therefore, that it were some suitable pæan, if we should piously celebrate this hour by exploring the *method of nature.* Let us see *that,* as nearly as we can, and try how far it is transferable to the literary life. Every earnest glance we give to the realities around us, with intent to learn, proceeds from a holy impulse, and is really songs of praise. What difference can it make whether it take the shape of exhortation, or of passionate exclamation, or of scientific statement? These are forms merely. Through them we express, at last, the fact, that God has done thus or thus.

In treating a subject so large, in which we must necessarily appeal to the intuition, and aim much more to suggest, than to describe, I know it is not easy to speak with the precision attainable on topics of less scope. I have no taste for partial statements: they disgust me also. I do not wish in attempting to paint a man, to describe an air-fed, unimpassioned, impossible ghost. My eyes and ears are revolted by any neglect of the physical facts, the limitations of man. And yet one who conceives the true order of nature, and beholds the visible as proceeding from the invisible, cannot state his thought, without seeming to those who study the physical laws, to do them some injustice. There is an intrinsic defect in the organ. Language overstates. Statements of the infinite are usually felt to be unjust to the finite, and blasphemous. Empedocles undoubtedly spoke a truth of thought, when he said, 'I am God;' but the moment it was out of his mouth, it became a lie to the ear; and the world revenged itself for the seeming arrogance, by the good story about his shoe. How can I hope for better hap in my attempts to enunciate spiritual facts? Thus only; as far as I share the influx of truth, so far shall I be felt by every true person to say what is just.

The method of nature: who could ever analyze it? That rushing stream will not stop to be observed. We can never surprise nature in a corner; never find the end of a thread; never tell where to set the first stone. The bird hastens to lay her egg: the egg hastens to be a bird. The wholeness we admire in the order of the world, is the result of infinite distribution. Its smoothness is the smoothness of the pitch of the cataract. Its permanence is a perpetual inchoation. Every natural fact is an emanation, and that from which it emanates is an emanation also, and from every emanation is a new emanation. If anything could stand still, it would be crushed and dissipated by the torrent it resisted, and if it were a mind, would be crazed; as insane persons are those who hold fast to one thought, and do not flow with the course of nature. Not the cause, but an ever novel effect, nature descends always from above. It is unbroken obedience. The beauty of these fair objects is imported into them from a metaphysical and eternal spring. In all animal and vegetable forms, the physiologist concedes that no chemistry, no mechanics can account for the facts, but a mysterious principle of life must be assumed, which not only inhabits the organ, but makes the organ.

How silent, how spacious, what room for all, yet without place to insert an atom,—in graceful succession, in equal fulness, in balanced beauty, the dance of the hours goes forward still. Like an odor of incense, like a strain of music, like a sleep, it is inexact and boundless. It will not be dissected, nor unravelled, nor shown. Away profane philosopher! seekest thou in nature the cause? This refers to that, and that to the next, and the next to the third, and everything refers. Thou must ask in another mood, thou must feel it and love it, thou must behold it in a spirit as grand as that by which it exists, ere thou canst know the law. Known it will not be, but gladly beloved and enjoyed.

The simultaneous life throughout the whole body, the equal serving of innumerable ends without the least emphasis or preference to any, but the steady degradation of each to the success of all, allows the understanding no place to work. Nature can only be conceived as existing to a universal and not to a particular end, to a universe of ends, and not to one,—a work of *ecstasy,* to be represented by a circular movement, as intention might be signified by a straight line of definite length. Each effect strengthens every other. There is no revolt in all the kingdoms from the commonweal: no detachment of an individual. Hence the catholic character which makes every leaf an exponent of the world. When we behold the landscape in a poetic spirit, we do not reckon individuals. Nature knows neither palm nor oak, but only vegetable life, which sprouts into forests, and festoons the globe with a garland of grasses and vines.

That no single end may be selected and nature judged thereby, appears from this, that if man himself be considered as the end, and it be assumed that the final cause of the world is to make holy or wise or beautiful men, we see that it has not succeeded. Read alternately in natural and in civil history, a treatise of astronomy, for example, with a volume of French *Memoires pour servir.* When we have spent our wonder in computing this wasteful hospitality with which boon nature turns off new firmaments without end into her wide common, as fast as the madrepores make coral,—suns and planets hospitable to souls,— and then shorten the sight to look into this court of Louis Quatorze, and see the game that is played there,—duke and marshal, abbé and madame,—a gambling table where each is laying traps for the other, where the end is ever by some lie or fetch to outwit your rival and ruin him with this solemn fop in wig and stars—the king; one can hardly help asking if this planet is a fair specimen of the so generous astronomy, and if so, whether the experiment have not failed, and whether it be quite worth while to make more, and glut the innocent space with so poor an article.

I think we feel not much otherwise if, instead of beholding foolish nations, we take the great and wise men, the eminent souls, and narrowly inspect their biography. None of them seen by himself—and his performance compared with his promise or idea, will justify the cost of that enormous apparatus of means by which this spotted and defective person was at last procured.

To questions of this sort, nature replies, 'I grow, I grow.' All is nascent, infant. When we are dizzied with the arithmetic of the savant toiling to compute the length of her line, the return of her curve, we are steadied by the perception that a great deal is doing; that all seems just begun; remote aims are in active accomplishment. We can point nowhere to anything final; but tendency appears on all hands: planet, system, constellation, total nature is growing like a field of maize in July; is becoming somewhat else; is in rapid metamorphosis. The embryo does not more strive to be man than yonder burr of light we call a nebula tends to be a ring, a comet, a globe, and parent of new stars. Why should not then these messieurs of Versailles strut and plot for tabourets and ribbons, for a season, without prejudice to their faculty to run on better errands by and by?

But nature seems further to reply, 'I have ventured so great a stake as my success, in no single creature. I have not yet arrived at any end. The gardener aims to produce a fine peach or pear, but my aim is the health of the whole tree,—root, stem, leaf, flower, and seed,—and by no means the pampering of a monstrous pericarp at the expense of all the other functions.'

In short, the spirit and peculiarity of that impression nature makes on us, is this, that it does not exist to any one or to any number of particular ends, but to numberless and endless benefit, that there is in it no private will, no rebel leaf or limb, but the whole is oppressed by one superincumbent tendency, obeys that redundancy or excess of life which in conscious beings we call *ecstasy*.

With this conception of the genius or method of nature, let us go back to man. It is true, he pretends to give account of himself to himself, but, at the last, what has he to recite but the fact that there is a Life not to be described or known otherwise than by possession? What account can he give of his essence more than *so it was to be?* The *royal* reason, the Grace of God seems the only description of our multiform but ever identical fact. There is virtue, there is genius, there is success, or there is not. There is the incoming or the receding of God: that is all we can affirm; and we can show neither how nor why. Self-accusation, remorse, and the didactic morals of self-denial and strife with sin, are in the view we are constrained by our constitution to take of the fact seen from the platform of action; but seen from the platform of intel-lection, there is nothing for us but praise and wonder.

The fact of facts is the termination of the world in a man. This appears to be the last victory of intelligence. The universal does not attract us until housed in an individual. Who heeds the waste abyss of possibility? The ocean is everywhere the same, but it has no character until seen with the shore or the ship. Who would value any number of miles of Atlantic brine bounded by lines of latitude and longitude? Confine it by granite rocks, let it wash a shore where wise men dwell, and it is filled with expression; and the point of greatest interest is where the land and water meet. So must we admire in man, the form of the formless, the concentration of the vast, the house of reason, the cave of memory. See the play of thoughts! what nimble gigantic crea-tures are these! what saurians, what palaiotheria shall be named with these agile movers? The great Pan of old, who was clothed in a leopard skin to signify the beautiful variety of things, and the firmament, his coat of stars,—was but the representative of thee, O rich and various Man! thou palace of sight and sound, carrying in thy senses the morn-ing and the night and the unfathomable galaxy; in thy brain, the geom-etry of the City of God; in thy heart, the bower of love and the realms of right and wrong. An individual man is a fruit which it cost all the foregoing ages to form and ripen. He is strong not to do, but to live;

not in his arms, but in his heart; not as an agent, but as a fact. The history of the genesis or the old mythology repeats itself in the experience of every child. He too is a demon or god thrown into a particular chaos, where he strives ever to lead things from disorder into order. Each individual soul is such, in virtue of its being a power to translate the world into some particular language of its own; if not into a picture, a statue, or a dance,—why, then, into a trade, an art, a science, a mode of living, a conversation, a character, an influence. You admire pictures, but it is as impossible for you to paint a right picture as for grass to bear apples. But when the genius comes, it makes fingers: it is pliancy, and the power of transferring the affair in the street into oils and colors. Raphael must be born, and Salvator must be born.

There is no attractiveness like that of a new man. The sleepy nations are occupied with their political routine. England, France and America read Parliamentary Debates, which no high genius now enlivens; and nobody will read them who trusts his own eye: only they who are deceived by the popular repetition of distinguished names. But when Napoleon unrols his map, the eye is commanded by original power. When Chatham leads the debate, men may well listen, because they must listen. A man, a personal ascendency is the only great phenomenon. When nature has work to be done, she creates a genius to do it. Follow the great man, and you shall see what the world has at heart in these ages. There is no omen like that.

But what strikes us in the fine genius is that which belongs of right to every one. Let us speak plainly and with no false humility. The humility which is the ornament of man in the presence of the ideal good and fair, is not to cloud his perception of that energy which he is. A man should know himself for a necessary actor. A link was wanting between two craving parts of nature, and he was hurled into being as the bridge over that yawning need, the mediator betwixt two else unmarriageable facts. His two parents held each of one of the wants, and the union of foreign constitutions in him enables him to do gladly and gracefully what the assembled human race could not have sufficed to do. He knows his own materials; everywhere he applies himself to his work; he cannot read, he cannot think, he cannot look, but he unites the hitherto separated strands into a perfect cord. What are the thoughts we utter but the reason of our incarnation? To utter these thoughts we took flesh, missionaries of the everlasting word which will be spoken. Should not a man be sacred to himself and to men? Is it for him to account himself cheap and superfluous, or to linger by the way-side for opportunities? Did he not come into being because something must be done which he and no other is and does? If only he *sees,* the world will be visible enough. He need not study where to stand, nor to put things in favorable lights; in him is the light, from him all things are to their centre illuminated. What patron shall he ask for employment and reward? Hereto was he born, to deliver the thought of his heart from the universe to the universe, to do an office which nature could not forego, nor he be discharged from rendering, and then immerge again into the holy silence and eternity out of which as a man he arose. God is rich, and many more men than one he harbors in his bosom, biding their time and the needs and the beauty of all. Is not this the theory of every man's genius or faculty? Why then goest thou as some Boswell or listening worshipper to this saint or to that? That is the only lese-majesty. Here art thou with whom so long the universe travailed in labor; darest thou think meanly of thyself whom the stalwart Fate brought forth to unite his ragged sides, to shoot the gulf,—to reconcile the irreconcilable?

Whilst a necessity so great caused the man to exist, his health and erectness consist in the fidelity with which he transmits influences from the vast and universal to the point on which his genius can act. The ends are momentary: they are vents for the current of inward life which increases as it is spent. A man's wisdom is to know that all ends are momentary, that the best end must instantly be superseded by a better. But there is a mischievous tendency in him to transfer his thought from the life to the ends, to quit his agency and rest in his acts: the tool runs away with the workman, the human with the divine. I conceive a man as always spoken to from behind, and unable to turn his head and see the speaker. In all the millions who have heard the voice, none ever saw the face. As children in their play run behind each other, and seize one by the ears and make him walk before them, so is the spirit our unseen pilot. That well-known voice speaks in all languages, governs all men, and none ever caught a glimpse of its form.

If the man will exactly obey it, it will adopt him, so that he shall not any longer separate it from himself in his thought, he shall seem to be it, he shall be it. If he listen with insatiable ears, richer and greater wisdom is taught him, the sound swells to a ravishing music, he is borne away as with a flood, he becomes careless of his food and of his house, he is the drinker of ideas, and leads a heavenly life. But if his eye is set on the things to be done, and not on the truth that is still taught, and for the sake of which the things are to be done, then the voice grows faint, and at last is but a humming in his ears. His health and greatness consist in his being the channel through which heaven flows to earth, in short, in the fulness in which an ecstatical state takes place in him. It is pitiful to be an artist when by forbearing to be artists we might be vessels filled with the divine overflowings, enriched by the circulations of omniscience and omnipresence. Are there not moments in the history of heaven when the human race was not counted by individuals, but was only the Influenced, was God in distribution, God rushing into multiform benefit? It is sublime to receive, sublime to love, but this lust of imparting as from *us*, this desire to be loved, the wish to be recognized as individuals,—is finite, comes of a lower strain.

Shall I say, then, that, as far as we can trace the natural history of the soul, its health consists in the fulness of its reception,—call it piety, call it veneration—in the fact, that enthusiasm is organized therein. What is best in any work of art, but that part which the work itself seems to require and do; that which the man cannot do again, that which flows from the hour and the occasion, like the eloquence of men in a tumultuous debate? It was always the theory of literature, that the word of a poet was authoritative and final. He was supposed to be the mouth of a divine wisdom. We rather envied his circumstance than his talent. We too could have gladly prophesied standing in that place. We so quote our Scriptures; and the Greeks so quoted Homer, Theognis, Pindar, and the rest. If the theory has receded out of modern criticism, it is because we have not had poets. Whenever they appear, they will redeem their own credit.

This ecstatical state seems to direct a regard to the whole and not to the parts; to the cause and not to the ends; to the tendency, and not to the act. It respects genius and not talent; hope, and not possession:

the anticipation of all things by the intellect, and not the history itself; art, and not works of art; poetry, and not experiment; virtue, and not duties.

There is no office or function of man but is rightly discharged by this divine method, and nothing that is not noxious to him if detached from its universal relations. Is it his work in the world to study nature, or the laws of the world? Let him beware of proposing to himself any end. Is it for use? nature is debased, as if one looking at the ocean can remember only the price of fish. Or is it for pleasure? he is mocked: there is a certain infatuating air in woods and mountains which draws on the idler to want and misery. There is something social and intrusive in the nature of all things; they seek to penetrate and overpower, each the nature of every other creature, and itself alone in all modes and throughout space and spirit to prevail and possess. Every star in heaven is discontented and insatiable. Gravitation and chemistry cannot content them. Ever they woo and court the eye of every beholder. Every man who comes into the world they seek to fascinate and possess, to pass into his mind, for they desire to republish themselves in a more delicate world than that they occupy. It is not enough that they are Jove, Mars, Orion, and the North Star, in the gravitating firmament; they would have such poets as Newton, Herschel and Laplace, that they may re-exist and re-appear in the finer world of rational souls, and fill that realm with their fame. So is it with all immaterial objects. These beautiful basilisks set their brute, glorious eyes on the eye of every child, and, if they can, cause their nature to pass through his wondering eyes into him, and so all things are mixed.

Therefore man must be on his guard against this cup of enchantments, and must look at nature with a supernatural eye. By piety alone, by conversing with the cause of nature, is he safe and commands it. And because all knowledge is assimilation to the object of knowledge, as the power or genius of nature is ecstatic, so must its science or the description of it be. The poet must be a rhapsodist: his inspiration a sort of bright casualty: his will in it only the surrender of will to the Universal Power, which will not be seen face to face, but must be received and sympathetically known. It is remarkable that we have out of the deeps of antiquity in the oracles ascribed to the half fabulous

Zoroaster, a statement of this fact, which every lover and seeker of truth will recognize. "It is not proper," said Zoroaster, "to understand the Intelligible with vehemence, but if you incline your mind, you will apprehend it: not too earnestly, but bringing a pure and inquiring eye. You will not understand it as when understanding some particular thing, but with the flower of the mind. Things divine are not attainable by mortals who understand sensual things, but only the light-armed arrive at the summit."

And because ecstasy is the law and cause of nature, therefore you cannot interpret it in too high and deep a sense. Nature represents the best meaning of the wisest man. Does the sunset landscape seem to you the palace of Friendship,—those purple skies and lovely waters the amphitheatre dressed and garnished only for the exchange of thought and love of the purest souls? It is that. All the other meanings which base men have put on it are conjectural and false. "You cannot bathe twice in the same river," said Heraclitus, for it is renewed every moment; and I add, a man never sees the same object twice: with his own enlargement the object acquires new aspects.

Does not the same law hold for virtue? It is vitiated by too much will. He who aims at progress, should aim at an infinite, not at a special benefit. The reforms whose fame now fills the land with Temperance, Anti-Slavery, Non-Resistance, No Government, Equal Labor, fair and generous as each appears, are poor bitter things when prosecuted for themselves as an end. To every reform, in proportion to its energy, early disgusts are incident, so that the disciple is surprised at the very hour of his first triumphs, with chagrins and sickness and a general distrust: so that he shuns his associates, hates the enterprise which lately seemed so fair, and meditates to cast himself into the arms of that society and manner of life which he had newly abandoned with so much pride and hope. Is it that he attached the value of virtue to some particular practices, as, the denial of certain appetites in certain speci-fied indulgences, and, afterward, allowing the soul to depart, found himself still as wicked and as far from happiness in that abstinence, as he had been in the abuse? But the soul can be appeased not by a deed but by a tendency. It is in a hope that she feels her wings. You shall love rectitude, and not the disuse of money or the avoidance of trade:

an unimpeded mind, and not a monkish diet; sympathy and usefulness, and not hoeing or coopering. Tell me not how great your project is, or how pure,—the civil liberation of the world, its conversion into a christian church, the establishment of public education, cleaner diet, a new division of labor and of land, laws of love for laws of property;—I say to you plainly there is no end to which your practical faculty can aim, so sacred or so large, that, if pursued for itself, will not at last become carrion and an offence to the nostril. The imaginative faculty of the soul must be fed with objects immense and eternal. Your end should be one inapprehensible to the senses: then will it be a god always approached—never touched; always giving health. A man adorns himself with prayer and love as an aim adorns an action. What is strong but goodness, and what is energetic but the presence of a brave man? The doctrine in vegetable physiology of the *presence,* or the general influence of any substance over and above its chemical influence, as of an alkali or a living plant, is more predicable of man. You need not speak to me, I need not go where you are, that you should exert magnetism on me. Be you only whole and sufficient, and I shall feel you in every part of my life and fortune, and I can as easily dodge the gravitation of the globe as escape your influence.

But there are other examples of this total and supreme influence, besides Nature and the conscience. "From the poisonous tree, the world," say the Brahmins, "two species of fruit are produced, sweet as the waters of life Love or the society of beautiful souls, and Poetry, whose taste is like the immortal juice of Vishnu." What is Love, and why is it the chief good, but because it is an overpowering enthusiasm? Never self-possessed or prudent, it is all abandonment. Is it not a certain admirable wisdom, preferable to all other advantages, and whereof all others are only secondaries and indemnities, because this is that in which the individual is no longer his own foolish master, but inhales an odorous and celestial air, is wrapped round with awe of the object, blending for the time that object with the real and only good, and consults every omen in nature with tremulous interest? When we speak truly,—is not he only unhappy who is not in love? his fancied freedom and self-rule—is it not so much death? He who is in love is wise and is becoming wiser, seeth newly every time he looks at the object beloved, drawing from it with his eyes and his mind those virtues which it possesses. Therefore if the object be not itself a living and expanding soul, he presently exhausts it. But the love remains in his mind and the wisdom it brought him; and it craves a new and higher object. And the reason why all men honor love, is because it looks up and not down; aspires and not despairs.

And what is Genius but finer love, a love impersonal, a love of the flower and perfection of things, and a desire to draw a new picture or copy of the same? It looks to the cause and life: it proceeds from within outward, whilst Talent goes from without inward. Talent finds its models and methods and ends in society, exists for exhibition, and goes to the soul only for power to work. Genius is its own end, and draws its means and the style of its architecture from within, going abroad only for audience and spectator, as we adapt our voice and phrase to the distance and character of the ear we speak to. All your learning of all literatures would never enable you to anticipate one of its thoughts or expressions, and yet each is natural and familiar as household words. Here about us coils forever the ancient enigma, so old and so unutterable. Behold! there is the sun, and the rain, and the rocks: the old sun, the old stones. How easy were it to describe all this fitly: yet no word can pass. Nature is a mute, and man, her articulate speaking brother, lo! he also is a mute. Yet when Genius arrives, its speech is like a river, it has no straining to describe, more than there is straining in nature to exist. When thought is best, there is most of it. Genius sheds wisdom like perfume, and advertises us that it flows out of a deeper source than the foregoing silence, that it knows so deeply and speaks so musically because it is itself a mutation of the thing it describes. It is sun and moon and wave and fire in music, as astronomy is thought and harmony in masses of matter.

What is all history but the work of ideas, a record of the incomputable energy which his infinite aspirations infuse into man? Has any thing grand and lasting been done?—Who did it? Plainly not any man, but all men: it was the prevalence and inundation of an idea. What brought the Pilgrims here? One man says, civil liberty; and another, the desire of founding a church; and a third discovers that the motive force was plantation and trade. But if the Puritans could rise from the dust, they could not answer. It is to be seen in what they were, and not in what they designed: it was the growth, the budding and expansion of the human race, and resembled herein the sequent Revolution, which was not begun in Concord, or Lexington, or Virginia, but was the overflowing of the sense of natural right in every clear and active spirit of the period. Is a man boastful and knowing, and his own master?—we turn from him without hope; but let him be filled with awe and dread before the Vast and the Divine which uses him glad to be used, and our eye is riveted to the chain of events. What a debt is ours to that old religion which, in the childhood of most of us, still dwelt like a sabbath morning in the country of New England, teaching privation, self-denial and sorrow! A man was born not for prosperity, but to suffer for the benefit of others, like the noble rock-maple which all around our villages bleeds for the service of man. Not praise, not men's acceptance of our doing, but the spirit's holy errand through us absorbed the thought. How dignified was this! How all that is called talents and success in our noisy capitals becomes buzz and din before this man-worthiness. How our friendships and the complaisances we use, shame us now! Shall we not quit our companions, as if they were thieves and pot-companions, and betake ourselves to some desert cliff of mount Katahdin, some unvisited recess in Moosehead Lake, to bewail our innocency and to recover it, and with it the power to communicate again with these sharers of a more sacred idea?

And what is to replace for us the piety of that race? We cannot have theirs: it glides away from us day by day, but we also can bask in the great morning which rises forever out of the eastern sea, and be ourselves the children of the light. I stand here to say, Let us worship the mighty and transcendant Soul. It is the office, I doubt not, of this age to annul that adulterous divorce which the superstition of many ages has effected between the intellect and holiness. The lovers of goodness have been one class, the students of wisdom another, as if either could exist in any purity without the other. Truth is always holy, holiness always wise. I will that we keep terms with sin and a sinful literature and society no longer, but live a life of discovery and performance. Accept the intellect and it will accept us. Be the lowly ministers of that pure omniscience, and deny it not before men. It will burn up all profane literature, all base current opinions, all the false powers of the world as in a moment of time. I draw from nature the lesson of an intimate divinity. Our health and reason as men needs our respect to this fact against the heedlessness and against the contradiction of society. The sanity of man needs the poise of this immanent force. His nobility needs the assurance of this inexhaustible reserved power. How great soever have been its bounties, they are a drop to the sea whence they flow. If you say, 'the acceptance of the vision is also the act of God:'— I shall not seek to penetrate the mystery, I admit the force of what you say. If you ask, 'How can any rules be given for the attainment of gifts so sublime?'—I shall only remark that the solicitations of this spirit, as long as there is life, are never forborne. Tenderly, tenderly, they woo and court us from every object in nature, from every fact in life, from every thought in the mind. The one condition coupled with the gift of truth is its use. That man shall be learned who reduceth his learning to practice. Emanuel Swedenborg affirmed that it was opened to him "that the spirits who knew truth in this life, but did it not, at death shall lose their knowledge." "If knowledge," said Ali the Caliph, "calleth unto practice, well; if not, it goeth away." The only way into nature is to enact our best insight. Instantly we are higher poets and can speak a deeper law. Do what you know, and perception is converted into character, as islands and continents were built by invisible infusories, or as these forest leaves absorb light, electricity, and volatile gases, and the gnarled oak to live a thousand years is the arrest and fixation of the most volatile and etherial currents. The doctrine of this Supreme Presence is a cry of joy and exultation. Who shall dare think he has come late into nature, or has missed anything excellent in the past, who seeth the admirable stars of possibility, and the yet untouched continent of hope glittering with all its mountains in the vast West? I praise with wonder this great reality which seems to drown all things in the deluge of its light. What man seeing this, can lose it from his thoughts, or entertain a meaner subject? The entrance of this into his mind seems to be the birth of man. We cannot describe the natural history of the soul, but we know that it is divine. I cannot tell if these wonderful qualities which house to-day in this mortal frame, shall ever re-assemble in equal activity in a similar frame, or whether they have before had a natural history like that of this body you see before you; but this one thing I know, that these qualities did not now begin to exist, cannot be sick with my sickness nor buried in any grave; but that they circulate through the Universe: before the world was, they were. Nothing can bar them out, or shut them in, but they penetrate the ocean and land, space and time, form and essence, and hold the key to universal nature. I draw from this faith courage and hope. All things are known to the soul. It is not to be surprised by any communication. Nothing can be greater than it. Let those fear and those fawn who will. The soul is in her native realm, and it is wider than space, older than time, wide as hope, rich as love. Pusillanimity and fear she refuses with a beautiful scorn: they are not for her who putteth on her coronation robes and goes out through universal love to universal power.

◆ Nature

(1844)

"Nature" was first published in October 1844 as part of *Essays: Second Series.* Emerson wrote, edited, and compiled these essays sporadically between lecture tours during the three years following the publication of *Essays: First Series* in 1841. Although Emerson had written an early draft of "Nature" and briefly considered its inclusion in *Essays: First Series,* he decided to omit the essay in order to revise it further. Along with *Nature* (1836), the two volumes of *Essays* constitute the most lasting and influential writings of Emerson's career. During this time of prodigious output, Emerson's first child, Waldo, died suddenly of scarlet fever in 1842. Waldo's death at age five would haunt Emerson, testing his philosophical optimism. *Essays: Second Series* signals this transition from the unreserved idealism of *Nature* and his early writings to the pragmatism of his later career. In "Nature," this growing skepticism may be seen in his discussion of the inherent limitations of language. Contrary to the call to learn nature's language—a call that resounds throughout his earlier sermons and natural history lectures—Emerson now speculates that nature's constant state of dynamic creation frustrates any attempt to transcribe its order. The continual fluidity of nature ensures this inability, as it will never be quite the same as experienced in the moment of discernment. According to Emerson, individuals can train themselves to focus on the present and to perceive the dynamic processes of life in the minutiae of everyday experiences and places. However, the optimism of these moments of ecstatic insight is tempered by the recognition of our fundamental inability to represent them adequately in language.

For the Emerson of "Nature," our attempts to interpret the book
of nature often leave us with only a linguistic "system of approximations."

♥

The rounded world is fair to see,
Nine times folded in mystery:
Though baffled seers cannot impart
The secret of its laboring heart,
Throb thine with Nature's throbbing breast,
And all is clear from east to west.
Spirit that lurks each form within
Beckons to spirit of its kin;
Self-kindled every atom glows,
And hints the future which it owes.

There are days which occur in this climate, at almost any season of the
year, wherein the world reaches its perfection, when the air, the heavenly bodies, and the earth, make a harmony, as if nature would indulge
her offspring; when, in these bleak upper sides of the planet, nothing
is to desire that we have heard of the happiest latitudes, and we bask
in the shining hours of Florida and Cuba; when everything that has life
gives sign of satisfaction, and the cattle that lie on the ground seem to
have great and tranquil thoughts. These halcyons may be looked for
with a little more assurance in that pure October weather, which we
distinguish by the name of the Indian Summer. The day, immeasur-
ably long, sleeps over the broad hills and warm wide fields. To have
lived through all its sunny hours, seems longevity enough. The solitary places do not seem quite lonely. [At the gates of the forest, the
surprised man of the world is forced to leave his city estimates of great
and small, wise and foolish. The knapsack of custom falls off his back
with the first step he makes into these precincts. Here is sanctity which
shames our religions, and reality which discredits our heroes] Here we
find nature to be the circumstance which dwarfs every other circumstance, and judges like a god all men that come to her. We have crept

out of our close and crowded houses into the night and morning, and we see what majestic beauties daily wrap us in their bosom. How willingly we would escape the barriers which render them comparatively impotent, escape the sophistication and second thought, and suffer nature to entrance us. The tempered light of the woods is like a perpetual morning, and is stimulating and heroic. The anciently reported spells of these places creep on us. The stems of pines, hemlocks, and oaks, almost gleam like iron on the excited eye. The incommunicable trees begin to persuade us to live with them, and quit our life of solemn trifles. Here no history, or church, or state, is interpolated on the divine sky and the immortal year. How easily we might walk onward into the opening landscape, absorbed by new pictures, and by thoughts fast succeeding each other, until by degrees the recollection of home was crowded out of the mind, all memory obliterated by the tyranny of the present, and we were led in triumph by nature. *healing power*

These enchantments are medicinal, they sober and heal us. These are plain pleasures, kindly and native to us. We come to our own, and make friends with matter, which the ambitious chatter of the schools would persuade us to despise. We never can part with it; the mind loves *nature* its old home: as water to our thirst, so is the rock, the ground, to our *as* eyes, and hands, and feet. It is firm water: it is cold flame: what health, *necess* what affinity! Ever an old friend, ever like a dear friend and brother, *for* when we chat affectedly with strangers, comes in this honest face, and takes a grave liberty with us, and shames us out of our nonsense. Cities give not the human senses room enough. We go out daily and nightly to feed the eyes on the horizon, and require so much scope, just as we need water for our bath. There are all degrees of natural influence, from these quarantine powers of nature, up to her dearest and gravest ministrations to the imagination and the soul. There is the bucket of cold water from the spring, the wood-fire to which the chilled traveller rushes for safety,—and there is the sublime moral of autumn and of noon. We nestle in nature, and draw our living as parasites from her roots and grains, and we receive glances from the heavenly bodies, which call us to solitude, and foretell the remotest future. The blue zenith is the point in which romance and reality meet. I think, if we should be rapt away into all that we dream of heaven, and should converse with Gabriel and Uriel, the upper sky would be all that would remain of our furniture.

It seems as if the day was not wholly profane, in which we have given heed to some natural object. The fall of snowflakes in a still air, preserving to each crystal its perfect form; the blowing of sleet over a wide sheet of water, and over plains; the waving ryefield; the mimic waving of acres of houstonia, whose innumerable florets whiten and ripple before the eye; the reflections of trees and flowers in glassy lakes; the musical steaming odorous south wind, which converts all trees to wind-harps; the crackling and spurting of hemlock in the flames; or of pine logs, which yield glory to the walls and faces in the sitting-room,—these are the music and pictures of the most ancient religion. My house stands in low land, with limited outlook, and on the skirt of the village. But I go with my friend to the shore of our little river, and with one stroke of the paddle, I leave the village politics and personalities, yes, and the world of villages and personalities behind, and pass into a delicate realm of sunset and moonlight, too bright almost for spotted man to enter without noviciate and probation. We penetrate bodily this incredible beauty: we dip our hands in this painted element: our eyes are bathed in these lights and forms. A holiday, a villeggiatura, a royal revel, the proudest, most heart-rejoicing festival that valor and beauty, power and taste, ever decked and enjoyed, establishes itself on the instant. These sunset clouds, these delicately emerging stars, with their private and ineffable glances, signify it and proffer it. I am taught the poorness of our invention, the ugliness of towns and palaces. Art and luxury have early learned that they must work as enhancement and sequel to this original beauty. I am overinstructed for my return. Henceforth I shall be hard to please. I cannot go back to toys. I am grown expensive and sophisticated. I can no longer live without elegance: but a countryman shall be my master of revels. He who knows the most, he who knows what sweets and virtues are in the ground, the waters, the plants, the heavens, and how to come at these enchantments, is the rich and royal man. Only as far as the masters of the world have called in nature to their aid, can they reach the height of magnificence. This is the meaning of their hanging-gardens, villas, garden-houses, islands, parks, and preserves, to back their faulty personality with these strong accessories. I do not wonder that the landed interest should be invincible in the state with these dangerous auxiliaries. These bribe and invite; not kings, not palaces, not men, not women, but these tender and poetic stars, eloquent of secret promises. We heard what the rich man said, we knew of his villa, his grove, his wine, and his company, but the provocation and point of the invitation came out of these beguiling stars. In their soft glances, I see what men strove to realize in some Versailles, or Paphos, or Ctesiphon. Indeed, it is the magical lights of the horizon, and the blue sky for the background, which save all our works of art, which were otherwise bawbles. When the rich tax the poor with servility and obsequiousness, they should consider the effect of men reputed to be the possessors of nature, on imaginative minds. Ah! if the rich were rich as the poor fancy riches! A boy hears a military band play on the field at night, and he has kings and queens, and famous chivalry palpably before him. He hears the echoes of a horn in a hill country, in the Notch Mountains, for example, which converts the mountains into an Æolian harp, and this supernatural *tiralira* restores to him the Dorian mythology, Apollo, Diana, and all divine hunters and huntresses. Can a musical note be so lofty, so haughtily beautiful! To the poor young poet, thus fabulous is his picture of society; he is loyal; he respects the rich; they are rich for the sake of his imagination; how poor his fancy would be, if they were not rich! That they have some high-fenced grove, which they call a park; that they live in larger and better-garnished saloons than he has visited, and go in coaches, keeping only the society of the elegant, to watering-places, and to distant cities, are the groundwork from which he has delineated estates of romance, compared with which their actual possessions are shanties and paddocks. The muse herself betrays her son, and enhances the gifts of wealth and well-born beauty, by a radiation out of the air, and clouds, and forests that skirt the road,—a certain haughty favor, as if from patrician genii to patricians, a kind of aristocracy in nature, a prince of the power of the air.

The moral sensibility which makes Edens and Tempes so easily, may not be always found, but the material landscape is never far off. We can find these enchantments without visiting the Como Lake, or the Madeira Islands. We exaggerate the praises of local scenery. In every landscape, the point of astonishment is the meeting of the sky and the earth, and that is seen from the first hillock as well as from the top of the Alleghanies. The stars at night stoop down over the brownest, homeliest common, with all the spiritual magnificence which they shed on the Campagna, or on the marble deserts of Egypt. The uprolled clouds and the colors of morning and evening, will transfigure maples and alders. The difference between landscape and landscape is small, but there is great difference in the beholders. There is nothing so wonderful in any particular landscape, as the necessity of being beautiful under which every landscape lies. Nature cannot be surprised in undress. Beauty breaks in everywhere.

But it is very easy to outrun the sympathy of readers on this topic, which schoolmen called *natura naturata,* or nature passive. One can hardly speak directly of it without excess. It is as easy to broach in mixed companies what is called "the subject of religion." A susceptible person does not like to indulge his tastes in this kind, without the apology of some trivial necessity: he goes to see a wood-lot, or to look at the crops, or to fetch a plant or a mineral from a remote locality, or he carries a fowling-piece, or a fishing-rod. I suppose this shame must have a good reason. A dilettantism in nature is barren and unworthy. The fop of fields is no better than his brother of Broadway. Men are naturally hunters and inquisitive of wood-craft, and I suppose that such a gazetteer as wood-cutters and Indians should furnish facts for, would take place in the most sumptuous drawing-rooms of all the "Wreaths" and "Flora's chaplets" of the bookshops; yet ordinarily, whether we are too clumsy for so subtle a topic, or from whatever cause, as soon as men begin to write on nature, they fall into euphuism. Frivolity is a most unfit tribute to Pan, who ought to be represented in the mythology as the most continent of gods. I would not be frivolous before the admirable reserve and prudence of time, yet I cannot renounce the right of returning often to this old topic. The multitude of false churches accredits the true religion. Literature, poetry, science, are the homage of man to this unfathomed secret, concerning which no sane man can affect an indifference or incuriosity. Nature is loved by what is best in us. It is loved as the city of God, although, or rather because there is no citizen. The sunset is unlike anything that is underneath it: it wants

men. And the beauty of nature must always seem unreal and mocking, until the landscape has human figures, that are as good as itself.
If there were good men, there would never be this rapture in nature.
If the king is in the palace, nobody looks at the walls. It is when he is
gone, and the house is filled with grooms and gazers, that we turn from
the people, to find relief in the majestic men that are suggested by the
pictures and the architecture. The critics who complain of the sickly
separation of the beauty of nature from the thing to be done, must
consider that our hunting of the picturesque is inseparable from our
protest against false society. Man is fallen; nature is erect, and serves
as a differential thermometer, detecting the presence or absence of the
divine sentiment in man. By fault of our dulness and selfishness, we are
looking up to nature, but when we are convalescent, nature will look
up to us. We see the foaming brook with compunction: if our own life
flowed with the right energy, we should shame the brook. The stream
of zeal sparkles with real fire, and not with reflex rays of sun and moon.
Nature may be as selfishly studied as trade. Astronomy to the selfish
becomes astrology; psychology, mesmerism (with intent to show where
our spoons are gone); and anatomy and physiology become phrenology
and palmistry.

But taking timely warning, and leaving many things unsaid on this
topic, let us not longer omit our homage to the Efficient Nature,
natura naturans, the quick cause, before which all forms flee as the
driven snows, itself secret, its works driven before it in flocks and multitudes, (as the ancients represented nature by Proteus, a shepherd,)
and in undescribable variety. It publishes itself in creatures, reaching
from particles and spicula, through transformation on transformation
to the highest symmetries, arriving at consummate results without a
shock or a leap. A little heat, that is, a little motion, is all that differences the bald, dazzling white, and deadly cold poles of the earth from
the prolific tropical climates. All changes pass without violence, by reason of the two cardinal conditions of boundless space and boundless
time. Geology has initiated us into the secularity of nature, and taught
us to disuse our dame-school measures, and exchange our Mosaic and
Ptolemaic schemes for her large style. We knew nothing rightly, for
want of perspective. Now we learn what patient periods must round

themselves before the rock is formed, then before the rock is broken, and the first lichen race has disintegrated the thinnest external plate into soil, and opened the door for the remote Flora, Fauna, Ceres, and Pomona, to come in. How far off yet is the trilobite! how far the quadruped! how inconceivably remote is man! All duly arrive, and then race after race of men. It is a long way from granite to the oyster; farther yet to Plato, and the preaching of the immortality of the soul. Yet all must come, as surely as the first atom has two sides. *Preliminary theory of evolution*

Motion or change, and identity or rest, are the first and second secrets of nature: Motion and Rest. The whole code of her laws may be written on the thumbnail, or the signet of a ring. The whirling bubble on the surface of a brook, admits us to the secret of the mechanics of the sky. Every shell on the beach is a key to it. A little water made to rotate in a cup explains the formation of the simpler shells; the addition of matter from year to year, arrives at last at the most complex forms; and yet so poor is nature with all her craft, that, from the beginning to the end of the universe, she has but one stuff,—but one stuff with its two ends, to serve up all her dream-like variety. Compound it how she will, star, sand, fire, water, tree, man, it is still one stuff, and betrays the same properties.

Nature is always consistent, though she feigns to contravene her own laws. She keeps her laws, and seems to transcend them. She arms and equips an animal to find its place and living in the earth, and, at the same time, she arms and equips another animal to destroy it. Space exists to divide creatures; but by clothing the sides of a bird with a few feathers, she gives him a petty omnipresence. The direction is forever onward, but the artist still goes back for materials, and begins again with the first elements on the most advanced stage: otherwise, all goes to ruin. If we look at her work, we seem to catch a glance of a system in transition. Plants are the young of the world, vessels of health and vigor; but they grope ever upward towards consciousness; the trees are imperfect men, and seem to bemoan their imprisonment, rooted in the ground. The animal is the novice and probationer of a more advanced order. The men, though young, having tasted the first drop from the cup of thought, are already dissipated: the maples and ferns are still uncorrupt; yet no doubt, when they come to consciousness, they too will curse and swear. Flowers so strictly belong to youth, that we adult men soon come to feel, that their beautiful generations concern not us: we have had our day; now let the children have theirs. The flowers jilt us, and we are old bachelors with our ridiculous tenderness.

Things are so strictly related, that according to the skill of the eye, from any one object the parts and properties of any other may be predicted. If we had eyes to see it, a bit of stone from the city wall would certify us of the necessity that man must exist, as readily as the city. That identity makes us all one, and reduces to nothing great intervals on our customary scale[We talk of deviations from natural life, as if artificial life were not also natural. The smoothest curled courtier in the boudoirs of a palace has an animal nature, rude and aboriginal as a white bear, omnipotent to its own ends, and is directly related, there amid essences and billetsdoux, to Himmaleh mountain-chains, and the axis of the globe. If we consider how much we are nature's, we need not be superstitious about towns, as if that terrific or benefic force did not find us there also, and fashion cities. Nature who made the mason, made the house.]We may easily hear too much of rural influences. The cool disengaged air of natural objects, makes them enviable to us chafed and irritable creatures with red faces, and we think we shall be as grand as they, if we camp out and eat roots; but let us be men instead of woodchucks, and the oak and the elm shall gladly serve us, though we sit in chairs of ivory on carpets of silk.

This guiding identity runs through all the surprises and contrasts of the piece, and characterizes every law. Man carries the world in his head, the whole astronomy and chemistry suspended in a thought. Because the history of nature is charactered in his brain, therefore is he the prophet and discoverer of her secrets. Every known fact in natural science was divined by the presentiment of somebody, before it was actually verified. A man does not tie his shoe without recognizing laws which bind the farthest regions of nature: moon, plant, gas, crystal, are concrete geometry and numbers. Common sense knows its own, and recognizes the fact at first sight in chemical experiment. The common sense of Franklin, Dalton, Davy, and Black, is the same common sense which made the arrangements which now it discovers.

If the identity expresses organized rest, the counter action runs also into organization. The astronomers said, 'Give us matter, and a little motion, and we will construct the universe. It is not enough that we should have matter, we must also have a single impulse, one shove to launch the mass, and generate the harmony of the centrifugal and centripetal forces. Once heave the ball from the hand, and we can show how all this mighty order grew.'—'A very unreasonable postulate,' said the metaphysicians, 'and a plain begging of the question. Could you not prevail to know the genesis of projection, as well as the continuation of it?' Nature, meanwhile, had not waited for the discussion, but, right or wrong, bestowed the impulse, and the balls rolled. It was no great affair, a mere push, but the astronomers were right in making much of it, for there is no end to the consequences of the act. That famous aboriginal push propagates itself through all the balls of the system, and through every atom of every ball, through all the races of creatures, and through the history and performances of every individual. Exaggeration is in the course of things. Nature sends no creature, no man into the world, without adding a small excess of his proper quality. Given the planet, it is still necessary to add the impulse; so, to every creature nature added a little violence of direction in its proper path, a shove to put it on its way; in every instance, a slight generosity, a drop too much. Without electricity the air would rot, and without this violence of direction, which men and women have, without a spice of bigot and fanatic, no excitement, no efficiency. We aim above the mark, to hit the mark. Every act hath some falsehood of exaggeration in it. And when now and then comes along some sad, sharp-eyed man, who sees how paltry a game is played, and refuses to play, but blabs the secret;—how then? is the bird flown? O no, the wary Nature sends a new troop of fairer forms, of lordlier youths, with a little more excess of direction to hold them fast to their several aim; makes them a little wrongheaded in that direction in which they are rightest, and on goes the game again with new whirl, for a generation or two more. The child with his sweet pranks, the fool of his senses, commanded by every sight and sound, without any power to compare and rank his sensations, abandoned to a whistle or a painted chip, to a lead dragoon, or a gingerbread-dog, individualizing everything, generalizing nothing, delighted with every new thing, lies down at night overpowered by the fatigue, which this day of continual pretty madness has incurred. But Nature has answered her purpose with the curly, dimpled lunatic. She has tasked every faculty, and has secured the symmetrical growth of the bodily frame, by all these attitudes and exertions,—an end of the first importance, which could not be trusted to any care less perfect than her own. This glitter, this opaline lustre plays round the top of every toy to his eye, to ensure his fidelity, and he is deceived to his good. We are made alive and kept alive by the same arts. Let the stoics say what they please, we do not eat for the good of living, but because the meat is savory and the appetite is keen. The vegetable life does not content itself with casting from the flower or the tree a single seed, but it fills the air and earth with a prodigality of seeds, that, if thousands perish, thousands may plant themselves, that hundreds may come up, that tens may live to maturity, that, at least, one may replace the parent. All things betray the same calculated profusion. The excess of fear with which the animal frame is hedged round, shrinking from cold, starting at sight of a snake, or at a sudden noise, protects us, through a multitude of groundless alarms, from some one real danger at last. The lover seeks in marriage his private felicity and perfection, with no prospective end; and nature hides in his happiness her own end, namely, progeny, or the perpetuity of the race.

But the craft with which the world is made, runs also into the mind and character of men. No man is quite sane; each has a vein of folly in his composition, a slight determination of blood to the head, to make sure of holding him hard to some one point which nature had taken to heart. Great causes are never tried on their merits; but the cause is reduced to particulars to suit the size of the partisans, and the contention is ever hottest on minor matters. Not less remarkable is the overfaith of each man in the importance of what he has to do or say. The poet, the prophet, has a higher value for what he utters than any hearer, and therefore it gets spoken. The strong, self-complacent Luther declares with an emphasis, not to be mistaken, that "God himself cannot do without wise men." Jacob Behmen and George Fox betray their egotism in the pertinacity of their controversial tracts, and James Naylor once suffered himself to be worshipped as the Christ. Each prophet comes presently to identify himself with his thought, and to esteem his hat and shoes sacred. However this may discredit such persons with the judicious, it helps them with the people, as it gives heat, pungency, and publicity to their words. A similar experience is not infrequent in private life. Each young and ardent person writes a diary, in which, when the hours of prayer and penitence arrive, he inscribes his soul. The pages thus written are, to him, burning and fragrant: he reads them on his knees by midnight and by the morning star; he wets them with his tears: they are sacred; too good for the world, and hardly yet to be shown to the dearest friend. This is the man-child that is born to the soul, and her life still circulates in the babe. The umbilical cord has not yet been cut. After some time has elapsed, he begins to wish to admit his friend to this hallowed experience, and with hesitation, yet with firmness, exposes the pages to his eye. Will they not burn his eyes? The friend coldly turns them over, and passes from the writing to conversation, with easy transition, which strikes the other party with astonishment and vexation. He cannot suspect the writing itself. Days and nights of fervid life, of communion with angels of darkness and of light, have engraved their shadowy characters on that tear-stained book. He suspects the intelligence or the heart of his friend. Is there then no friend? He cannot yet credit that one may have impressive experience, and yet may not know how to put his private fact into literature; and perhaps the discovery that wisdom has other tongues and ministers than we, that though we should hold our peace, the truth would not the less be spoken, might check injuriously the flames of our zeal. A man can only speak, so long as he does not feel his speech to be partial and inadequate. It is partial, but he does not see it to be so, whilst he utters it. As soon as he is released from the instinctive and particular, and sees its partiality, he shuts his mouth in disgust. For, no man can write anything, who does not think that what he writes is for the time the history of the world; or do anything well, who does not esteem his work to be of importance. My work may be of none, but I must not think it of none, or I shall not do it with impunity.

In like manner, there is throughout nature something mocking, something that leads us on and on, but arrives nowhere, keeps no faith with us. All promise outruns the performance. We live in a system of approximations. Every end is prospective of some other end, which is also temporary; a round and final success nowhere. We are encamped in nature, not domesticated. Hunger and thirst lead us on to eat and to drink; but bread and wine, mix and cook them how you will, leave us hungry and thirsty, after the stomach is full. It is the same with all our arts and performances. Our music, our poetry, our language itself are not satisfactions, but suggestions. The hunger for wealth, which reduces the planet to a garden, fools the eager pursuer. <u>What is the</u> <u>end sought</u>? Plainly to secure the ends of good sense and beauty, from the intrusion of deformity or vulgarity of any kind. But what an operose method! What a train of means to secure a little conversation! This palace of brick and stone, these servants, this kitchen, these stables, horses and equipage, this bank-stock, and file of mortgages; trade to all the world, country-house and cottage by the waterside, all for a little conversation, high, clear, and spiritual! Could it not be had as well by beggars on the highway? No, all these things came from successive efforts of these beggars to remove friction from the wheels of life, and give opportunity. Conversation, character, were the avowed ends; wealth was good as it appeased the animal cravings, cured the smoky chimney, silenced the creaking door, brought friends together in a warm and quiet room, and kept the children and the dinner-table in a different apartment. Thought, virtue, beauty, were the ends; but it was known that men of thought and virtue sometimes had the headache, or wet feet, or could lose good time whilst the room was getting warm in winter days. Unluckily, in the exertions necessary to remove these inconveniences, the main attention has been diverted to this object; the old aims have been lost sight of, and to remove friction has come to be the end. That is the ridicule of rich men, and Boston, London, Vienna, and now the governments generally of the world, are cities and governments of the rich, and the masses are not men, but *poor men*, that is, men who would be rich; this is the ridicule of the class, that they arrive with pains and sweat and fury nowhere; when all is done, it is for nothing. They are like one who has interrupted the conversation of a company to make his speech, and now has forgotten what he went to say. The appearance strikes the eye everywhere of an aimless society, of aimless nations. Were the ends of nature so great and cogent, as to exact this immense sacrifice of men?

Quite analogous to the deceits in life, there is, as might be expected, a similar effect on the eye from the face of external nature. There is in woods and waters a certain enticement and flattery, together with a failure to yield a present satisfaction. This disappointment is felt in every landscape. I have seen the softness and beauty of the summer-clouds floating feathery overhead, enjoying, as it seemed, their height and privilege of motion, whilst yet they appeared not so much the drapery of this place and hour, as forelooking to some pavilions and gardens of festivity beyond. It is an odd jealousy: but the poet finds himself not near enough to his object. The pine-tree, the river, the bank of flowers before him, does not seem to be nature. Nature is still elsewhere. This or this is but outskirt and far-off reflection and echo of the triumph that has passed by, and is now at its glancing splendor and heyday, perchance in the neighboring fields, or, if you stand in the field, then in the adjacent woods. The present object shall give you this sense of stillness that follows a pageant which has just gone by. What splendid distance, what recesses of ineffable pomp and loveliness in the sunset! But who can go where they are, or lay his hand or plant his foot thereon? Off they fall from the round world forever and ever. It is the same among the men and women, as among the silent trees; always a referred existence, an absence, never a presence and satisfaction. Is it, that beauty can never be grasped? in persons and in landscape is equally inaccessible? The accepted and betrothed lover has lost the wildest charm of his maiden in her acceptance of him. She was heaven whilst he pursued her as a star: she cannot be heaven, if she stoops to such a one as he.

What shall we say of this omnipresent appearance of that first projectile impulse, of this flattery and baulking of so many well-meaning creatures? Must we not suppose somewhere in the universe a slight treachery and derision? Are we not engaged to a serious resentment of this use that is made of us? Are we tickled trout, and fools of nature? One look at the face of heaven and earth lays all petulance at rest, and soothes us to wiser convictions. To the intelligent, nature converts itself into a vast promise, and will not be rashly explained. Her secret is untold. Many and many an Œdipus arrives: he has the whole mystery teeming in his brain. Alas! the same sorcery has spoiled his skill; no syllable can he shape on his lips. Her mighty orbit vaults like the fresh rainbow into the deep, but no archangel's wing was yet strong enough to follow it, and report of the return of the curve. But it also appears, that our actions are seconded and disposed to greater conclusions than we designed. We are escorted on every hand through life by spiritual agents, and a beneficent purpose lies in wait for us. We cannot bandy words with nature, or deal with her as we deal with persons. If we measure our individual forces against hers, we may easily feel as if we were the sport of an insuperable destiny. But if, instead of identifying ourselves with the work, we feel that the soul of the workman streams through us, we shall find the peace of the morning dwelling first in our hearts, and the fathomless powers of gravity and chemistry, and, over them, of life, preëxisting within us in their highest form.

The uneasiness which the thought of our helplessness in the chain of causes occasions us, results from looking too much at one condition of nature, namely, Motion. But the drag is never taken from the wheel. Wherever the impulse exceeds, the Rest or Identity insinuates its compensation. All over the wide fields of earth grows the prunella or self-heal. After every foolish day we sleep off the fumes and furies of its hours; and though we are always engaged with particulars, and often enslaved to them, we bring with us to every experiment the innate universal laws. These, while they exist in the mind as ideas, stand around us in nature forever embodied, a present sanity to expose and cure the insanity of men. Our servitude to particulars betrays us into a hundred foolish expectations. We anticipate a new era from the invention of a locomotive, or a balloon; the new engine brings with it the old checks. They say that by electro-magnetism, your salad shall be grown from the seed, whilst your fowl is roasting for dinner: it is a symbol of our modern aims and endeavors,—of our condensation and acceleration of objects: but nothing is gained: nature cannot be cheated: man's life is but seventy salads long, grow they swift or grow they slow. In these checks and impossibilities, however, we find our advantage, not less than in the impulses. Let the victory fall where it will, we are on that side. And the knowledge that we traverse the whole scale of being, from the centre to the poles of nature, and have some stake in every possibility, lends that sublime lustre to death, which philosophy and religion have too outwardly and literally striven to express in the popular doctrine of the immortality of the soul. The reality is more excellent than the report. Here is no ruin, no discontinuity, no spent ball. The divine circulations never rest nor linger. Nature is the incarnation of a thought, and turns to a thought again, as ice becomes water and gas. The world is mind precipitated, and the volatile essence is forever escaping again into the state of free thought. Hence the virtue and pungency of the influence on the mind, of natural objects, whether inorganic or organized. Man imprisoned, man crystallized, man vegetative, speaks to man impersonated. That power which does not respect quantity, which makes the whole and the particle its equal channel, delegates its smile to the morning, and distils its essence into every drop of rain. Every moment instructs, and every object: for wisdom is infused into every form. It has been poured into us as blood; it convulsed us as pain; it slid into us as pleasure; it enveloped us in dull, melancholy days, or in days of cheerful labor; we did not guess its essence, until after a long time.

The Relation of Intellect to Natural Science

(1848)

E merson delivered "The Relation of Intellect to
Natural Science" to the Literary and Scientific
Institution in London's Portman Square on June 8, 1848. Emerson
had returned to Europe after an uncharacteristic period of profes-
sional uncertainty. Having published *Poems* in late 1846, he spent the
following months creating an enormous, eight-hundred-page index of
his journals. Still lacking a clear direction for new work, he accepted
an invitation for a lecture tour in England in July 1847. Inspired by
material rediscovered during his indexing process, Emerson wrote a
few miscellaneous lectures upon his arrival in England before beginning what he referred to in a letter to his wife as "a kind of 'Natural
History of the Intellect'"—a project that would ultimately include
"The Relation of Intellect to Natural Science." Arguing for his version
of the "Doctrine of Correspondence," Emerson articulates a renewed
idealism in poetic possibility, the foundation for what he would later
call his "New Metaphysics." Seeking an understanding of mental
processes through an exploration of correspondent phenomena in
nature, Emerson's metaphysics confronts the inability of language to
bridge the gaps between people's respective experiential knowledge.
For scientific insight to benefit humanity, the scientist needs to be
able to communicate across both the "barriers of language" and the
"barriers of society." Into this apparent impasse, Emerson interjects a
poetic principle capable of circumventing the limitations of language
and creating meaningful connections between individuals, as well
as between people and nature. The individual capable of employing
these poetics is reminiscent of the poetic naturalist that he called for

in "The Naturalist" and "Humanity of Science." Here, Emerson adds the caveat that this genius must be a solitary figure capable of surmounting linguistic limitations in order to communicate a profound sense of interrelation. Emerson would revise and deliver this lecture a number of times in the following years and would return to this material in 1870 for Natural History of the Intellect, the final lecture series of his career.

♣

In the last lecture, I proposed to attempt a simple enumeration of some of the mental laws; I spoke of their commanding interest for all men, notwithstanding the frequent ruin of the inquirers, through one of the vices insidiously born with him like the weevil in the wheat. I spoke of the Excellency of Knowledge and Thought; of the Intellect pure, whose sign was declared to be Beauty and Cheerfulness. I proceed now with that description and have to consider, first, the Identity of the Intellect with Nature and, second, some of the Statutes or Byelaws of the Mind.

The first fact in the Natural History of the Intellect, is its similarity, in so many remarkable points, to the history of material atoms; indicating a profound identity with all the parts of Nature. All seem to come of one stock. What is the interest of tropes and symbols to men? I think it is that; unexpected relationship. Each remote part corresponds to each other, can represent the other; because all spring from one root. Nature is a chamber lined with mirrors, and look where we will in botany, mechanics, chemistry, numbers, the image of man comes throbbing back to us. From whatever side we look at nature, we seem to be exploring the figure of a disguised man. We still see the old law gleaming through as the sense of a poem in a language imperfectly understood. Shall I say that the world may be reeled off from any one of its laws like a ball of yarn; that a chemist can explain by his analogies the processes of the Intellect; the physician from his; the geometer, and the mechanician, respectively from theirs?

Thus the idea of Vegetation is irresistible in considering mental activity. Man seems a higher plant. What happens here in mankind, is matched by what happens out there in the history of grass and wheat: an identity long ago observed or, I may say, never not observed, suggesting that the planter among his vines is in the presence of his ancestors; or, shall I say, that the orchardist is a pear raised to the highest power? In this mind, the Persian poet wrote,

> "The gardener's beauty is not of himself,
> His hue the rose's, and his form the palm's."

This curious resemblance to the vegetable pervades human nature, and repeats, in the mental function, the germination, growth, state of melioration, crossings, blights, parasites, and, in short, all the accidents of the plant. The analogy is so thorough, that I shall detain you a few minutes on some of the points.

It appears as if a good work did itself; as if whatever is good, in proportion as it is good, had a certain self-existence or self-organizing power. The new study, the good book, advances, whether the writer is awake or asleep; its subject and order are not chosen, but pre-appointed. It is observed, that our mental processes go forward, even when they seem suspended. Scholars say, that, if they return to the study of a new language after some intermission, the intelligence of it is more and not less. A subject of thought to which we return from month to month, from year to year, has always some ripeness, of which we can give no account. Hence we say, the book grew in the author's mind.

Under every leaf, is the bud of a new leaf; and, not less, under every thought, is a newer thought. Every reform is only a mask, under cover of which a more terrible reform, which dares not yet name itself, advances.

The plant absorbs much nourishment from the ground, in order to repair its own waste by exhalation, and keep itself good. Increase its food, and it becomes fertile. The mind is first only receptive. Surcharge it with thoughts, in which it delights, and it becomes active. The moment a man begins not to be convinced, that moment he begins to convince.

In the orchard, many trees send out a moderate shoot in the first summer heat, and stop. They look, all summer, as if they would presently burst the bud again, and grow; but they do not. The fine tree continues to grow. The same thing happens in the man. The commonest remark, if the man could only extend it a little, would make him a genius; but the thought is prematurely checked and grows no more.

All great masters are chiefly distinguished by the power of adding a second, a third, and perhaps a fourth step, in a continuous line. Many a man had taken their first step. With every additional step, you enhance immensely the value of your first. It is like the rising premium which is sometimes set on a horse by farmers. A price is agreed on in the stable; then he is turned into a pasture, and allowed to roll; and every time he shall roll himself quite over, adds ten dollars to the value.

Van Mons, the inventor of pears, discovered that under favorable circumstances, and at a certain age, the tree was in a state of variation, or state of melioration; as Newton had already observed the fits of easy transmission and easy refraction in light. And there is not less in the human mind, in certain favorable times and relations, a creative saliency, a habit of saliency, which is a sort of importation and domestication of the Divine Effort in a man; a habit of originating, a habit of initiating action, instead of following custom.

See how many men are near a capital discovery; or how near all men are, for years, for ages,—and only one man leaps the invisible fence, and arrives at it. Bichat remarks, "Nothing is more simple than the fact discovered yesterday: Nothing more difficult, than that which will be discovered tomorrow."

The botanist discovered long ago, that nature loves mixtures, and nothing grows well on the Crab Stock; but the bloods of two trees being mixed, a new and excellent fruit is produced. Our flower and fruit gardens are the result of that experiment.

And not less in human history, aboriginal races are incapable of improvement; the dull, melancholy Pelasgi arrive at no civility until the Phoenicians and Ionians come in. The Briton, the Pict, is nothing, until the Roman, the Saxon, the Norman arrives. The Indian of North America is barbarous. And, in the conduct of the mind, the blending of two tendencies or streams of thought, the union of two brains, is a happy result. And usually every mind of a remarkable efficiency owes it to some new combination of traits not observed to have met before.

All that delight which the eye owes to complemental colours, for example, those two harmonies of colour which our winter scenery so frequently offers, in the contrast of snow lying under green pine-trees; and of snow lying under the dead oak-leaves; each of which contrasts gives the eye a lively pleasure; and also that delight which the ear owes to the complemental sounds,—the beautiful surprises of music,— delights us still more in the combinations of human life, and gives rise to love and joy.

It is quite easy to indicate these analogies to any extent, as, for instance, in the special cultivation. The education of the garden is like the education of the college, or the bound apprentice; its aim is to produce, not sap, but plums or quinces; not the health of the tree, but an overgrown pericarp; and it is too apparent in much old history of Universities, not less, which will train a grammarian, though it dry up the man. We will hope that the mended humanity of Republics will save us from this peril.

As thus, it is easy to take vegetation as the type of power; to represent the world as a plant, and the particles plants,—and the vegetable function may be easily traced through all parts of nature, and even in the functions of mind, where Freedom seems to suspend the brute organic action, so it would be easy, with the ancient mythologists, and early theorists, to find the world an animal, which repeats in colossal the economy of animation, which has locomotion, perspiration, inspiring and expiring of air and water, assimilates food, and draws to it with intelligence all that suits its constitution. Its particles were animals, and endowed with appetences, and the whole order of things exhibits the analogy of sex. Kepler looked at the world as a single animal which roared in caverns, and breathed in sea tides; and Goethe represents it as sucking in and ejecting water to make the alternations of weather as well as of tides. It was then, of course, easy to represent all the metaphysical facts by animal analogies; and, indeed, so many of our mental words are derived from the animal body; as, grasp, carry, leap, digest, swallow, run, sleep, wake, hear. It admits too the most exact analogy. Saint Augustine says, "The memory is, as it were, the belly of the mind, and joy and sadness like sweet and bitter food, which, when committed to the memory, are, as it were, passed into the belly, where they may be stowed, but cannot taste. Ridiculous is it to imagine these to be alike, and yet they are not utterly unlike."

It would be as easy to draw our terms of describing mental science from the secret activity of crystallization and its self-determined affinity and form; or, from electricity, which lies already in so many minds as the sufficient theory for explaining creation.

And, in general, all the secrets of natural laws are repeated in mental experience.

Or, the like analogies might be shown between the chemical action of bodies and the intellectual chemistry. The affinity of particles accurately translates the affinity of thoughts; and, what a modern experimenter calls "the contagious influence of chemical action," is so true of minds, that I have only to read the law, that its application may be evident. It is thus. "A body in the act of combination or decomposition, enables another body with which it may be in contact, to enter into the same state." "A substance which would not of itself yield to a particular chemical attraction, will nevertheless do so, if placed in contact with some other body, which is in the act of yielding to the same force."

And if one remembers how contagious are the moral states of men, if one remembers how much we are braced by the presence and actions of any Spartan soul;—it does not need vigour of our own kind; but the spectacle of vigour of any kind, of any prodigious power of performance, wonderfully arms and recruits us.

On the other hand, how many men are degraded only by their sympathies. Their native aims and genius are high enough, but their relation all too tender to the gross people about them.

In unfit company, the finest powers are paralysed. No ambition, no opposition, no friendly attention and fostering kindness, no wine, music, or exhilarating aids, neither warm fireside, nor fresh air, walking, or riding, avail at all to resist the palsy of misassociation. Genius is mute, is dull; there is no Genius. We have tried every variety of appliance, and failed with all, to elicit a spark. Misalliance. Ask your flowers to open, when you have let in on them a freezing wind.

This singular exactness of analogy between all the parts of nature,—this copula or tie between all the sciences,—has been and remains the highest problem which men have to solve. You all know the Platonic solution of the Reminiscence. Show us what facts you will, and we are agitated with dim sentiments that we already know somewhat of this.

The mechanical laws might as easily be shown pervading the kingdom of mind, as the vegetative. A man has been in Spain. The facts and thoughts which the traveller has found in that country gradually settle themselves into a determinate heap of one size and form, and not another. That is what he knows and has to say of Spain. He cannot say it truly, until a sufficient time for the settling and fermenting has passed, and for the disappearing of whatever is accidental and not essential. Then how obvious is the momentum in our mental history! The momentum which increases by exact law in falling bodies, increases by the same rate in the intellectual action. Every scholar knows that he applies himself coldly and slowly at first to his task, but, with the progress of the work, the mind itself becomes heated, and sees far and wide, as it approaches the end of its task: so that it is the common remark of the student, 'Could I only have begun with the same fire which I had on the last day, I should have done something.'

It is true, there is a striking, and, if you will, a certain ridiculous resemblance between a man and a woodchuck; between a man and a pineapple; between a man and a sponge; or whatever natural creature. The gentleman stands in his garden by his vines; gentleman and vine: the one can make a railroad, or a Canton voyage, or an oration; the other can make a watermelon. Each is a caricature of the other, the man of the vine, the vine of the man. A sort of Hudibrastic rhyme. Well, the man discovers that resemblance in all things he looks at,— the sun, the moon, or the salt, or metal, in his crucible. They all mock him, mimic him;—there is the oddest parody always going forward. What can it mean? Every thing he looks at, seems to be humming,

"For auld lang syne, my dear,
For auld lang syne!"

Well, here are two explanations.

Plato explains the intuitive knowledge which all souls have of the truths of geometry, by reminiscence. They have all been through the mill before: they are horribly old: and, on first meeting with a new truth, the soul shakes its head with a knowing look, "Old fellow, I knew your grandfather." And certainly, it were very desirable, as we have histories entitled "Adventures of a cent," "History of a velvet cushion," "Adventures of an old soldier," and the like; that we should have the veracious "Adventures of an old Soul." The history of one of these eternal Jews on the high road of eternity must supersede Malebranche, Locke, Stewart, and Hegel.

That is Plato's doctrine, *that,* the souls learned it all long ago by experience; have been everywhere; and are soaked and saturated with nature, and, in short, have quite sucked the apple of Eden.

The other theory of this relation is the *Omoiomeria* (or like atoms) of Leucippus and Lucretius; the *"leasts"* of Malpighi and Swedenborg; that, fire is made of little fires; and water, of little waters; and man, of manikins; drops make the ocean, sands compose its shores. A drop of water and a grain of sand give you the whole economy. A man is a developed animalcule; animalcule is an arrested Man, but animalcule, again, is made up of atoms, the same atoms of which water, fire, or sand are composed, and, on each atom, the whole atomic power is impressed. A violence of direction is given to it, a genius belongs to it, which, in all its career of combination, it never loses, but still manages to express in a man, in an orange, in a ruby, in a peacock, in a moss: it is still atom, and holds hard by the honest manners and aims of atom.

It is certain that however we may conceive of the wonderful little bricks of which the world is builded, we must suppose a similarity, and fitting, and identity in their frame. It is necessary to suppose that every hose in nature fits every hydrant; that every atom screws to every atom. So only is combination, chemistry, vegetation, animation, intellection, possible. Without identity at base, chaos must be forever.

Identity at the base. It need not be atoms: Modern theory sets aside atoms as unphilosophical, and the first of English physical philosophers, Faraday, propounds that we do not arrive at last at atoms, but at spherules of force. But, in the initial forms or creations, be they what they may, we must find monads that have already all the properties which in any combination they afterwards exhibit. (And this is the fruitful fact whence the sense of relation and the intellectual facts also must be explained.)

It is very easy to push the doctrine into vagaries and into burlesque.

Pythagoras and Plato taught it in grave earnest: The comic Poets and the Hindoo priests exaggerated it into the transmigration of Souls who remembered in one state what befel them in another. But the necessities of the human mind, of logic, and of nature, require the admission of a profound identity at the base of things to account for our skill, and even for our desire of knowledge.

Somewhere, sometime, some eternity, we have played this game before, and have retained some vague memory of the thing, which, though not sufficient to furnish an account of it, yet enables us to understand it better, now that we are here.

If we go through the British Museum, or the *Jardin des Plantes* in Paris, or any cabinet where is some representation of all the kingdoms of nature, we are surprised with occult sympathies, and feel as if looking at our own bone and flesh through colouring and distorting glasses. Is it not a little startling to see with what genius some people take to hunting; with what genius some men fish; what knowledge they still have of the creature they hunt, (the robber, as the police reports say, must have been intimately acquainted with the premises,) how lately the hunter was the poor creature's organic enemy: a presumption *inflamed,* (as lawyers say,)—by observing how many faces in the street still remind us of visages in the forest;—the escape from the quadruped type is not yet perfectly accomplished.

I see the same fact everywhere. The chemist has a frightful intimacy with the secret architecture of bodies; as the fisherman follows the fish, because *he* was *fish;* so the chemist divines the way of alkali, because he was alkali.

As we cannot go into the Zoological Museum without feeling our family ties, and every rhomb, and vesicle, and spicule claiming old acquaintance, so neither can a tender Soul stand under the starry heaven, and explore the solar and stellar arrangements, without the wish to mix with them by knowledge. If men are analogons of acids and salts, and of beast and bird, so are they of geometric laws, and of astronomic galaxies. I have read that "The first of mortals was formed according to all the art, image, and connexion of the world.—"

This knowledge and sympathy only needs augmentation, and it becomes active or creative. The love of the stars becomes inventive and constructive. Descartes, Kepler, Newton, Swedenborg, Laplace, Schelling, wrestle with the problem of genesis, and occupy themselves with constructing cosmogonies.

Nature is saturated with Deity; the particle is saturated with the elixir of the Universe. Little men just born Copernicise. They cannot radiate as suns, or revolve as planets, and so they do it in effigy, by building the orrery in their brain.

Who can see the profuse wealth of Raphaelle's or Angelo's designs, without feeling how near these were to the secret of structure, how little added power it needs to convert this rush of thoughts and forms into bodies? Nay, who can recall the manifold creations of his own fancy in his dreams, without feeling his own readiness to be an artist and creator? And we are very conscious that this identity reaches farther than we know,—has no limits; or none that we can ascertain; as appears in the language men use in regard to men of extraordinary genius. For, the signal performances of great men seem only an extension of the same art that built animal bodies, applied to toys or miniatures. Thus in Laplace and Napoleon, is the old planetary arithmetic now walking in a man: in the builder of Egyptian, or in the designer of Gothic piles, is a reduction of nature's great aspects in caverns and forests, to a scale of human convenience. And there is a conviction in the mind, that some such impulse is constant; that, if the solar system is good art and architecture, the same achievement is in our brain also, if only we can be kept in height of health, and hindered from any interference with our great instincts.

This theory is the root of all the great arts of picture, music, sculpture, architecture, poetry. And the history of the highest genius will warrant the conclusion, that, in proportion as a man's life comes into union with nature, his thoughts run parallel with the creative law.

The act of Imagination is the sharing of the ethereal currents. The poet beholds the central identity, and sees an ocean of power roll and stream this way and that, through million channels, and, following it, can detect essential resemblances in things never before named together. The poet can distribute things after true classes. His own body also is a fleeing apparition, his personality as fugitive as any type, as fugitive as the trope he employs. In certain hours, we can almost pass our hand through our own bodies. I think the last use or value of poetry to be, the suggestion it affords of the flux or fugaciousness of the poet.

The act of Imagination is, the sharing of the real circulations of the Universe; and the value of a symbol or trope, on which, as we know, religions and philosophies are built, is, the evidence it affords that the thought was just.

I had rather have a good symbol of my thought, or a good analogy, than the suffrage of Kant and Plato. If you agree with me, or if Locke, or Montesquieu, or Spinoza agree, I may yet be wrong. But if the elm tree thinks the same thing, if running water, if burning coal; if crystals and alkalies, in their several fashions, say what I say, it must be true.

A good symbol or image therefore is worth more than any argument. A good symbol is a missionary to persuade thousands and millions. The Vedas, the Edda, the Koran, and each new religion and philosophy, what else have they been than the expansion of some happy figure?

Thus, "One touch of nature makes the whole world kin." Intellect agrees with nature. Thought is a finer chemistry, a finer vegetation, a finer animal action. The act of imagination is an obedience of the private spirit to the currents of the world. The act of memory is only the right polarity of the individual or the private mind adjusted to the poles of the world; then it easily commands, as at the centre, the past and the present.

It is not strange that the workman should appear in the work. The world exists for the thought. It is to make appear things which hide. Plants, crystals, animals, are seen; that which makes them such, is not seen. These, then, are "apparent copies of unapparent natures."

Thought agrees also with the moral code of the universe. There is nothing anomalous or antinomian in its higher properties, but as complete a normality or allegiance to general laws, as is shown by the moss or the egg.

The same laws which are kept in the lower parts, in the mines and workshops of nature, are kept in these palaces and council chambers. One police is good for snails and for seraphim. Nature is a shop of one price,—*prix fixé*. Great advantages are bought at great cost. It is good to see the stern terms on which all these high prizes of fortune are obtained, and which parallel in their exactness the rigour of material laws.

If you will suffer me to express somewhat mathematically,—that is, somewhat materially,—the relation of Knowledge, Wisdom, and Virtue, I should say, Knowledge is the straight line, Wisdom is the power of the straight line, that is, the Square. Virtue is the power of the Square, that is, the Solid. A man reads in the "Cultivator," the method of planting and hoeing potatoes, or follows a farmer hoeing along the row of potato hills. That is knowledge. At last, he seizes the hoe, and, at first, with care and heed, pulls up every root of sorrel and witch grass. The day grows hot, the row is long; he says to himself, "This is wisdom,—but one hill is like another,—I have mastered the art: It is trifling to do many times the same thing;" and he desists. But the last lesson was still unlearned. The moral power lay in the continuance, in fortitude, in working against pleasure, to the excellent end, and conquering all opposition. He has knowledge; he has wisdom; but he has missed Virtue, which he only acquires who endures routine, and sweat, and postponement of ease, to the achievement of a worthy end.

The whole history of man is a series of conspiracies to win from nature some advantage without paying for it. Especially, the history of Arts, and of Education. We need not go back to old Sophists. We have had some signal instances in our own times.

It is very curious to see what grand powers we have a hint of, and are mad to grasp, yet how slow Heaven is to trust us with edge-tools.

We found insuperable difficulty in the old way to obtain the knowledge which others all around us possessed, and were willing enough to impart, and which we wanted. Barriers of society,—barriers of language,—inadequacy of the channels of communication, all choked up and disused. Lawyers say, Speech is to conceal. Each man has facts I am looking for, and, though I talk with him, I cannot get at them, for want of the clew. I do not know enough to ask the right question. He does not know what to do with his facts. I know, if I could only get them. But I cannot get society on my own terms. If I want his facts, I must use his keys,—his keys,—that is his arrangements and reserves.

Here is all Boston, all railroads, all manufactures and trade, in the head of this merchant at my side. What would I not give for a peep at his rows, and files, and systems of facts?—Cuvier is gone, and Humboldt is gone, but here is another man who is the heir of all their faculty, with the whole theory of anatomy and Nature: I am in his chamber, and I do not know what question to put.—Here is the king of chemists, whom I have known so long, who knows so much; and I through my ignorance of the vocabulary have never been able to get anything truly valuable from him.—

Here is all Fourier, with his brilliant social schemes, in the head of his disciple.—Here is a philologist, who knows all languages.—Here is all anatomy in the mind of Richard Owen, all electromagnetism in Faraday's, all geology in Lyell's, all mechanism in Stephenson's, all Swedenborg in yonder mystic, all American History in Bancroft's or Sumner's head; and I cannot, with all my avarice of these facts, appropriate any fragment of all their experience. I would fain see their picture-books as they see them. Now, said the adept, if I could cast a spell on this man, and see his pictures by myself, without his inter-vention,—I see them, and not he report them,—that were science and power. And, having learned that lesson, then turn the spell on another, lift up the cover of another hive, and see the cells and suck the honey; and then another; and so without limit, they were not the poorer, and I were rich indeed. This was the expedient of mesmerism,—by way of suction-pump to draw the most unwilling and valuable mass of expe-rience from every extraordinary individual at pleasure. It is not to be told with what joy we began to put this experiment in practice. The eyes of Lynceus who saw through the earth the ingots of gold that were lying a rod or two under the surface; or of the diver who comes suddenly down on a bed of pearl-oysters, that were all pearl;—were not to be compared to his, which put him in possession of men. He was the man-diver. He was the thought-vampyre. He became at once ten, twenty, a thousand men, as he stood gorged with knowledges and turning his fierce eyes on the multitude of masters in all departments of human skill, and hesitating on which mass of action and adventure to turn his all-commanding introspection.

Unhappily, on trial, this bubble broke. Nature was too quick for us. It was found, that the old conditions were invariably enforced; that, if he would arrive at their pictures by the short cut proposed, he must still be imprisoned in their minds by dedication to their experience, and lose so much career of his own, or so much sympathy with still higher souls than theirs: that the condition of participation in any man's thought, is, entering the gate of that life. No man can be intellectually apprehended;—as long as you see only with your eyes, you do not see him. You must be committed, before you shall be intrusted with the secrets of any party.

Besides, he found that really and truly there were no short cuts, that every perception costs houses and lands. Every word of the man of Genius, apprises me how much he has turned his back upon. Every image, every truth, cost him a great neglect; the loss of an estate; the loss of brilliant career opened to him; the loss of friend; wife; child; the flat negation of a duty. Alas! The whole must come by his own proper growth, and not by addition; by education not by induction. If it could be pumped into him, what prices would not be paid! Money, diamonds, houses, counties, for that costly power that commands and creates all these. But no,—the art of arts, the power of thought, Genius, cannot be taught.

In speaking of identity, I said, All things grow; in a living mind, the thoughts live and grow; and what happens in the vegetable happens to them. There are always individuals under generals, not stagnant, not childless, but everything alive reproduces, and each has its progeny which fast emerge into light, or what seemed one truth, presently multiplies itself into many.

Of course, this detachment the intellect contemplates. The intellect forever watches and foresees this detachment.

'Tis an infinite series. Every detachment prepares a new detachment. Of course, the prophecy becomes habitual and reaches to all things. Having seen one thing that once was firmament enter into the kingdom of change and growth, the conclusion is irresistible, there is no fixture in the Universe. Everything was moved, did spin, and will spin again. This changes once for all his view of things. Hint of dialectic: Things appear as seeds of an immense future. Whilst the dull man seems to himself always to live in a finished world, the thinker always finds himself in the early ages; the world lies to him in heaps and gathered materials;—materials of a structure that is yet to be built.

But, what is very curious, this intellect that sees the interval, partakes of it; and the fact of intellectual perception severs, once for all, the man from the things with which he converses. Affection blends, Intellect disjoins the subject and object. For weal or for woe we clear ourselves from the thing we contemplate. We grieve, but are not the grief; we love, but are not love. If we converse with low things, with crimes, with mischances, we are not compromised: and if with high things, with heroic actions, with virtues, the interval becomes a gulf, and we cannot enter into the highest good. "Artist natures do not weep." Goethe, the surpassing intellect of modern times, is spiritual, but not a spiritualist.

You may see it in any home in which the boy of genius is born: it makes him strange among his housemates. He can take what interest he pleases in their interests and pursuits,—he cannot be mixed with them. He holds a Gyges ring in his hand, and can disappear from them at will.

"Many are the ways," said Mahomet to Ali, "by which men enter into Paradise; but thou, by thy intellect, art created near, and standest above them by many degrees of approach." Bonaparte, by force of intellect, is raised out of all comparison with the strong men around him. His marshals, though able, are as horses and oxen; he alone is a fine tragic figure, related to the daemons, and to all time. Add as much force of intellect again, to repair the large defects of his *morale,* and he would have been in harmony with the ideal world.

This inevitable interval is one of the remarkable facts in the natural history of man; a fact fraught with good and evil. It is only those who have this detachment, who interest us. If we go to any nation, who are those whom we seek? Who, but the men of thought. If we go to any society, though of seraphim, he only would engage us, who comprehended and could interpret the thought and theory of it; and that act does instantly detach him from them. That thought is the unfolding of wings at his shoulders.

The poet, in celebrating his hero, celebrates to the wise ear, his superiority to his hero, and announces to the intelligent the lowness of that he magnifies. Shall I say, 'tis an exquisite luxury,—for so I feel it,—the speech of those who treat of things by the genius of the things, and not by the facts themselves? What is vulgar but the laying of the emphasis on persons and facts, instead of on the quality of the fact?

Mr. Prose and Mr. Hoarse-as-crows inform me that their respected grandmothers died this morning, in this very room, an hour ago. I cannot bring myself to say, Alas! No, not if they should both suffer as their grandmothers did. But an engineer draws my notice to the electricity on a shred of paper; a mote may show the secret of gravity; or one of the masters of the world may show me how a feature of the human face obeys a moral rule; and open to me a new scale of means and agencies.

It is not to be concealed, that the gods have guarded this god-like privilege with costly penalty. This slight discontinuity which perception effects between the mind and the object, paralyses the will. If you cut or break in two a block of wood or stone, and unite the parts, you can indeed bring the particles very near, but never again so near that they shall attract each other, so that you can take up the block as one. That indescribably small interval is as good as a thousand miles, and has forever severed the practical unity. Such too is the immense deduction from power by discontinuity. There is a story in the nursery books (which always seemed to me to be a covert satire directed at the Universities and men of thought,) of Velent, who had a sword so wonderfully sharp, that its entrance into the body was hardly to be perceived.—"I feel thy sword," cried Æmilius, "like cold water gliding through my body." "Shake thyself," said Velent; he shook himself, and fell down dead in two pieces.

This interval even comes between the thinker and his conversation,—which he cannot inform with his genius.

There is, indeed, this vice about men of thought, that, you cannot quite trust them, not as much as other men of the same natural probity without intellect, because they have a hankering to play Providence, and make a distinction in favour of themselves, from the rules which they apply to all the human race. The correction for this insubordination is herein,—that religion runs in true and parallel lines, through the Intellect, as through Morals. All the powers and rewards of Faith, which we find in the *Good,* hold equally in the region of the *True.* Integrity is really the fountain of power, in one as in the other.

In regard to a poem of mine in which hints were given how the national Destinies would be likely to work out the problem of Mexican War, I remember something like this was objected.

It is the office of the poet to justify the moral sentiment and establish its eternal independence on demoniacal agencies. It is the merit of New England that it believes and knows, that Slavery must be abolished. That faith and the expression of it, we demand of the poet.

In a poem for modern men, in these days of subserviency and adulation, the possibility of emancipation should have been made indubitable. There is a God to propitiate against this duality in Nature;—and the poet, whilst admitting the facts as they lie in nature, owes to that worship of the Best in the best men, the celebration of his own and the reader's faith in the possible reconciliation of things, that is, the bad force of things, with mankind.

This interval or discontinuity is every way a remarkable trait of intellectual action. I pointed out some of the many analogies between vegetation and intellection. Certainly, this is not the least. In the growth of the plant, cell grows out of cell, the walls bend inwards, and make two. In the instinct of progress, the mind is always passing—by successive leaps,—forward into new states, and, in that transition, is its health and power. The detachment which thought effects is the preparation for this step.

The brain and hands are hardly contemporaries. The brain is the ancestor of the man. The Intellect is the watchman, the Angel in the sun, and announces the far off age. All its laws it can read before yet the happy men arrive who enter into Power. But the rest of men must follow their heads; and if I can see their eyes, I will trust that they will soon be able to disengage their hands.

Every truth tends to become a power. Every idea from the moment of its emergence, begins to gather material forces, and, after a little while makes itself known in the spheres of politics and commerce. It works first on thoughts, then on things; it makes feet, and afterward shoes; first, hands; then, gloves; makes the men, and so the age and its *materiel* soon after. Astronomy is of no use, unless I can carry it into shops and sitting-rooms. He only is immortal to whom all things are immortal.

As certainly as water falls in rain on the tops of mountains, and runs down into valleys, plains, and pits, so does thought fall first on the best minds, and run down from class to class, until it reaches the masses, and works revolution. Let the river roll which way it will, cities will rise on its banks.

Nature obeys a truth. The earth, the stones, stir to own their law. See a political revolution dogging a book. See armies, and institutions, and literatures appearing in the train of some wild Arabian's dream. See all the ponderous instrumentalities which follow a speech in Parliament. What is personal power but the immense terror and love that follow a thought.

From the steamboat I like to mark the long wake in the sea, whitening the water for a mile or two astern. I like that the brain of the animal should be produced to a goodly length of tail. I like long hair, I like longevity, I like every sign of riches and extent of nature in an individual; but most of all, I like a great memory: "Stability of knowledge." I hate this fatal shortness of memory, these docked men whom I behold. We knew of Assyria and Egypt, of Dorians and Etruscans, of Macedon and Rome, and Gaul and England. We knew of geography, and natural philosophy, geology, chemistry, magnetism. We knew of poets and painters, we knew of hundreds of private persons, their lives, relations, fortunes. We gathered up what a rolling snowball as we came along, much of it professedly for the future as capital stock of knowledge.

Where is it all now? Look behind you. I cannot see that your train is any longer than it was in childhood. The facts of the last two or three days are all you have with you: the reading of the last month's books. Your conversation, your action, your face and manners report of no more, of no greater wealth of mind. Alas, you have lost something for every thing you have gained, and cannot grow. You are a lead stone put through steel-shavings, only so much iron will it draw. It gains new particles, all the way, as you move it, but one falls off for every one that adheres. The reason of the short memory is the shallow thought. As deep as the thought, so great is the attraction. An act of the understanding will marshal and concatenate a few facts. A new principle, will thrill, magnetise, and new divide the whole world. Yet 'tis amusing to see the astonishment of people over any new fact, as mesmerism. You would think they knew everything but this one, and there is no one thing they knew.

A deeper thought would hold in solution more facts. It is the law of nature that you shall keep no more than you use. The fishes that swim in the waters of the Mammoth Cave in Kentucky in darkness are blind. When the eye was useless, it ceased to exist. It is the eternal relation between power and use.

A man should not be rich by having what is superfluous, but by having what is essential to him like a manufacturer, or engineer, or astronomer who has a great capital invested in his machines. The question is, How to animate all his possessions? If he have any not animated by his quality and energy, let him sell them and buy things nearer to his nature. Such a rich man excites no envy. He has no more than he needs or uses. Give us a deeper nature, increase our affinities, and you add organs and powers. The oyster has few wants and is a poor creature. The Mammalia with their manifold wants are rich men.

The complex animals are the highest: the more wants the richer men. Men want everything. They are made of hooks and eyes and put the universe under contribution. Man is rich as he is much-related.

The more rich, the more expensive, the better. I would have vaster demands made, and rich men shown how to be rich. I never saw a rich man who was rich enough, as rich as all men ought to be. Rich men are powerless and unskilful spenders. Very few understand that art. It needs truly great wants to be greatly gratified. One would like that thoughts should spend! What an apparatus does not every high genius require! No handloom, no watch-wheel, but wheels that roll like the solar system. I think you must give him gardens, towns, courts, kings, earth itself and astronomies, a freedom of the whole City of God.

I like to see rich men seem rightly rich when I see them take more hold on the world, possess Niagara; possess the sea, the mountains.

Every truth leads in another. The bud extrudes the old leaf, and every truth brings that which will supplant it. In the true and real world the judge sits over the culprit, but in the same hour, the judge also stands as culprit before a true tribunal. Every judge is culprit, every law an abuse. Every fort has been taken. Every scholar has his superior. Life is on platforms. Montaigne kills off bigots as cowage kills worms, but there is a higher muse there, sitting where he durst not soar, of wing so swift and eye so keen, that it can follow the flowing Power, follow that which flies, and report of a realm in which all the wit and learning of the Frenchman is no more than the cunning of a beast.

The ground of hope is in the infinity of the world, which infinity reappears in every particle. The man truly conversant with life, knows against all appearances, that there is a remedy for every wrong, and that every wall is a gate.

Everyone's reading will have furnished him with how many examples of the parentage of those thoughts that make the value of literature. Every thought begets sons and daughters. In like manner, the history of politics, of philanthropy, for a short term of years shows a rapid filiation. From the Society for Abolition of Slavery sprang within a few years a Temperance, a Non-Resistance, an Anti-Church and Anti-Sabbath Movement.

Every truth is universally applicable, thousand-sided. Every drop of blood has great talents; the original vesicle, the original cellule, seems identical in all animals, and only varied in its growth by the varying circumstance which opens now this kind of cell and now that, causing in the remote effect now horns, now wings, now scales, now hair; and the same numerical atom, it would seem, was equally ready to be a particle of the eye or brain of man, or of the claw of a tiger. In the body of a man, all those terrific energies which belong to it, the capability of being developed into a *saurus*, or a mammoth, a baboon that would twist off heads, or a grampus that tears a square foot of flesh from the whale or grampus that swims by him,—are held in check, and subordinated to the human genius and destiny. But it is ready at any time to pass into other circles and take its part in baser or in better forms. Nay, it seems that the animal and the vegetable texture at last are alike. Well, as thus the drop of blood has many talents lurking in it, so every truth is much more rich.

Every law detected in any part of nature holds in every other part. The law of music is law of anatomy, of algebra, of astronomy, of human life and social order. The Greek statues of the ancient temples of Jove, Mars, Venus, Diana, and Apollo are observed to have a family likeness.

It is certain that these laws are all versions of each other. The symmetry and coordination of things is such that from any creature well and inly known the law of any other might be legitimately deduced. Palmistry, phrenology, astrology rest on a real basis. 'Tis certain that there is a relation between the stars and your wedding day, between the lines of your hand and the works done by it, between the activity of your brain and its outward figure,—there is a relation,—though you may easily fail to find it. The world, the Universe, may be reeled off from any idea, like a ball of yarn. Just see how the chemist, how the Christian, how the negro, each disposes of it with the greatest ease, after his own peculiar habit, and finds all the facts fit and confirm his view.

And each science and law is in like manner prospective and fruitful. Astronomy is not yet astronomy whilst it only counts the stars in the sky. It must come nearer and be related to men and their life, and interpret the moral laws. In learning one thing you learn all. Egg and stratum go together, as the naturalist found that the order of changes in form of the embryo in the egg from day to day determined the right succession of the fossil remains of species which had occupied the surface of the globe for geologic ages.

I had intended to add to these a few examples of specific laws; as, that every thought ranks itself; that there is a constant effort at ascension of state; that a certain motive force is the aim of education: a whip for our top. I but shall continue the inquiry in the next lecture.

Country Life

(1858)

The little-known lecture "Country Life" was delivered on March 3, 1858, at the Freeman Place Chapel in Boston. It was the first in Emerson's six-part Natural Method of Mental Philosophy lecture series, which focused on his metaphysical philosophy and was delivered in March and April 1858. The mid- to late 1850s were a reflective period for Emerson, a time when he often returned to and reconsidered central themes of his career in light of his accumulated life experiences. This recursive tendency is evident in "Country Life," in which he uses a philosophical meditation on walking as an opportunity to return to the key insights of earlier pieces contained in this collection. Quoting Rousseau's claim that walking "has something which animates and vivifies my ideas," Emerson endorses rambles in nature as beneficial in providing the walker the opportunity to hone their own perceptual skills. As he did in his discussion of the transcendent experience in his 1844 essay "Nature," Emerson emphasizes that ecstatic moments in nature result from a mode of perception that is not innate but rather acquired through the sustained practice of attention and engagement. As in "The Uses of Natural History," Emerson asserts that the transcendent experience arises from discerning the grand design revealed in the particular natural elements encountered. Walking cultivates this new way of seeing nature by creating a sense of familiarity with the landscape through continued exposure. Out of this intimacy with the land, the walker begins to discern the constant creation at work within an ecological system and, in so doing, avoids the overly narrow focus of the myopic scientist Emerson first identified in "The Naturalist." In addition to revisiting Emerson's own earlier work, "Country Life" may also allude to the work of his friend Henry David Thoreau, whose peripatetic spirit seems to animate Emerson's endorsement of the art of rambling. Like Thoreau's remarkable essay "Walking" (1862), "Country Life" is a testimonial to the physical, aesthetic, and spiritual value of sauntering. Walking is of the utmost importance to Emerson because it exposes the walker to the "soothing and expanding influences" of the natural world and also fosters an intellectual acuity, both of which are necessary for a transformative encounter with nature.

The Teutonic race have been marked in all ages by a trait which has received the name of *Earth-hunger*, a love of possessing land. It is not less visible in that branch of the family which inhabits America. Nor is it confined to farmers, speculators, and *fillibusters*, or conquerors. The land, the care of land, seems to be the calling of the people of this new country, of those, at least, who have not some decided bias, driving them to a particular craft, as a born sailor or machinist. The capable and generous,—let them spend their talent on the land. Plant it; adorn it; study it. It will develop in the cultivator the talent it requires.

The avarice of real estate,—native to us all,—covers instincts of great generosity, namely, all that is called the love of nature, comprising the largest use and the whole beauty of a farm or landed estate; and I wish to call your attention to the pursuits of country-life, not so much to farmers, as to a class of the population in which this attribute of the Teutonic family takes a liberal and artistic form, and is stripped of all its malignant features,—the class of peripatetics, or walkers.

Travel and walking have this apology, that nature has impressed on savage men periodical or secular impulses to emigrate, as upon lemmings, rats, and birds. The Indians go in summer to the coast, for fishing; in winter, to the woods. The nomads wander over vast territory, to find their pasture.

Other impulses hold us to other habits. As the increasing population finds new values in the ground, the nomad life is given up for settled homes. But the necessity of exercise and the nomadic instinct are always stirring the wish to travel, and in spring and summer, it commonly gets the victory. Chaucer notes of the month of April,

"Then long the folk to go on pilgrimages,
And palmers for to seeken stranger strands,
To serve the saints beknown in sondry lands."

And, in the country, nature is always inviting to the compromise of walking as soon as we are released from severe labor. Linnaeus, early in life, read a discourse at the University of Uppsala, *on the necessity of travelling in one's own country,* based on the conviction that nature was inexhaustibly rich, and that in every district were swamps, or beaches, or rocks, or mountains, which were now nuisances, but, if explored, and turned to account, were capable of yielding immense benefit. At Uppsala, therefore, he instituted what were called *herborizations;* he summoned his class to go with him on excursions on foot into the country, to collect plants, and insects, birds, and eggs. These parties started at seven in the morning, and stayed out, till nine in the evening; the professor was generally attended by two hundred students, and, when they returned, they marched through the streets of Uppsala in a festive procession, with flowers in their hats, to the music of drums and trumpets, and with loads of natural productions collected on the way.

Let me remind you what this walker found in his walks. He went to Öland, and found that the farms on the shore were perpetually encroached on by the sea, and ruined by blowing sand. He discovered that the *arundo arenaria,* or beach grass, had long firm roots, and he taught them to plant it for the protection of their shores. In Torneå, he found the people suffering every spring from the loss of their cattle, which died by some frightful distemper, to the number of fifty or a hundred in a year. Linnaeus walked out to examine the meadow into which they were first turned out to grass, and found it a bog, where the *water hemlock* grew in abundance, and had evidently been cropped plentifully by the animals in feeding. He found the plant also dried in their cut hay. He showed them, that the whole evil might be prevented by employing a woman for a month to eradicate the noxious plants.

When the shipyards were infested with rot, Linnaeus was sent to provide some remedy. He studied the insects that infested the timber, and found that they laid their eggs in the logs within certain days in April. And he directed that during ten days, at that time of the year, the logs should be immersed under water in the docks, which, being done, the timber was found to be uninjured. He found that the gout, to which he was subject, was cured by wood strawberries. He had other remedies. When Kalm returned from America, Linnaeus was laid up with severe gout. But the joy in his return and the curiosity to see his plants restored him instantly, and he found an old friend as good as the treatment by wood strawberries. He learned the secret of making pearls in the river-pearl-muscle. He found out that a terrible distemper which sometimes proves fatal in the north of Europe, was occasioned by an animalcule, which he called *Furia infernalis,* which falls from the air on the face, or hand, or other uncovered part, burrows into it, multiplies, and kills the sufferer. By timely attention, it is easily extracted.

He examined eight thousand plants; and examined fishes, insects, birds, and quadrupeds; and distributed the animal, vegetable, and mineral kingdoms. And if, instead of running about in the hotels and theatres of Europe, we would man-like see what grows, or might grow, in Massachusetts, stock its gardens, drain its bogs, plant its miles and miles of barren waste with oak and pine; and,—following what is usually the natural suggestion of these pursuits,—ponder the moral secrets which in her solitudes Nature has to whisper to us, we were better patriots and happier men.

In June, man feels the blood of thousands in his body, and his heart pumps the sap of all this forest through his arteries. What fugitive summer flower, papilionaeceous, is he, among these longevities! Gladly he would spread himself abroad among them, as if he were their father, borrow,—by his love,—the manners of his trees, and, with nature's patience, watch the giants from their youth to the age of golden fruit, or gnarled timber, nor think it long.

We have the finest climate in the world, for this purpose, in Massachusetts. If we have coarse days, and dog days, and white-days, and days that are like ice-blinks, we have also yellow days, and crystal days,—days which are neither hot nor cold,—but the perfection of temperature. New England has a good climate,—yet, in choosing a farm, we like a southern exposure, whilst Massachusetts, it must be owned, is on the northern slope, towards the Arctic Circle, and the Pole. Our climate is a series of surprises, and, among our many prognostics of the weather, the only trustworthy one that I know, is, that, when it is warm, it is a sign that it is going to be cold. The climate needs, therefore, to be corrected by a little anthracite coal;—a little coal in-doors, during much of the year; and thick coats and shoes must be recommended to walkers. I own, I prefer the solar to the polar climates. "I have no enthusiasm for nature," said a French writer, "which the slightest chill will not instantly destroy."

But we cannot overpraise the comfort and the beauty of the climate in the best days of the year. In summer, we have for weeks a sky of Calcutta, yielding the richest growth, maturing plants which require strongest sunshine. And scores of days when the heat is so rich, and yet so tempered, that it is delicious to live.

The importance to the intellect of exposing the body and brain to the fine mineral and imponderable agents of the air makes the chief interest in the subject. "So exquisite is the structure of the cortical glands," said the old physiologist Malphigi, "that when the atmosphere is ever so slightly vitiated or altered, the brain is the first part to sympathize and to undergo a change of state." We are very sensible of this, when, in midsummer, we go to the seashore, or to mountains, or when, after much confinement to the house, we go abroad into the landscape, with any leisure to attend to its soothing and expanding influences. The old physiologists were much more attentive than we, to the effects of air. "There is in the air," they said, "a hidden food of life;" and they watched the different effect of certain climates. They believed the air of mountains and the seashore a potent and great predisposer to rebellion. The air was a famous republican; And, it was remarked, that "insulary people are extremely versatile and obnoxious to change, both in religious and secular affairs."

The power of the air, was the first explanation offered by the early philosophers of the mutual understanding that men have. "The air," said Anaximenes, "is the Soul, and the essence of life. By breathing it, we become intelligent, and, because we breathe the same air, understand one another." Plutarch thought it contained the knowledge of the future: "that souls are naturally endued with the faculty of prediction, and that the chief cause that excites that faculty, is a certain temperature of air and winds.—" Even Lord Bacon said, "the stars inject their imagination or influence into the air."

The air that we breathe is an exhalation of all the solid material of the globe. An aerial fluid of some kind streams all day, all night, from every flower and leaf, yes, and from every mineral substance. It is the last finish of the work of the Creator. We might say, the Rock of Ages dissolves himself into the mineral air to build up this mystic constitution of man's mind and body.

Walking has the best value as gymnastics for the mind. "You shall never break down in a speech," said Sydney Smith, "on the day on which you have walked twelve miles." In the English universities, the reading men are daily performing their punctual training in the boat-clubs, or a long gallop of many miles in the saddle, or, taking their famed "constitutionals," walks of eight and ten miles. "Walking," said Rousseau, "has something which animates and vivifies my ideas." And Plato said of exercise, that, "it would almost cure a guilty conscience." "For the living out of doors, and simple fare, and gymnastic exercises, and the morals of companions, produce the greatest effect in the way of virtue and of vice."

Few men know how to take a walk. The qualifications of a professor are endurance, plain clothes, old shoes, an eye for nature, good humor, vast curiosity, good speech, good silence, and nothing too much. If a man tells me that he has an intense love of nature, I know, of course, that he has none. Good observers have the manners of trees and animals, their patient good sense, and if they add words, 'tis only when words are better than silence. But a loud singer, or a story teller, or a vain talker profanes the river and the forest, and is nothing like so good company as a dog.

There is an effect also on beauty.

"I have seen Wordsworth's eyes sometimes affected powerfully in this respect. His eyes are not under any circumstances bright, lustrous, or piercing, but, after a long day's toil in walking, I have seen them assume an appearance the most solemn and spiritual that it is possible for the human eye to wear. The light which resides in them is at no time a superficial light, but, under favorable accidents, it is a light which seems to come from depths below all depths; in fact, it is more truly entitled to be held 'the light that never was on land, or sea,' a light radiating from some far spiritual world, than any that can be named."

But De Quincey prefixes to this description of Wordsworth, a little piece of advice, which, I wonder has not attracted more attention. "The depth and subtlety of the eyes varies exceedingly with the state of the stomach, and, if young ladies were aware of the magical transformations which can be wrought in the depth and sweetness of the eye, by a few weeks' exercise, I fancy we should see their habits in this point altered greatly for the better."

For walking, you must have a broken country. In Illinois, everybody rides. There is no good walk in that state. The reason is, a square yard of it is as good as a hundred miles. A man on the prairie called my attention to the fact that you can distinguish from the cows a horse feeding, at the distance of five miles, with the naked eye. Hence, you have the monotony of Holland, and when you step out of the door, can see all that you will have seen when you come home. In Massachusetts, our land is agreeably broken, and, is permeable like a park, and not like some towns in the more broken country of New Hampshire, built on three or four hills having each one side at forty-five degrees, and the other side perpendicular; so that if you go a mile, you have only the choice whether you will climb the hill on your way out, or on your way back. The more reason we have to be content with the felicity of our slopes in Massachusetts—undulating, rocky, broken, and surprising, but without this Alpine inconveniency.

Twenty years ago, in northern Wisconsin the pinery was composed of trees so big, and so many of them, that it was impossible to walk in the country, and the traveller had nothing for it, but to wade in the streams.—One more inconveniency, I remember, they showed me in Illinois, that, in the bottom lands, the grass was fourteen feet high.

We may well enumerate what compensating advantages we have over that country for, 'tis a commonplace, which I have frequently heard spoken in Illinois, that, it was a manifest leading of the Divine Providence, that the New England states should have been first settled, before the western country was known, or they would never have been settled at all.

The privilege of the country-man is the culture of the land, the laying out of grounds, and gardens, the orchard, and the forest. The Rosaceous tribe in botany, including the apple, pear, peach, and cherry, are coeval with man. The apple is our national fruit. In October, the country is covered with its ornamental harvest. The color of the apple heaps, more lively and varied than the orange, give a depth to our russet Massachusetts. The American sun paints itself in these glowing balls amid the green leaves the social fruit, in which nature has deposited every possible flavor; whole zones and climates she has concentrated into apples.

I am afraid you do not understand values. Look over the fence at the farmer who stands there. He makes every cloud in the sky, and every beam of the sun, serve him. His trees are full of brandy. He saves every drop of sap, as if it were wine. A few years ago, those trees were whipsticks. Now, every one of them is worth a hundred dollars. Observe their form; not a branch, nor a twig, is to spare. They look as if they were arms and fingers, holding out to you balls of fire and gold. One tree yields the rent of an acre of land.

Yonder pear has every property which should belong to a tree. It is hardy, and almost immortal. It accepts every species of nourishment, and yet could live, like an Arab, on air and water. It grows like the ash Igdrasil. There is no chemist like that tree, which has the art, out of all kinds of refuse rubbish, to manufacture Virgalieus, Bergamots, and Seckles, in a manner which no chemist and no confectioner can approach, and his way of working is as beautiful as the result.

In old towns, there are always certain paradises known to the pedestrian, old and deserted farms, where the neglected orchard has been left to itself, and, whilst some of its trees decay, the hardier have held their own. I know a whole district made up of wide straggling orchards, where the apple trees strive with, and hold their ground against, the native forest trees: the apple growing with a profusion that mocks the pains taken by careful Cockneys, who come out into the country, plant young trees, and watch them dwindling. Here, no hedges are wanted; the wide distance from any population is fence enough: the fence is a mile wide. Here are varieties of apple not found in Downing or London;—the "Tartaric" variety, and "Cow" apple, and the "Bite me if you dare," and the "Beware of this." The ground is strewn with red and yellow heaps. They grew for their own pleasure, and almost lost price. Apples of a kind which I remember in boyhood: the farmer bragged each contained a barrel of wind, and half a barrel of cider.

But here was a contest between the old orchard and the invading forest-trees for the possession of the ground, of the whites against the Pequots, and if the handsome savages win, we shall not be losers. A grove of trees,—what benefit or ornament is so fair and great? They make the landscape. They keep the earth habitable. Their roots run down, like cattle, to the watercourses. Their heads expand to feed the atmosphere. The life of a tree is a hundred and a thousand years; its decays ornamental; its repairs self-made. They grow, when we sleep; they grew, when we were unborn. Man is a moth among these longevities. He plants too the next millennium. Shadows haunt them. All that ever lived about them, clings to them. You can almost see, behind these pines, the Indian with bow and arrow lurking yet, exploring the traces of the old trail.

There is no ornament, no architecture, alone, so sumptuous, as well-disposed woods and waters, where art has been employed only to remove superfluities, and bring out the natural advantages. What work of man will compare with the plantation of a park? It dignifies life. It is a seat for friendship, counsel, taste, and religion. I do not wonder that parks are the chosen badge and point of pride of European nobility. But how much more are they needed by us, anxious, over-driven Americans, to staunch and appease that fury of temperament which our climate bestows!

According to the common estimate of farmers, the woodlot yields its gentle rent of six percent, without any care or thought, when the owner sleeps or travels, and is subject to no enemy but fire. Evelyn quotes Lord Caernarvon's saying, "Wood is an excrescence of the earth provided by God for the payment of debts." I admire in trees the creation of property so clean of tears, or crime, or even care. No lesson of chemistry is more impressive than this: Nineteen-twentieths of the timber is drawn from the atmosphere. We knew the root was sucking juices from the ground; the top of the tree is also a taproot thrust into the public pocket of the world. This is a *highwayman,* to be sure. And I am always glad to remember, that, in proportion to the foliation is the addition of wood. There they grow, when you wake, and, when you sleep, at nobody's cost, and for everybody's comfort. Lord Abercorn, when someone praised the rapid growth of his trees, replied, "Sir, they have nothing else to do."

When Nero advertised for a new luxury, a walk in the woods should have been offered. 'Tis one of the secrets for dodging old age. For Nature makes a like impression on age as on youth. Then, I recommend it to people who are growing old against their will. A man in that predicament, if he stands before a mirror, or among young people, is made quite too sensible of the fact; but the forest awakes in him the same feeling it did when he was a boy: And he may draw a moral from the fact that 'tis the old trees that have all the beauty and grandeur.

I admire the taste which makes the avenue to a house, were the house, never so small, through a wood; besides the beauty, it has a positive effect on manners, as it disposes the mind of the inhabitant and of his guests to the deference due to each. Some English reformers thought the cattle made all this wide space necessary between house and house, and, that, if there were no cows to pasture, less land would suffice. But a cow does not need so much land as the owner's eyes require between him and his neighbor.

Our Aryan progenitors in Asia celebrated the Winds as the conveying *Maruts,* traversers of places difficult of access. Stable is their birthplace in the sky, but they are agitators of heaven and earth, who shake all around like the top of a tree. Because they drive the clouds, they have harnessed the spotted deer to their chariot; they are coming with weapons, war-cries, and decorations. I hear the cracking of the whips in their hands. I praise their sportive, resistless strength; they are generators of speech. They drive before them in their course the long, vast, uninjurable, rain-retaining cloud. Wherever they pass, they fill the way with clamor. Everyone hears their noise. The lightning roars like a parent cow that bellows for its calf, and the rain is set free by the *Maruts. Maruts,* as you have vigor, invigorate mankind.

Aswins, Waters, long-armed, good-looking *Aswins*! bearers of wealth, guides of men, harness your car! Ambrosia is in you; in you are medicinal herbs.

The Hindoos called Fire *Agni,* born in the woods, bearer of oblations, smoke-bannered and light-shedding, lord of red coursers; the guest of man; protector of people in villages; the sacrificer visible to all, thousand-eyed, all-beholding, of graceful form, and whose countenance is turned on all sides.

[What uses that we know belong to the forest, and what countless uses that we know not! How an Indian helps himself with fibre of milkweed, or white bush, or wild hemp, or root of spruce, black or white, for strings; making his bow of hickory, birch, or even a fir-bough, at a pinch; white birch for hat and leggings; hemlock bark for his roof; hair moss or fern for his bed. He goes to a tree, and can fit his leg with a seamless boot, or a hat for his head. He can draw sugar from the maple, food and antidotes from a hundred plants. He knows his way in a straight line from watercourse to watercourse, and you cannot lose him in the woods. He consults, by way of natural compass, when he travels, first, large pine trees, which bear more numerous branches on their southern side; second, ant hills, which have grass on their south; and, third, whortleberries on the north, and aspens, whose bark is rough on the north, and smooth on the south, side. <u>All his knowledge is for use, and it only appears in use; whilst white men have theirs also for talking purposes.</u>]

I am a very indifferent botanist, but I admire that perennial four-petalled flower, which has one grey petal, one green, one red, and one white. I think sometimes, how many days could Methusalem go out and find something new. In January, the new snow has changed the woods so that he does not know them; has built sudden cathedrals in a night. In the familiar forest, he finds Norway and Russia in the masses of overloading snow which break all that they cannot bend. In March, the thaw, and the sounding of the south wind, and the splendor of the icicles. On the pond there is a cannonade of a hundred guns, but it is not in honor of the election of any president. He goes forth again after the rain; in the cold swamp, the buds are swollen, the *ictodes* prepares its flower, and the mallows, and mouse-ear. The mallows the Greeks held sacred as giving the first sign of the sympathy of the earth with the celestial influences. The next day, the Hylas are piping in every pool, and a new activity among the hardy birds, the premature arrival of the bluebird, and the first northward flight of the geese, who cannot keep their joy to themselves, and fly low over the farms. In May, the bursting of the leaf,—the oak and maple are red with the same colors on the new leaf which they will resume in autumn, when it is ripe. In June, the miracle works faster,

> Painting with white and red the moors,
> To draw the nations out of doors.

Man feels the blood of thousands in his body, and pumps the sap of all this forest through his arteries; the loquacity of all birds in the morning; and the immensity of life seems to make the world deep and wide. In August, when the corn is grown to be a resort and protection to woodcocks and small birds, and when the leaves whisper to each other in the wind, we observe already that the leaf is sear, that a change has passed on the landscape.

The world has nothing to offer more rich or entertaining than the days which October always brings us, when, after the first frosts, a steady shower of gold falls in the strong southwind from the chestnuts, maples, and hickories: All the trees are wind harps, filling the air with music; and all men become poets, and walk to the measures of rhymes they make or remember. The dullest churl begins to quaver. The forest in its coat of many colors reflects its varied splendor through the softest haze. The witch-hazel blooms to mark the last hour arrived, and that nature has played out her summer scene. The dry leaves rustle so loud, as we go rummaging through them, that we can hear nothing else. The leaf in our dry climate gets fully ripe, and, like the fruit when fully ripe, acquires fine color; whilst, in Europe, the damper climate decomposes it too soon.

But the pleasures of garden, orchard, and wood, must be alternated.

We know the healing effect on the sick, of change of air; the action of new scenery on the mind is not less fruitful. We must remember that man is a natural nomad, and his old propensities will stir at midsummer, and send him, like an Indian, to the sea. The influence of the ocean on the love of liberty, I mentioned already. Its power on the mind in sharpening the perceptions, has made the sea the famous educator of our race. The history of the world,—what is it, but the doings about the shores of the Mediterranean Sea, and the Atlantic?

I have heard with much sympathy the story of the old lady, who, coming from the interior to the seaside, delighted in looking at the ocean, and said, "She was glad at last to see in the world something that there was enough of." On the seashore, the play of the Atlantic with the coast. Every wave reached a quarter of a mile along shore, as it broke. Who is rich to compare with these sea gods? What a hint for wealth is here! Every wave is a fortune. One thinks of Etzlers and great projectors, who will turn this waste strength to account. What freedom and grace has the sea with all this might! The wind blew back the foam from the top of each billow, as it rolled in, like the hair of a woman in the wind.

The freedom makes the observer feel as a slave. Our expression is so thin and cramp. Can we not learn here a generous eloquence? This was the lesson our starving poverty wanted. This was the disciplinary Pythagorean music, which should be medicine. The seeing so excellent a spectacle, is a certificate that all imaginable good shall yet be realized.

At Niagara, I have noticed, that, as quick as I got out of the wetting of the 'Fall, all the grandeur changed into beauty. You cannot keep it grand, 'tis so quickly beautiful; and the sea gave me the same experience. 'Tis great and formidable, when you lie down in it, among the rocks. But, on the shore, at one rod's distance, 'tis changed into a beauty as of gems and clouds.

Shores in sight of each other in a warm climate, make boat builders; and wherever we find a coast broken up into bays and harbors, we find an instant effect on the intellect and industry of the people.

The sea is a noble, friendly power, and seems to say, Why so late and slow to come? Am I not always here, thy proper summer home? Is not my voice thy needful music; my breath thy healthful climate in the heats? My touch, thy cure? Was ever building like my terraces? Was ever couch magnificent as mine? Lie down on my warm ledges, and learn that a little tent is all you need. I make your civic architecture needless; it is paltry beside mine. Here are Romes, Ninevehs, and Karnaks; Obelisk, pyramid, and Giant's Causeway, prostrate or half-piled.

And behold the sea! the opaline, plentiful and strong, yet beautiful as the rose or the rainbow; full of food, nourisher of men, purger of the world, creating a sweet climate, and, in its mathematic ebb and flow, giving a hint of that which changes not and is perfect.

The sea is the chemist that dissolves the mountain and the rock; pulverises old continents, and builds new;—forever re-distributing the solid matter of the globe; and performs an analogous office in perpetual new transplanting of the races of men over the surface—Exodus of nations.

We may well yield us for a time to its lessons. But the nomad instinct, as I said, persists to drive us to fresh fields and pastures new. Indeed, the variety of our moods has an answering variety in the face of the world, and the sea drives us back to the hills.

Dr. Johnson said of the Scotch Mountains, "The appearance is that of matter incapable of form or usefulness, dismissed by nature from her care." The poor, blear-eyed doctor was no poet. Like Charles Lamb, he loved the sweet security of streets. It was said of him, that, "he preferred the Strand to the Garden of the Hesperides." But this is not the experience of imaginative men, nor of men with good eyes, and susceptible organization.

"It is customary," says Linnaeus, "in our part of Sweden, for those who fancy themselves indisposed, to frequent watering places or mineral springs, during the heat of summer." "For my part," says Linnaeus, "I have enjoyed good health, except a slight languor:—but as soon as I got upon the Norway Alps, I seemed to have acquired a new existence. I felt as if relieved from a heavy burden. Then spending a few days in the low country of Norway, though without committing the least excess, my languor or heaviness returned. When I again ascended the

Alps, I revived as before." And he celebrates the health and performance of the Laps, as the best walkers of Europe.

> "Not without admiration, I have watched my two Lap companions, in my journey to Finmark, one, my conductor, the other, my interpreter. For after having climbed the Alps, whilst I, a youth of twenty-five years was spent and tired, like one dead, and lay down as if to die in those ends of the world, these two old men, one fifty, one seventy years, running and playing like boys, felt none of the inconveniences of the road, although they were both loaded heavily enough with my baggage. I saw men more than seventy years old put their heel on their own neck, without any exertion. O holy simplicity of diet, past all praise!"

But beside their sanitary and gymnastic benefit, mountains are silent poets, and a view from a cliff over a wide country reinstates us wronged men in our rights. The imagination is touched. There is some pinch and narrowness to us, and we are glad to see the world, and what amplitudes it has, of meadow, stream, upland, forest, and sea, which yet are lanes and crevices to the great space in which the world swims like a coch-boat in the sea.

Of the finer influences, I shall say, that they are not less positive, if they are indescribable. If you wish to know the shortcomings of poetry and language, try to reproduce the October pictures to a city company,—and see what you make of it. There is somewhat finer in the sky, than we have senses to appreciate. It escapes us, and yet is only just beyond our reach. Tantalus must have finer senses. Is all this beauty to perish? Where is he who is to save the present moment, and cause that this beauty shall not be lost? Where is he who has senses fine enough to catch the inspirations of the landscape? The mountains in the horizon acquaint us with finer relations to our friends than any we sustain.

I think 'tis the best of humanity, that goes out to walk. In happy hours, I think all affairs may be wisely postponed for this walking. Can you hear what the morning says to you, and believe *that*? Can you bring home the summits of Wachusett, Greylock, and the New Hampshire hills? The Savin groves of Middlesex? the sedgy ripples of the Old

Colony Ponds? the sunny shores of your own bay, and the low Indian hills of Rhode Island? the savageness of pine woods? Can you bottle the efflux of a June noon, and bring home the tops of Uncanoonuc?

The landscape is vast, complete, alive. We step about, dibble, and dot, and attempt in poor linear ways to hobble after those angelic radiations. The gulf between our seeing and our doing is a symbol of that between faith and experience.

Linnaeus says of the *Andromeda Tetragona* which he found on the mountain of Wallivari, in Luleå,

> Whilst I was walking quickly along, in a profuse perspiration, facing the cold wind at midnight, if I may call it night, when the sun was shining without setting at all, still anxiously inquiring of my interpreter how near we were to a Lapland dwelling, which I had been for two hours expecting, casting my eager eyes around me in all directions, I perceived, as it were, the shadow of this plant, but did not stop to examine it, taking it for the *Empetrum*. But, after going a few steps further, an idea of its being something I was unacquainted with, came across my mind, and I turned back, when I should again have taken it for the *Empetrum,* had not its greater height caused me to consider it with more attention. I know not what it is that so deceives the sight in our Alps at night, as to render objects far less distinct than in the middle of the day, though the sun shines equally bright, and so forth. Having gathered one of these plants, I looked about, and found several more in the neighborhood, but I never met with the same in any other place afterwards. As they had lost their flowers, it was not till I had sought a very long time, that I met with a single flower, which was white, shaped like a lily of the valley, but with five sharper divisions.

Our schools and colleges strangely neglect the general education of the eye. Every acquisition we make in the science of beauty is so sweet, that I think it is cheaply paid for by what accompanies it, of course,— the prating and affectation of connoisseurship. The facts disclosed by Winckelmann, Goethe, Bell, Greenough, Ruskin, Garbett, Penrose, are joyful possessions, which we cannot spare, and which we rank close beside the disclosures of natural history.

There are probably many in this audience who have tried the experiment on a hill-top, and many who have not, of bending the head so as to look at the landscape with your eyes upside down. What new softness in the picture! It changes the landscape from November into June. My companion and I had remarked from the hill-top the prevailing sobriety of color, and agreed that russet was the hue of Massachusetts, but on trying this experiment of inverting the view, he said, "There is the Campagna! and Italy is Massachusetts upside down."

The effect is remarkable, and perhaps is not explained. An ingenious friend of mine suggested, that it was because the upper part of the eye is little used, and therefore retains more susceptibility than the lower, and returns more delicate impressions.

Dr. Johnson said, "Few men know how to take a walk," and it is certain that Dr. Johnson was not one of the few. It is a fine art, requiring rare gifts and much experience. No man is suddenly a good walker. Many men begin with good resolution, but they do not hold out. These we call apprentices. And I have sometimes thought it would be well to publish an *Art of Walking, with easy lessons for beginners.* Those who persist from year to year, and obtain at last an intimacy with the country, and know all the good points within ten miles, with the seasons for visiting each, know the lakes, the hills, where grapes, berries, and nuts,—where the rare plants are; where the best botanic ground and where the noblest landscapes are seen; and are learning all the time;—these we call professors.

There are two companions, with one or other of whom 'tis desireable to go out on a tramp. One is an artist, or one who has an eye for beauty. 'Tis sometimes good to carry a telescope in your pocket, specially for birds. And as you take a telescope, that you may see what your eyes cannot reach, so, if you use a good and skilful companion, you shall see through his eyes, and, if they be of great discernment, you will learn wonderful secrets. In walking with Allston, you shall see what was never before shown to the eye of man. And as the perception of beauty always exhilarates, if one is so happy as to find the company of a true artist, he is a perpetual holiday, and ought only to be used, like an oroflamme or a garland, for feasts and may-days, and parliaments of wit and love. The other is a naturalist, for the reason that it is much better to learn the elements of geology, of botany, of ornithology, and astronomy, by word of mouth from a companion, than drily by book. There is so much, too, which a book cannot teach, which an old friend can.

A man should carry nature in his head; should know the hour of the day or night, and the time of the year, by the sun and stars; should know the solstice, and the equinox, the quarter of the moon, and the daily tides. Nature kills egotism, and conceit; deals strictly with us; and gives sanity; so that it was the practice of the Orientals, especially of the Persians, to let insane persons wander at their own will out of the towns, into the desert, and, if they liked, to associate with wild animals. In their belief, wild beasts, especially gazelles, collect around an insane person, and live with him on a friendly footing. The patient found something curative in that intercourse, by which he was quieted, and sometimes restored.

But there are more insane persons than are called so, or are under treatment in hospitals. The crowd in the cities, at the hotels, theatres, card-tables, the speculators who rush for investment at ten percent,—twenty percent,—are all more or less mad,—I need not say it now in the crash of bankruptcy. These point the moral, and persuade us to seek in the fields the health of the mind.

I hold all these opinions on the power of the air, to be substantially true. The poet affirms them; the religious man, going abroad, affirms them; the patriot on his mountains or his prairie affirms them; the contemplative man affirms them.

You know that physical geography shows us that the highest mountains are the newest formed; that the oldest have been all worn down, or are crumbling down every day by the action of sun, and frost, and water; that the sea is always destroying the land, preying on every shore, and that hundreds of miles of land are every year sunk in the ocean. Meantime, the repairers of all this waste are the volcanoes that, when the pressure of the mountain's weight is taken off, and the crust is thin, the internal fires burst up, lifting new masses above the surface to be island and continent, making good the loss of the old.

Nature tells everything once. Our microscopes are not necessary. She shows every fact in large bodies somewhere. On the seashore, she reveals to the eye, by the sea-line, the true curve of the globe. It does not need a barometer to find the height of mountains. The line of snow is surer than the barometer: and the zones of plants, the savin, the pine, vernal gentian, geum, linnaea, and the various lichens and grapes, are all thermometers which cannot be deceived, and will not lie. They are instruments by the best maker. The earthquake is the first chemist, goldsmith, and brazier: he wrought to purpose in craters, and we borrowed the hint in crucibles.

When I look at natural structures, as at a tree, or the teeth of a shark, or the anatomy of an elephant, I know that I am seeing an architecture and carpentry which has no sham, is solid and conscientious, which perfectly answers its end, and has nothing to spare. But in all works of human art, there is deduction to be made for blunder and falsehood. Therefore Goethe, whose whole life was a study of the theory of art, said, No man should be admitted to his Republic, who was not versed in Natural History.

The college is not so wise as the mechanic's shop, nor the quarter-deck as the forecastle. Witness the insatiable interest of the white man about the Indian, the trapper, the hunter, and sailor. In a water-party, in which many scholars joined, I noted that the skipper of the boat was much the best companion. The scholars made puns. The skipper saw instructive facts on every side, and there was no trifle to him. How startling are the hints of wit we detect in the horse and dog, and in the wild animals! By what compass the geese steer, and the herrings migrate, we would so gladly know. What the dog knows, and how he knows it, piques us more than all we heard from the Chair of Metaphysics.

Is it not an eminent convenience to have in your town a person who knows where Arnica grows, or sassafras, or penny-royal, and the mints, or the scented-goldenrod, or punk for glow match; or the slippery elm; or wild cherries or wild pears? Where are the best hazel-nuts, chestnuts, and shag barks? Where the white grapes? Where is the choice apple tree, and what are the poisons? Where is the Norway pine; where the beech; where the epigaea; the linnaea, or sanguinaria, or orchis pulcherrima; or sundew; or laurus benzoin, or pink huckle-berry? Where trout, woodcocks, wild bees, pigeons, where the bittern (stake driver), can be seen and heard; where the Wilson's plover can be seen and heard?

The true naturalist can go wherever woods and waters go; almost where a squirrel or a bee can go, he can; and no man is asked for leave. Sometimes the farmer withstands him in crossing his lots, but 'tis to no purpose: the farmer could as well hope to prevent the sparrows or tortoises. It was their land, before it was his, and their title was precedent. My naturalist knew what was on their land, and the farmers did not, and sometimes he brought them ostentatiously gifts of flowers, fruits, or rare shrubs, they would gladly have paid a price for, and did not tell them that he gathered them in their own woods. Moreover, the very time at which he used their land and water, for his boat glided like a trout everywhere unseen, was in hours when they were sound asleep. Before the sun was up, he went up and down to survey his possessions, and passed onward, and left them, before the second owners, as he called them, were awake.

If we should now say a few words on the advantages that belong to the conversation with nature, I might set them so high as to make it a religious duty. 'Tis the greatest use and the greatest beauty. One thing, the lover of nature cannot tell the best things he knows. 'Tis the lesson we were sent hither to learn. What truth, and what elegance, belong to every fact of nature we know. And the study of them awakens the like truth and elegance in the student.

Who does not see the farmer with pleasure and respect, knowing what powers and utilities are so meekly worn? They know every secret of work; they change the face of landscape, and put it in a new planet; yet there is no arrogance in their bearing, but a perfect gentleness. The farmer stands well on the world, as Adam did, as an Indian does, or as Homer's heroes. He is a person whom a poet of any clime, Milton, or Firdousi, would appreciate, as being really a piece of the old nature, comparable to sun and moon, to rainbow and flood, because he is, as all natural persons are, only metamorphoses of these things. Why a writer should be vain, and a farmer not,—though the writer admires the farmer, and the farmer does not admire the writer,—does not appear.

But the principal benefit of conversation with nature is to foster the peculiar genius of each man. That uncorrupted behaviour which we admire in the animals, and in young children, belongs also to the farmer, the hunter, the sailor, the man, who lives in the presence of nature. Cities force the growth, and make him talkative and entertaining, but they make him artificial and false. What alone possesses interest for us is the *naturel* of each man. This is that which is the saliency, or principle of levity, the antagonist of matter and gravitation, and as good as they. This is forever a surprise, and engaging, and lovely. We can't be satiated with knowing it, and about it. It is related to the secret of the world, to gravity, the growth of grass, and the angles of crystals.

Nature speaks to the imagination; first, through her grand style,—the hint of immense force and unity which her works convey;—secondly, because her visible productions and changes are the nouns of language, and our only means of uttering the invisible thought.

Every new perception of the method and beauty of nature gives a new shock of surprise and pleasure; and always for this double reason; first, because they are so excellent in their primary fact, as frost, or cloud, or fire, or animal; and, secondly, because we have an instinct that they express a grander law.

'Tis not easy to say again what nature says to us. But it is the best part of poetry, merely to name natural objects well. A farmer's boy finds delight in reading the verses under the Zodiackal vignettes in the *Almanac*. What is the merit of Thomson's "Seasons," but copying a few of the pictures out of this vast book into words, without a hint of what they signify, and the best passages of great poets, old and new, are often simple enumerations of some features of landscape.

And, as man is the object of Nature, so what we study in nature is man. 'Tis true, that man only interests us. We are not to be imposed upon by the apparatus and the nomenclature of the physiologist. Agassiz studies, year after year, fishes and fossil anatomy of saurian, and lizard, and pterodactyl. But whatever he says, we know very well what he means. He pretends to be only busy with the foldings of the yolk of a turtle's egg. I can see very well what he is driving at, he means men and women. He talks about lizard, shellfish, and squid; he means John and Mary, Thomas and Ann. For Nature is only a mirror in which man is reflected colossally. Swedenborg, or Behmen, or Plato tried to decipher this hieroglyphic, and explain what rock, what sand, what wood, what fire signified in regard to man.

They may have been right or wrong in any particulars of their interpretation, but it is only our ineradicable belief that the world answers to man, and part to part, that gives any interest in the subject. If we believed that nature was foreign and unrelated,—some rock on which souls wandering in the Universe were ship-wrecked, we should think all exploration of it frivolous waste of time. No, it is bone of our bone, flesh of our flesh, made of us, as we of it.

External nature is only a half. The geology, the astronomy, the anatomy, are all good, but 'tis all a half, and,—enlarge it by astronomy never so far,—remains a half. It requires a will as perfectly organized,—requires man. Astronomy is a cold desert science, with all its pompous figures,—depends a little too much on the glass grinder, too little on the mind. 'Tis of no use to show us more planets and systems. We know already what matter is, and more or less of it does not signify. Man can dispose in his thought of more worlds, just as readily as of few, or one. It is his relation to one, to the first, that imports. Nay, I will say, of the two facts, the world and man, man is by much the largest half.

It by no means happens that the imagination is excited whenever we are in the presence of nature. If that were so, it were a cheap and inestimable recipe. No, it is a coy, capricious power, and does not impart its secret to inquisitive persons. Sometimes a parlor in which fine persons are found, with beauty, culture, and sensibility, answers our purpose still better,

Striking the electric chain with which we are darkly bound.

But that again is nature, and there we have again the charm which landscape gives us, in a finer form; but the persons must have had the influence of nature, must know her simple and cheap pleasures, must know what Pindar means when he says, that, "Water is the best of things," and have manners that speak of reality and great elements, or we shall have no Olympus.

[Matter, how immensely soever enlarged by the telescope, remains the lesser half. The very science by which it is shown to you—argues the force of Man. Nature is vast and strong, but as soon as Man knows himself as its interpreter, knows that Nature and he are from one source, and that he, when humble and obedient, is nearer to the source, then all things fly into place, then is there a rider to the horse,—an organized will,—then nature has a lord.

The Natural Method of
Mental Philosophy

(1858)

Emerson first delivered "The Natural Method of Mental Philosophy" on March 24, 1858, at the Freeman Chapel in Boston. The six-part Natural Method of Mental Philosophy lecture series was the second iteration of Emerson's "Natural History of the Intellect" project, which began in London with the Mind and Manners of the Nineteenth Century lecture series in 1848 and culminated in the 1870 Natural History of the Intellect lecture series at Harvard. Emerson begins by replacing his advocacy of the "Doctrine of Correspondence" with a claim for analogy as the foundational principle of nature. This shift to an analogous relationship between nature and the mind allows for a richer understanding of how the diversity of nature adheres to and reflects the same governing laws, because analogy simultaneously implies similarity and difference. This model allows Emerson to explicate how the most minute elements in nature are capable of reflecting the laws that regulate both the human mind and the cosmos. He grounds this assertion in the observation that the forces of centrality and polarity govern all things. This effort to amend philosophic claims about the mind with scientific laws is an overt attempt to draw together a number of his career-spanning inquiries that are evident throughout the sermons, lectures, and essays contained in this volume. He also argues for the role of imagination in perceiving this analogy in spite of the constant flux that is visible in the natural world. In an extension of both his renewed idealism and his turn toward the poetic in "The Relation of Intellect to Natural Science," here the imagination mediates and unifies nature and the mind. For Emerson, "[t]he imagination gives value to the day" by inspiring the intellect and revealing the mind's inherent connection to nature. This is perhaps the most profound of the uses of natural history that Emerson began searching for at the outset of his career as a natural history writer in 1833.

Knowing is the measure of the man. By how much we know, so much we are. It is the measure of the man, because it is the measure of God. In all men, the first notion of God, is, the Omniscient. Homer says of his gods, "But Jove is the eldest, and knows the most." I quoted Plato as saying, "it is the law of Adrastia, that he who has known any truth shall be safe from harm until another period." The Buddhists, in the East, say, "he who has well made Bana, (truths,) shall never be born into any hell."

We are to each other as our perception is. It is the distinction of man to think and know. Otherwise, how can a man compare with a steam engine, or a self-acting mule, which stands up all day to work, never tires, and makes no fault?

We are getting to be proud of our Scandinavian descent, and the more, as we learn more of that race, and find they were always a sensible family. They thought, that he who could answer a question so as not to admit of any further answer, was the best man. In the Edda, the gods and heroes test their divinity by propounding questions to each other; and the one who cannot answer loses his life to the other. 'Tis like the riddles of the Sphinx, and on the same conditions; the heads of the speakers are at stake. So Thor is put to his wit at Asgard; Odin, in the Wastbrudius Hall; and Svend Vonved is a terrible champion who rides up and down, putting conundrums, and killing such as take time to guess them.

It is very easy to see, that this game goes on in all societies of men, from the prize questions of Academies and Institutes; to the rivalries of the senate and the bar; the polished competition of wits at the dinner table; and the boisterous sally and retort of the swaggerers in the bar-room. We are to each other as our perception is. The nobility of a company, or of a period, is to be estimated by the depth of the ideas from which they live, and to which they appeal.

In that pure glory, what geometer can come with his angles? What astronomer can enter and plant his instruments, and take some instant measurement and inventory of this dome, in whose light forms, and substances, and sciences are dissolved? What chemist can analyse these subtle elements, or find the metre of mind, whereon readily, as on our thermometer, we may say, this one had ten degrees, twenty degrees, one hundred degrees of intellect?

Now the method, the metaphysician, who can best help us, is, natural science. The German Steffens said, "The view of nature generally prevailing, at any determined time, in a nation, is the foundation of their whole Science; and its influence spreads over every department of life. It has an important influence on all social order, on morals, nay even on religion. 'Tis the peculiar mode of viewing nature which imparts a marked peculiarity to certain periods."

We are always finding language wiser than we; and our best thought is already anticipated by the popular use of some word which covers it. After a man has made great progress, and fancies he has come to heights hitherto unscaled, the common words still fit his thought: Nay, he only now finds how wise they were:—for instance, 'Reason,' 'Conscience,' 'Substance,' 'Relation,' 'Nature,' 'Fortune,' 'Fate,' 'Person.'

After the student has waked all night, speculating on his relations to the world, and to the starry heaven, perhaps the first words he meets in the book he opens in the morning, are, *macrocosm* and *microcosm;* that is, the great world of nature, and the miniature world in man, showing him that some old thinker or nations of thinkers have thought his thoughts ages ago; that wherever he goes, men have been before him. What has Carlyle written about heroism, which the word *hero* did not already say to a gentle soul? The word *Genius* still is better than any definition of it.

The Greeks were the subtlest makers of words. It was a characteristic of the Athenians, that they were anticipators of what the orator would say. And of these, the most eminent is Plato, who gave us many important words. *Poet* or *Maker* was one. And what a step was taken by the word *Analogy*, which he defined, "identity of ratio, the most beautiful of all bonds." Not of facts, or of results, but of method. That was a perception of a few laws, of one law, streaming through nature, variously effecting a like result.

"There is a certain common bond that unites all the sciences together," said Cicero. The highest value of natural history, and, mainly, of the new results of geology, and the discovery of parallax, and the resolution of nebulae, is its translation into an universal cipher applicable to the Intellect. "All the languages should be studied abreast," said Kraitser. And all the sciences should be, and all illuminate each other. Teach me the laws of Music, said Fourier, and I can tell you any secret in any part of the Universe,—in anatomy, for instance, or in astronomy. Kepler thought as much.

We are intent on Meteorology, and wish to find the law of the variable winds, and not get our hay wet. Winds and Tides, to be sure! I wish an Almanac for *my* farm. Tides indeed! What ebb and flow of power! as if life were a thunderstorm wherein we could now see by a flash the whole horizon, and then cannot see your hand. I wish to predict these, and not waste my time in attempting work which the soul today refuses.

Intellect; 'Tis a finer vegetation. It has, like that, germination, maturation, crossing, blight, and parasite. Reminiscence is only the perception of identity. Imagination is the being guided to the true symbol, by sharing the circulations of the universe. The intellect also finds its analogon in the atoms of chemistry, of electricity. Solitude is the father,—conversation the mother of thought.

Nature works after the same method as the human Imagination. Organic matter and mind go from the same law, and so correspond. Metaphysics might anticipate Jussieu.

And in the impenetrable mystery which hides (through absolute transparency) the mental nature, I await the insight which our advancing knowledge of material laws shall furnish. Thus, the laws of fluids, of the atmosphere, of light, heat, electricity, and galvanism, the law of undulation and polarity, are symbolical statements of the laws of memory and of thinking.

A physiologist told me, when he was at a loss in his study of embryos, he would go and talk with astronomers about the nebular theory, and what occurred in such and such conditions of the forming planet; and presently he got the analogic hint he wanted. Homology is the great gain of modern science. And it reaches much wider, not only through matter, but through mind. He who enunciates a law of nature, enunciates a law of the mind.

The game of intellect is the perception that whatever befals (or can be stated,) is a universal proposition; and, contrariwise, that every general statement is poetical again, by being particularized or impersonated. Napoleon sees the same law running through all things. "Whatever they may tell you, believe that one fights with cannon as with fists." And J. Kemble said, steam carriages, Scythe chariots, Macedonian Phalanx, nay squadrons of horse are only larger bullets. The scholar can easily translate all of Bonaparte's technics into all of his, and Carnot's and Maupertuis' laws of dynamics, and the laws of architecture and the rest. Every breath of air is a carrier of the Universal Mind. So it is that every natural law enunciates a law of the mind. For all difference is quantitative. The quality is one.

All thought analogizes. Mental faculties are the transcendency of the physical. All above, as below, is organized. The symbolism of nature exists, because the mental series exactly tallies with the material series. And who enunciates a law of nature, enunciates a law of the mind.

Carnot added a new theorem to Dynamics, which was, in sum, that sudden alterations of speed are to be avoided in machinery, because all the power that, in the moment of stoppage, is taken from the legitimate action of the machine, goes to tear the machine asunder. When he was counselled to break up the French Directory, he replied, "No," for "sudden losses of speed are damaging." He too was a poet, and universalized his propositions, not only applied them to engines, but carried the hint up into higher planes of life.

Maupertuis taught, "that the quantity of action employed in nature to produce a change in the movement of bodies, is always a minimum." And I have heard it announced as a thesis in zoology, that in nature there is a minimum of pain; that the bird of prey seizes its victim in the manner that kills with the least suffering.

In reference to men, we learn this lesson early. We have an instinct, that in spite of seeming difference, men are all of one pattern. We readily assume this, with our mates, with those with whom we talk and deal, and are disappointed and angry, if we find we are premature, and that their watches are slower than ours. In fact, the only sin which we never forgive in each other, is difference of opinion.

If we extend this identification, as we must,—beyond man, to the system of animals,—we trace, on a lower plane, or in accommodation to some tyrannic circumstance, a repetition of our own properties and powers. Thus, if man has organs for breathing, for sight, for locomotion, for taking food, for digesting, for protection by house building, by attack and defence, for reproduction, and love, and care of his young, you shall find all the same in the brute. You shall find all the same in the muskrat.

There is perfect correspondence, or, 'tis, only man modified to live in a mud-bank. A fish, in like manner, is man furnished to live in the sea; a thrush, to fly in the air; and a mollusk is a cheap edition, with a suppression of the costlier illustrations, designed for dingy circulation or shelving in an oyster bank, or among the seaweed.

And as man and man are superficially unlike, but radically identical,—leaves of one tree,—and men and animals are modifications of one idea, so, in a larger generalization, the animal creation and the globe on which they live, or,—to take man as the representative,—man and his planet: these have great common relations, the man being only a sort of compend of the globe with its centrifugence and centripetence, with its chemistry, with its polarity, with its undulation. And, lastly, as man and men, man and animals, man and planet, are analogous, so, the same laws which these obey and express, run up into the invisible world of the mind, namely, chemistry, polarity, undulation, gravity, centrifugence, periodicity, and, that, hereby we acquire a key to these sublimities which skulk and hide in the caverns of human consciousness; namely; by the solar microscope of *Analogy*. 'Tis the key that opens the Universe. Nature shows every thing once,—shows every thing in coarse or colossal lines somewhere; and here, by extending into our dreams the same law by which tides ebb and flow, moons wax and wane, trees grow, and stones fall.

All difference is quantitative: quality one. However we may conceive of the wonderful little bricks of which the world is builded, we must suppose similarity, and fitting, in their make. We must believe, that every hose in nature fits every hydrant, every atom screws to every atom. So only is chemistry, vegetation, animation, intellection, possible. Without identity at base, chaos must be forever. In the initial forms or forces, be they what they may, we must have already all the properties, which, in any combination, they afterwards exhibit.

Wonderful pranks this identity plays with us. It is because of this, that nothing comes quite strange to us: As we knew our friends, before we were introduced to them, and, at first sight distinguished them as ours; so to know, is to re-know, or to recognize. We hail each discovery of science as the most natural thing in the world.

"All things she knoweth are herself, and she is all that she knoweth." All knowledge is assimilation to the object of knowledge. "The understanding transforms itself into the image of the thing understood.— The very understandingness of a thing is nothing but a coming to and immediate approach of the unity of the understanding, and of the thing understood; So as the things themselves seem to talk with us without words."

An angel who was present at the Creation saw, that from each man, as he was formed, a piece of the clay whereof he was made was taken, and set apart for him, as goods, or property; and it was allowed him to receive this in whatever form he desired, whether as wife, friend, son, daughter, or as house, land, warehouses, merchandize, horses, libraries, gardens, ships; also, he might have it now in one of these forms, and, at his will, it was converted into another. But, because it was one and the same lump, out of which all these were fashioned, and, as that was the clay of his own body, all these things had one and the same taste and quality to him, and he died at last of *ennui*.

We have shown that our help must be in that identity of ratio or design, which through all the variety of structure and element appears. What we see once, we see again; what is here, that is there: And it makes little difference what I learn; learn one thing thoroughly, and I have the key to all existences. This is that which the Indian sages, that which Plato, and Plotinus found. And we say, that, in the mind, all the laws of each department of nature, whether Botany, Anatomy, Chemistry, or Cosmology, are duly found repeated on a higher plane.

Thus, the first quality we know in matter, is, Centrality, which we commonly call gravity, and which holds the Universe together; which remains pure, and entire, and indestructible in each mote, as in masses and planets, and from each atom rays out illimitable influence. To this central essence answers Truth, in the intellectual world, Truth, whose centre is everywhere and its circumference nowhere, whose existence we cannot disimagine; Truth, the soundness and health of things against which no blow can be struck, but it recoils on the striker, and no fraud can prosper. Liars also are true. Let a man begin where he will, and work in whatever direction, he is sure to be found instantly afterwards arriving at a right result! Truth, which we cannot wound; on whose side we always heartily are.

The mind is always true. Though the premises are false, the conclusions are right. And the self-reliance which belongs to every healthy human being is proof of it; proof that not he, but the soul of the world is in him; and, in proportion as it penetrates his crust of partiality, saith, 'Here am I; here is the whole.' Therefore, we require absoluteness in every man, absoluteness in the orator, in the poet, in the hero, in all manners; and if they have it not, they simulate it.

And if we are looking for intellectual metres, the first measure of a mind is its centrality, its veracity, its capacity of truth and its adhesion to the same. Every man is strong and mighty in proportion to his penetration of the facts of nature. And it would be easy to show, in intellectual action, the analogon of the momentum of falling bodies. The power of the mind, and its pace, increases as it approaches the end of its task.

How obvious is the momentum in our mental history! The momentum, which increases by exact law in falling bodies, increases by the like rate in intellectual action. Every scholar knows, that he applies coldly and slowly, at first, to his task; but, with the progress of the work, the mind becomes heated, and sees far and wide, as it approaches the end of the task, so that, it is the common remark of the student, 'Could I only have begun with the same fire I had on the last day, I should have done something.' Then, to do something well we must have done it often.

When we have *Gravity* or *Centrality* in Nature, then we have *Polarity*. As one is the principle of rest and permanence, so is this the principle of *difference*, of *generation*, of change. In the imponderable fluids, it shows itself in circulation, in undulation, in fits of easy transmission and reflection: In chemistry it appears in the affinities: In organized matter, in sex.

Well, this property is also the essential property of mental life,—the flowing, the generation, the melioration. The advance, everlasting. All things flow, said the Ancient; all flows; παντα ρει. The Universe is only in transit, or, we behold it shooting the gulf from past to future: And this the mind shares. Transition is the attitude of power, and the essential act of life. The whole history of the mind is passage, pulsation, dark and light, preparation and arrival; and again, preparation and arrival. And as we only truly possess what we mentally possess, that is, what we understand, we are passing into new earths and new heavens,—into new earths, by chemistry; into new heavens, in fact, by the movement of our solar system, and, in thought, by our better knowledge. The habit of saliency, of not pausing, but going on, is a sort of importation and domestication of the Divine effort into a man.

It is true, that, whilst it is the distinction of man to think, few men think truly. But there are in every society of well-born men, souls which apprehend things so correctly, that they seem to have been in the counsel of Nature. Their understanding seems to transform itself into the image of the thing understood, and that, not as a passive mirror, but as a living cause, so that they can not only describe the thing as it is, but can follow its genesis as a creator. They have the generalizing and ascending effort, which, even in chemistry, finds not atoms, at last, but spherules of force,—which measures and differences minds as they can take strides of advancing, as if one mind could only take one step, another could take two or three, another many. And there are minds which do not sit down in any finality, which neither gold, nor love of antiquity, nor old age, can tame or clip the wings of, but which, like Ulysses, sail the sea, and discover and project as long as they remain in our sight.

For man does not love fences. Each farmer covets the land that joins his own. And in mind there is always a better thought awaiting for us. What we call bounds of nature are only the limits of our organs. The microscope detects the eye of an invisible infusory, but it cannot reach to what the infusory sees. The microscope saw far; the infusory sees farther. There are no finalities in nature. The Torricellian tube was thought to make a vacuum. But no, over the mercury is the vapor of mercury. The pores of glass, the pores of gold, are as wide to the mysterious ether and the elemental forces, as the chimney of a volcano. Our Arctic voyagers, as if obeying the laws of the mind, are now seeking beyond the polar barrier a Polynia, or open sea, north of the north. And, in mind, every thought leads in another thought by the hand. Every generalization shows the way to a larger; and every reform is only a cover, under which a larger reform, that dares not yet name itself, advances.

Transition, shooting the gulf, becoming somewhat else, is the whole game of nature: and death, the penalty of standing still. 'Tis not less in thought. I cannot conceive of any good in a thought which ends and stagnates. Liberty is the power to flow. To continue is to flow. Life is unceasing parturition.

"His very flight is presence in disguise."

Inspiration is power to carry on and complete the metamorphosis, which, in the imperfect kinds is arrested for ages, and in the perfecter proceeds rapidly in the same individual.

Power of generalizing differences men, and it shows the rudeness of our metaphysics, though this is not down in the books. The number of successive saltations the nimble thought can make, measures the difference between the highest and lowest of mankind.

The nearness with which a man deals with his experiences, ranks him. If he go to antiquity, or to Europe for his subject, he avows incapacity. Therefore, I think that the poet consults his ease rather than his ability when he takes an ancient or a foreign subject.

The commonest remark, if the man could extend it a little, would make him a genius; but the thought is prematurely checked. All masters are distinguished by the power to add a second, a third, and perhaps, a fourth step, in a continuous line. Many a man had taken the first: with every additional step, you enhance immensely the value of the first.

So one would say of the force exerted at any one time in the works of nature, all depends on the battery. If it can give one shock, we shall get to the fish-form, and there stop; if two shocks, to the bird; if three, to the quadruped; if four, to the man. A great word was that which John Hunter introduced into Zoology,—*"arrested development,"* and which is now the commonplace of savans. And the measure of a mind is its fluidity, its sharing of the circulations,—of generalization,—of passing to interior and intimate thought, of watching the metamorphosis, the ascension into new forms, which is so dear a law of outward and inward nature.

See how the organism of mind corresponds to that of the body. There is the same hunger for food,—we call it curiosity; there is the same swiftness of seizing it,—we call it perception. The same assimilation of food to the eater, we call it culture; for simple recipiency is the virtue of space, not of a man.

The phenomena of sex reappear,—as, creation, in one mind, apprehension, in the other;—though I may remark, the sex of the mind does by no means always follow the sex of the body, or, we often meet masculine minds in many women, and feminine minds in men. But as it is a law that, "Two great sexes animate the world," we note that a powerful mind impresses itself on a whole nation of minds; and is the parent of an innumerable spiritual progeny. What do you suppose is the census of the Platonists? or of the Aristotelian minds? What of the followers of Saint Paul? or of Luther? or of Descartes? or of Voltaire? or of Swedenborg? or Goethe? Nature loves to cross her stocks, and does the variety and blending of talents less appear in new minds that have been bred under varied and antagonistic influence, under Napoleon and under Goethe? Composite minds, like Burke, which blend two tendencies or streams of thought, give a rich result; And, usually, every mind of remarkable efficiency owes it to new combination of traits.

The gestation or bringing forth of the mind is seen in the act of detachment. Life is incessant parturition. There are viviparous and oviparous minds, minds that produce their thoughts complete men, like armed soldiers, ready and swift to go out to resist and conquer all the armies of error; and others, that deposit their dangerous, unripe thoughts here and there to lie still, for a time, and be brooded in other minds, and the shell shall not be broken until the next age, for them to begin, as new individuals, their career.

Some minds suffocate from too much store, too little vent. Kvasir, in the Norse legend, was a man so wise that none asked him any things which he knew not how to answer; but the dwarves said, that he had choked in his wisdom, there being none wise enow to ask him enough about learning. Health consists in the balance between knowing and expression; in keeping the channels open. Some minds choke from too much, some pine from too little communion. Some discharge their thought in volleys; and some would be invaluable, if you could attach to them a self-acting siphon, that would tap and draw them off, as now they carry about with them a perilous wisdom which they have no talent to impart. These are all related to the law of sex.

All natural functions are attended by their own pleasure: so are metaphysical. Perception gives pleasure; classification gives a keen pleasure; memory does; imagination intoxicates.

See how nature has secured the communication of knowledge. 'Tis certain that money does not more burn in a boy's pocket, than a piece of news burns in our memory, until we can tell it. And, in higher activity of the mind, every new perception is attended with a thrill of pleasure; and the imparting of it to others is also attended with pleasure. Thought is the child of the intellect; and the child is conceived with joy, and born with joy.

Conversation is the laboratory and workshop of the student. The affection or sympathy helps. The wish to speak to the want of another mind,—assists to clear your own. A certain truth possesses us, which we in all ways labor to utter. Every time we say a thing in conversation, we get a certain mechanical advantage in detaching it well and deliverly. I value the mechanics of conversation. 'Tis pulley, and lever, and screw. To fairly disengage the mass, and find it jingling down, a good boulder, a block of quartz and gold, to be worked up at leisure in the useful arts.

Porosity is the best quality of matter. Every material possession must pass into the intellect, to become of real value. Until we have intellectual property, in a thing, we can have no right property in it. So works the poor little blockhead manikin. He must arrange and dignify his shop or farm, the best he can. At last, he must be able to tell you it, or write it, or to himself translate it all clumsily enough into the new sky-language he calls thought. Say not, 'tis bungling; he can't help it. The irresistible meliorations bear him forward; the fermentations go on, saccharine and vinous now; acetous by and by; upward to gas, and the imponderables at last.

Intellectual activity is contagious like the superinductions of chemistry. The boy becomes the hero of whom he reads: the man assimilates to the master he admires. Napoleon Napoleonizes and Plato Platonizes you. It is sufficient to set one in the mood of writing verses, at any time, to read any original poetry. And it is only necessary to look at the current literature, to see how one masterpiece brings into vogue a whole catalogue of books in the same style. What an impulse Cuvier, or Davy, or Liebig, or de Candolle, or Fresnel, or von Buch, has given to science!

The spectacle of vigor of any kind recruits us. In like manner, a blockhead makes a blockhead of you. In unfit company, the finest powers are benumbed; and no aids avail to resist the palsy of misassociation.

What's the use of telegraphs, what of newspapers? To know how men feel in Wisconsin, in Illinois, in Minnesota, I wait for no mails, no telegraphs. I ask my own heart. My interest tells me how their selfishness works; my honor what their honor dictates.

And this endless passing of one element into new forms, this incessant metamorphosis, explains the importance which the Imagination holds in all our catalogue of mental powers. The Imagination is the reader of these forms; the Imagination accounts all productions and changes of nature as the nouns of language. The Imagination uses all the objects of nature representatively, too well pleased with their ulterior meaning to value their primary meaning much.

Now what is the drift of all this? What, but this:—that, Nature in every part is one,—that, in every particle is a hint of every mass, and of the Universe; every atom, a miniature of the world. That, the progress of all recent science has been, in the closet of each student, a tying together,—a study of one detail, under concentrating lamps of all the sciences and histories, and the total experience of a million observers.

I know there is a wisdom and love outside of all the liberty and vice of man, which redresses the disturbed balance. It is observed, that, as there are times of famine, of pest, and cholera, in races; so there are epochs of decline of genius, and destitution of thought. It has been noticed that these times precede as a cause such national calamities. It is a hybernation or sleep of the mind. But it appears also that the same periodicity which governs the ebb and flow of seas, and the astronomical motion, reaches also into the laws of thought. Each produces the other: the mind now retires inward; sheds her plumes; hoards by coarse activity; to be freed again for new power in science and art. And this alternation of animal and of intellectual eras follows one the other.

Not less large, not less exact, are the mysterious circulations in the realm we are exploring. The perceptions of a soul, its wondrous progeny, are born by the conversation, the marriage of Souls, so nourished, so enlarged. They are detached from their parent, they pass into other minds; ripened and unfolded by many, they hasten to incarnate themselves in action to take body, only to carry forward the will which sent them out: they take to them wood, and stone, and iron, and ships, and cities, and armies, and nations of men, and ages of duration, and the pomps of religion; the armaments of war, the codes and heraldry of states; agriculture, trade, colonies,—these are the ponderous instrumentalities, into which these nimble thoughts pass; and which they animate and alter. And, presently, antagonized by other thoughts which they first aroused, or by thoughts which are sons and daughters of these, the thought buries itself only in the new thought of larger scope which sprung from it—its new creations and forwarder triumphs, whilst the old instrumentalities and incarnations are decomposed and recomposed into new.

The first illusion that is put upon us in the world is the amusing miscellany of colors, forms, and properties. Our education is through surfaces and particulars. Nature masks, under ostentatious subdivisions and manifold particulars, the poverty of her elements, and the rigid economy of her rules. Each has its enemy: brewer, sour fermentation; iron, rust; furrier, moths; orchardists, insects; farmer, frost; ice-man, heat. And as infants and children are occupied wholly with surface differences, so multitudes of people remain in the infant or animal estate, and never see or know more. They pass their whole existence in devotion to some huckster of fusty details; haberdasher in tape; fisher with his fish; grocer in candles; Cincinnati man in corn and bacon; Southern planter in short-staple and sea-island, and the rise and fall of a farthing or half-penny in cotton; towns of people live by shoes, or pails, or combs, or buttons, and so with countless trades, and trades-men, and tradeswomen, all occupied in making much of small differences, to see which is nowise exhilarating to the student of man.

But in the measure in which there is wit, men leave looking at these trivial differences in things, and come to see that one ware is like another ware; nor at the difference between themselves and their customers and neighbors, friends and enemies, but perceive, that they are alike, that a fundamental unity or agreement exists, without which there could be neither marriage, nor conversation, politics, trade, literature, nor science.

And, lastly, Nature speaks to the imagination. Nature provides us in her changes and her productions with words to express every experience and thought of our own. The impressions made on our imagination make the great days in our life,—the book, poem, person, walk, which did not stay on the surface of the eye or ear, but penetrated to the inward senses, sets the whole man in movement, and is not forgotten. The imagination gives value to the day. Walking, working, or talking,—it is, how many strokes vibrate on the mystic string,—how many diameters are drawn quite through from matter to spirit; for, whenever you enunciate a natural law, you enunciate a law of the mind.

The spiritual crises are periods of as certain recurrence in some form to every mind as are dentition and puberty. The moment of early consciousness, when the young child first finds himself, as we say; the great day in youth, when the mind begins to render account to itself; when it assumes its own vows; when its religious convictions befall; the day of love, when it joins itself to its kind; and the day of reason, when it sees all its partial and fiery experiences as elements of genius and destiny;—The *va et vient*, the ebb and flow, the pendulum, the alter-nation, the sleep and waking, the fits of easy transmission and reflec-tion, the pulsation, the undulation, which shows itself as a fundamental secret of nature, exists in intellect.

The circulation of the waters: the rain falls, the brook runs into the river; the river into the sea; the sea exhales all day its mighty stream into the air; the universal vegetation sucks the stream, and gives it again to the atmosphere. It gathers into clouds, and drifts to moun-tains, and falls in rain, to renew its round.

The circulation of the gas locked up in blocks of basalt, in globe-crusts of granite, in beds of coal that floor counties and states, then heaved, in new ages, and unlocked by chemic affinities, and the joyful vesicle, with all its eternal properties safe and sound, there is no tear or wear to it,—through all its changes indestructible;—millions of years old, but as good as new,—sails away to enter into new combining; to make part of the plant, then part of the animal that feeds on it; then part of the man that feeds on the animal; then, by and by, buried once more in stone; inundated by new seas, for more millions of years; to wait for new fires to lift it again, to repeat the like circulation.

The circulation of the blood in the little world of man, food into chyme, chyme into chyle, chyle into blood, hurled from the heart in endless spasm, to rush through the system, carrying nutriment to every organ and every extremity.

Every discovery in any part gets recorded. It makes new instru-ments at the mathematical and philosophical shop: it requires and obtains a new modification in the construction of the observatory, in the coast-survey. It lets in some new light for the reading of ancient observations. Then the eyes of analogy bring it to the students of other sciences. Animal and vegetable structures correspond, and any new light on one is sure to suggest and to find some parallel provision by which analogous function in the other is worked. Even embryology, I have learned from its students, is served by the results of astronomy. Thus the most delicate and perishable improvement, gets recorded.

'Tis indifferent whether you say, All is matter, or, All is Spirit, and 'tis plain, there is a tendency in the times to an identity-philosophy. Once, we were timorous at allowing any dignity to matter. Matter was the principle of evil. Let there be no commerce between that Gentile and these Jews. Now, we are reconciling them in phrenology, the new German physiology, and in the new unproven sciences.

You do not degrade man by saying, Spirit is only finer body; nor exalt him by saying, Matter is phenomenal merely; all rests on the affection of the theorist, on the question whether his aim is noble. You will observe that it makes no difference herein whether you call yourself materialist or spiritualist. If there be but one substance or reality, and that is body, and it has the quality of creating the sublime astronomy, of converting itself into brain, and geometry, and reason; if it can reason in Newton, and sing in Homer and Shakspeare, and love and serve as saints and angels, then I have no objection to transfer to body all my wonder and allegiance.

Thoreau

(1862)

E merson delivered this eulogy at the funeral of
his close friend Henry David Thoreau on May 9,
1862, in Concord, Massachusetts. Thoreau had died three days
earlier of tuberculosis at the age of forty-four. Emerson would later
revise this eulogy for publication in the August 1862 issue of *Atlantic
Monthly,* and it would also become the introduction to Thoreau's
posthumous essay collection, *Excursions,* the following year. Emerson
served a formative role in Thoreau's adult life. He delivered "The
American Scholar" address to Thoreau's graduating class at Harvard
in 1837, invited Thoreau to live with his family in 1841, published
Thoreau's first essay in *The Dial* in 1842, and provided the land for
the famous life experiment that would be recounted in *Walden.* The
sketch of Thoreau that emerges in the eulogy is one of a true Transcendentalist. Emerson praises Thoreau's keen perception of and
relation to nature, qualities that "showed him the material world as
a means and symbol." However, he tempers this admiration with a
critique of Thoreau's lack of poetic skill and his oppositional nature.
While this may seem inappropriate or unkind, it can be read as a
moving tribute when considered alongside Emerson's other biograph-
ical writings. In his 1850 collection *Representative Men,* Emerson
would exercise a similarly critical eye toward Plato, Shakespeare,
Goethe, and others, all of whom he identifies as intellectual heroes.
Furthermore, Emerson assesses Thoreau according to the rubric of
the ideal poetic naturalist that he established in "The Uses of Natural
History," "The Naturalist," and "Humanity of Science." By holding
Thoreau to his own elevated standard of genius, Emerson expresses

his esteem for him. Within this context, Emerson's eulogy may be understood as a flattering testament to his closest friend—an eloquent, honest attempt to elucidate "how great a son [America] has lost" with the passing of Thoreau.

♣

Henry D. Thoreau was the last male descendant of a French ancestor who came to this country from the isle of Guernsey. His character exhibited occasional traits drawn from this blood in singular combination with a very strong Saxon genius.

He was born in Concord, Massachusetts, on the 12th of July, 1817. He was graduated at Harvard College, in 1837, but without any literary distinction. An iconoclast in literature, he seldom thanked colleges for their service to him, holding them in small esteem, whilst yet his debt to them was important. After leaving the University, he joined his brother in teaching a private school, which he soon renounced. His father was a manufacturer of lead pencils, and Henry applied himself for a time to this craft, believing he could make a better pencil than was then in use. After completing his experiments, he exhibited his work to chemists and artists in Boston, and having obtained their certificates to its excellence and to its equality with the best London manufacture, he returned home contented. His friends congratulated him that he had now opened his way to fortune. But he replied, that he should never make another pencil. "Why should I? I would not do again what I have done once." He resumed his endless walks, and miscellaneous studies, making every day some new acquaintance with Nature, though as yet never speaking of zoology or botany, since, though very studious of natural facts, he was incurious of technical and textual science.

At this time, a strong, healthy youth fresh from college, whilst all his companions were choosing their profession, or eager to begin some lucrative employment, it was inevitable that his thoughts should be exercised on the same question, and it required rare decision to refuse all the accustomed paths, and keep his solitary freedom at the cost of disappointing the natural expectations of his family and friends. All the more difficult that he had a perfect probity, was exact in securing his own independence, and in holding every man to the like duty. But Thoreau never faltered. He was a born protestant. He declined to give up his large ambition of knowledge and action for any narrow craft or profession, aiming at a much more comprehensive calling, the art of living well. If he slighted and defied the opinions of others, it was only that he was more intent to reconcile his practice with his own belief. Never idle or self-indulgent, he preferred when he wanted money, earning it by some piece of manual labor agreeable to him, as building a boat or a fence, planting, grafting, surveying, or other short work, to any long engagements. With his hardy habits and few wants, his skill in wood-craft, and his powerful arithmetic, he was very competent to live in any part of the world. It would cost him less time to supply his wants than another. He was therefore secure of his leisure.

A natural skill for mensuration, growing out of his mathematical knowledge, and his habit of ascertaining the measures and distances of objects which interested him, the size of trees, the depth and extent of ponds and rivers, the height of mountains and the air-line distance of his favorite summits,—this, and his intimate knowledge of the territory about Concord, made him drift into the profession of land-surveyor. It had the advantage for him that it led him continually into new and secluded grounds, and helped his studies of nature. His accuracy and skill in this work were readily appreciated, and he found all the employment he wanted.

He could easily solve the problems of the surveyor, but he was daily beset with graver questions which he manfully confronted. He interrogated every custom, and wished to settle all his practice on an ideal foundation. He was a protestant *à l'outrance* and few lives contain so many renunciations. He was bred to no profession; he never married; he lived alone; he never went to church; he never voted; he refused to pay a tax to the state; he ate no flesh, he drank no wine, he never knew the use of tobacco; and, though a naturalist, he used neither trap nor gun. He chose wisely, no doubt, for himself to be the bachelor of thought and nature. He had no talent for wealth, and knew how to be poor without the least hint of squalor or inelegance. Perhaps he fell into his way of living, without forecasting it much, but approved it with later wisdom. "I am often reminded," he wrote in his journal, "that, if I had bestowed on me the wealth of Crœsus, my aims must be still the same, and my means essentially the same." He had no temptations to fight against; no appetites, no passions, no taste for elegant trifles. A fine house, dress, the manners and talk of highly cultivated people were all thrown away on him. He much preferred a good Indian, and considered these refinements as impediments to conversation, wishing to meet his companion on the simplest terms. He declined invitations to dinner-parties, because there each was in every one's way, and he could not meet the individuals to any purpose. "They make their pride," he said, "in making their dinner cost much: I make my pride in making my dinner cost little." When asked at table, what dish he preferred, he answered, "the nearest." He did not like the taste of wine, and never had a vice in his life. He said, "I have a faint recollection of pleasure derived from smoking dried lily stems, before I was a man. I had commonly a supply of these. I have never smoked any thing more noxious."

He chose to be rich by making his wants few, and supplying them himself. In his travels, he used the railroad only to get over so much country as was unimportant to the present purpose, walking hundreds of miles, avoiding taverns, buying a lodging in farmers' and fishermen's houses, as cheaper, and more agreeable to him, and because there he could better find the men and the information he wanted.

There was somewhat military in his nature not to be subdued, always manly and able, but rarely tender, as if he did not feel himself except in opposition. He wanted a fallacy to expose, a blunder to pillory, I may say, required a little sense of victory, a roll of the drum, to call his powers into full exercise. It cost him nothing to say No; indeed he found it much easier than to say Yes. It seemed as if his first instinct on hearing a proposition was to controvert it, so impatient was he of the limitations of our daily thought. This habit of course is a little chilling to the social affections; and though the companion would in the end acquit him of any malice or untruth, yet it mars conversation. Hence no equal companion stood in affectionate relations with one so pure and guileless. "I love Henry," said one of his friends, "but I cannot like him: and as for taking his arm, I should as soon think of taking the arm of an elm-tree."

Yet hermit and stoic as he was, he was really fond of sympathy, and threw himself heartily and childlike into the company of young people whom he loved, and whom he delighted to entertain, as he only could, with the varied and endless anecdotes of his experiences by field and river. And he was always ready to lead a huckleberry party or a search for chestnuts or grapes. Talking one day of a public discourse, Henry remarked, that whatever succeeded with the audience, was bad. I said, "Who would not like to write something which all can read, like 'Robinson Crusoe'; and who does not see with regret that his page is not solid with a right materialistic treatment, which delights everybody." Henry objected, of course, and vaunted the better lectures which reached only a few persons. But, at supper, a young girl, understanding that he was to lecture at the Lyceum, sharply asked him, "whether his lecture would be a nice, interesting story such as she wished to hear, or whether it was one of those old philosophical things that she did not care about?" Henry turned to her, and bethought himself, and, I saw, was trying to believe that he had matter that might fit her and her brother, who were to sit up and go to the lecture, if it was a good one for them.

He was a speaker and actor of the truth,—born such,—and was ever running into dramatic situations from this cause. In any circumstance, it interested all bystanders to know what part Henry would take, and what he would say: and he did not disappoint expectation, but used an original judgment on each emergency. In 1845, he built himself a small framed house on the shores of Walden Pond, and lived there two years alone, a life of labor and study. This action was quite native and fit for him. No one who knew him would tax him with affectation. He was more unlike his neighbors in his thought, than in his action. As soon as he had exhausted the advantages of that solitude, he abandoned it. In 1847, not approving some uses to which the public expenditure was applied, he refused to pay his town-tax, and was put in jail. A friend paid the tax for him, and he was released. The like annoyance was threatened the next year. But, as his friends paid the tax, notwithstanding his protest, I believe he ceased to resist. No opposition or ridicule had any weight with him. He coldly and fully stated his opinion without affecting to believe that it was the opinion of the company. It was of no consequence if every one present held the opposite opinion. On one occasion he went to the University Library to procure some books. The Librarian refused to lend them. Mr. Thoreau repaired to the President, who stated to him the rules and usages which permitted the loan of books to resident graduates, to clergymen who were alumni, and to some others resident within a circle of ten miles' radius from the College. Mr. Thoreau explained to the President that the railroad had destroyed the old scale of distances,—that the library was useless, yes, and President and College useless, on the terms of his rules,—that the one benefit he owed to the College was its library,—that at this moment, not only his want of books was imperative, but he wanted a large number of books, and assured him that he Thoreau, and not the Librarian, was the proper custodian of these. In short, the President found the petitioner so formidable and the rules getting to look so ridiculous, that he ended by giving him a privilege which in his hands proved unlimited thereafter.

No truer American existed than Thoreau. His preference of his country and condition was genuine, and his aversation from English and European manners and tastes almost reached contempt. He listened impatiently to news or bon mots gleaned from London circles; and, though he tried to be civil, these anecdotes fatigued him. The men were all imitating each other, and on a small mould. Why can they not live as far apart as possible, and each be a man by himself? What he sought was the most energetic nature, and he wished to go to Oregon, not to London. "In every part of Great Britain," he wrote in his diary, "are discovered traces of the Romans, their funereal urns, their camps, their roads, their dwellings. But New England, at least, is not based on any Roman ruins. We have not to lay the foundations of our houses on the ashes of a former civilization."

But idealist as he was, standing for abolition of slavery, abolition of tariffs, almost for abolition of government, it is needless to say he found himself not only unrepresented in actual politics, but almost equally opposed to every class of reformers. Yet he paid the tribute of his uniform respect to the anti-slavery party. One man, whose personal acquaintance he had formed, he honored with exceptional regard. Before the first friendly word had been spoken for Captain John

Brown, after the arrest, he sent notices to most houses in Concord, that he would speak in a public hall on the condition and character of John Brown, on Sunday Evening, and invited all people to come. The Republican committee, the abolitionist committee, sent him word that it was premature and not advisable. He replied, "I did not send to you for advice but to announce that I am to speak." The hall was filled at an early hour by people of all parties, and his earnest eulogy of the hero was heard by all respectfully, by many with a sympathy that surprised themselves.

It was said of Plotinus, that he was ashamed of his body, and 'tis very likely he had good reason for it; that his body was a bad servant, and he had not skill in dealing with the material world, as happens often to men of abstract intellect. But Mr. Thoreau was equipped with a most adapted and serviceable body. He was of short stature, firmly built, of light complexion, with strong, serious blue eyes, and a grave aspect; his face covered in the late years with a becoming beard. His senses were acute, his frame well-knit and hardy, his hands strong and skilful in the use of tools. And there was a wonderful fitness of body and mind. He could pace sixteen rods more accurately than another man could measure them with rod and chain. He could find his path in the woods at night, he said, better by his feet than his eyes. He could estimate the measure of a tree very well by his eye; he could estimate the weight of a calf or a pig, like a dealer. From a box containing a bushel or more of loose pencils, he could take up with his hands fast enough just a dozen pencils at every grasp. He was a good swimmer, runner, skater, boatman, and would probably out-walk most countrymen in a day's journey. And the relation of body to mind was still finer than we have indicated. He said, he wanted every stride his legs made. The length of his walk uniformly made the length of his writing. If shut up in the house, he did not write at all.

He had a strong common sense, like that which Rose Flammock, the weaver's daughter, in Scott's romance, commends in her father, as resembling a yardstick, which, whilst it measures dowlas and diaper, can equally well measure tapestry and cloth of gold. He had always a new resource. When I was planting forest trees, and had procured half a peck of acorns, he said, that only a small portion of them would be sound, and proceeded to examine them, and select the sound ones. But finding this took time, he said, "I think, if you put them all into water, the good ones will sink," which experiment we tried with success. He could plan a garden, or a house, or a barn; would have been competent to lead a "Pacific Exploring Expedition"; could give judicious counsel in the gravest private or public affairs. He lived for the day, not cumbered and mortified by his memory. If he brought you yesterday a new proposition, he would bring you to-day another not less revolutionary. A very industrious man, and setting, like all highly organized men, a high value on his time, he seemed the only man of leisure in town, always ready for any excursion that promised well, or for conversation prolonged into late hours. His trenchant sense was never stopped by his rules of daily prudence, but was always up to the new occasion. He liked and used the simplest food, yet, when some one urged a vegetable diet, Thoreau thought all diets a very small matter; saying, that "the man who shoots the buffalo lives better than the man who boards at the Graham house." He said, "You can sleep near the railroad, and never be disturbed. Nature knows very well what sounds are worth attending to, and has made up her mind not to hear the railroad-whistle. But things respect the devout mind, and a mental ecstacy was never interrupted."

He noted what repeatedly befel him, that, after receiving from a distance a rare plant, he would presently find the same in his own haunts. And those pieces of luck which happen only to good players happened to him. One day walking with a stranger who inquired, where Indian arrowheads could be found, he replied, "Every where," and stooping forward, picked one on the instant from the ground. At Mount Washington, in Tuckerman's Ravine, Thoreau had a bad fall, and sprained his foot. As he was in the act of getting up from his fall, he saw for the first time, the leaves of the *Arnica mollis*.

His robust common sense, armed with stout hands, keen perceptions, and strong will, cannot yet account for the superiority which shone in his simple and hidden life. I must add the cardinal fact that there was an excellent wisdom in him, proper to a rare class of men, which showed him the material world as a means and symbol. This discovery, which sometimes yields to poets a certain casual and interrupted light serving for the ornament of their writing, was in him an unsleeping insight; and, whatever faults or obstructions of temperament might cloud it, he was not disobedient to the heavenly vision. In his youth, he said, one day, "The other world is all my art: my pencils will draw no other; my jack-knife will cut nothing else; I do not use it as a means." This was the muse and genius that ruled his opinions, conversation, studies, work, and course of life. This made him a searching judge of men. At first glance, he measured his companion, and, though insensible to some fine traits of culture, could very well report his weight and calibre. And this made the impression of genius which his conversation often gave.

He understood the matter in hand at a glance, and saw the limitations and poverty of those he talked with, so that nothing seemed concealed from such terrible eyes. I have repeatedly known young men of sensibility converted in a moment to the belief that this was the man they were in search of, the man of men, who could tell them all they should do. His own dealing with them was never affectionate, but superior, didactic; scorning their petty ways; very slowly conceding or not conceding at all the promise of his society at their houses or even at his own. "Would he not walk with them?"—He did not know. There was nothing so important to him as his walk; he had no walks to throw away on company. Visits were offered him from respectful parties, but he declined them. Admiring friends offered to carry him at their own cost to the Yellow Stone River; to the West Indies; to South America. But though nothing could be more grave or considered than his refusals, they remind one in quite new relations of that fop Brummel's reply to the gentleman who offered him his carriage in a shower, "But where will *you* ride then?" And what accusing silences, and what searching and irresistible speeches battering down all defences, his companions can remember!

Mr. Thoreau dedicated his genius with such entire love to the fields, hills, and waters of his native town, that he made them known and interesting to all reading Americans, and to people over the sea. The river on whose banks he was born and died, he knew from its springs to its confluence with the Merrimack. He had made summer and winter observations on it for many years, and at every hour of the day and the night. The result of the recent survey of the Water Commissioners appointed by the State of Massachusetts, he had reached by his private experiments, several years earlier. Every fact which occurs in the bed, on the banks, or in the air over it; the fishes, and their spawning and nests, their manners, their food; the shad-flies which fill the air on a certain evening once a year, and which are snapped at by the fishes so ravenously, that many of these die of repletion; the conical heaps of small stones on the river shallows, one of which heaps will sometimes overfill a cart,—these heaps the huge nests of small fishes; the birds which frequent the stream, heron, duck, sheldrake, loon, osprey; the snake, muskrat, otter, woodchuck, and fox, on the banks; the turtle, frog, hyla, and cricket, which make the banks vocal,—were all known to him, and, as it were, townsmen and fellow-creatures: so that he felt an absurdity or violence in any narrative of one of these by itself apart, and still more of its dimensions on an inch-rule, or in the exhibition of its skeleton, or the specimen of a squirrel or a bird in brandy. He liked to speak of the manners of the river, as itself a lawful creature, yet with exactness, and always to an observed fact. As he knew the river, so the ponds in this region.

One of the weapons he used, more important than microscope or alcohol receiver, to other investigators, was a whim which grew on him by indulgence, yet appeared in gravest statement, namely, of extolling his own town and neighborhood as the most favored centre for natural observation. He remarked that the Flora of Massachusetts embraced almost all the important plants of America,—most of the oaks, most of the willows, the best pines, the ash, the maple, the beech, the nuts. He returned Kane's "Arctic Voyage" to a friend of whom he had borrowed it with the remark, that "most of the phenomena noted might be observed in Concord." He seemed a little envious of the Pole, for the coincident sunrise and sunset, or five minutes' day after six months. A splendid fact which Annursnuc had never afforded him. He found red snow in one of his walks; and told me that he expected to find yet the *Victoria regia* in Concord. He was the attorney of the indigenous plants, and owned to a preference of the weeds to the imported plants, as of the Indian to the civilized man: and noticed with pleasure that the willow bean-poles of his neighbor had grown more than his beans.

"See these weeds," he said, "which have been hoed at by a million farmers all spring and summer, and yet have prevailed, and just now come out triumphant over all lanes, pastures, fields, and gardens, such is their vigor. We have insulted them with low names too, as pigweed, wormwood, chickweed, shad blossom." He says they have brave names too, ambrosia, stellaria, amelanchier, amaranth, etc.

I think his fancy for referring every thing to the meridian of Concord, did not grow out of any ignorance or depreciation of other longitudes or latitudes, but was rather a playful expression of his conviction of the indifferency of all places, and that the best place for each is where he stands. He expressed it once in this wise: "I think nothing is to be hoped from you, if this bit of mould under your feet is not sweeter to you to eat, than any other in this world, or in any world."

The other weapon with which he conquered all obstacles in science was patience. He knew how to sit immoveable, a part of the rock he rested on, until the bird, the reptile, the fish, which had retired from him, should come back, and resume its habits, nay, moved by curiosity should come to him and watch him.

It was a pleasure and a privilege to walk with him. He knew the country like a fox or a bird, and passed through it as freely by paths of his own. He knew every track in the snow, or on the ground, and what creature had taken this path before him. One must submit abjectly to such a guide, and the reward was great. Under his arm he carried an old music book to press plants; in his pocket, his diary and pencil, a spy-glass for birds, microscope, jack-knife, and twine. He wore straw hat, stout shoes, strong gray trowsers, to brave shrub-oaks and smilax, and to climb a tree for a hawk's or a squirrel's nest. He waded into the pool for the water-plants, and his strong legs were no insignificant part of his armour. On the day I speak of he looked for the menyanthes, detected it across the wide pool, and, on examination of the florets, decided that it had been in flower five days. He drew out of his breast-pocket his diary, and read the names of all the plants that should bloom on this day, whereof he kept account as a banker when his notes fall due. The cypripedium not due till tomorrow. He thought, that, if waked up from a trance, in this swamp, he could tell by the plants what time of the year it was within two days. The redstart was flying about and presently the fine grosbeaks, whose brilliant scarlet makes the rash gazer wipe his eye, and whose fine clear note Thoreau compared to that of a tanager which has got rid of its hoarseness. Presently he heard a note which he called that of the night-warbler, a bird he had never identified, had been in search of twelve years, which always, when he saw it, was in the act of diving down into a tree or bush, and which it was vain to seek; the only bird that sings indifferently by night and by day. I told him he must beware of finding and booking it, lest life should have nothing more to show him. He said, "What you seek in vain for, half your life, one day you come full upon all the family at dinner. You seek it like a dream, and, as soon as you find it, you become its prey."

His interest in the flower or the bird lay very deep in his mind, was connected with Nature,—and the meaning of Nature was never attempted to be defined by him. He would not offer a memoir of his observations to the Natural History Society. "Why should I? To detach the description from its connections in my mind, would make it no longer true or valuable to me: and they do not wish what belongs to it." His power of observation seemed to indicate additional senses. He saw as with microscope, heard as with ear-trumpet, and his memory was a photographic register of all he saw and heard. And yet none knew better than he that it is not the fact that imports, but the impression or effect of the fact on your mind. Every fact lay in glory in his mind, a type of the order and beauty of the whole.

His determination on Natural History was organic. He confessed that he sometimes felt like a hound or a panther, and, if born among Indians, would have been a fell hunter. But, restrained by his Massachusetts culture, he played out the game in this mild form of botany and ichthyology. His intimacy with animals suggested what Thomas Fuller records of Butler the apiologist, that "either he had told the bees things or the bees had told him." Snakes coiled round his leg; the fishes swam into his hand, and he took them out of the water; he pulled the woodchuck out of its hole by the tail, and took the foxes under his protection from the hunters. Our naturalist had perfect magnanimity; he had no secrets: he would carry you to the heron's haunt, or, even to his most prized botanical swamp;—possibly knowing that you could never find it again,—yet willing to take his risks.

No college ever offered him a diploma, or a professor's chair; no academy made him its corresponding secretary, its discoverer, or even its member. Whether these learned bodies feared the satire of his presence. Yet so much knowledge of nature's secret and genius few others possessed, none in a more large and religious synthesis. For not a particle of respect had he to the opinions of any man or body of men, but homage solely to the truth itself. And as he discovered everywhere among doctors some leaning of courtesy, it discredited them. He grew to be revered and admired by his townsmen, who had at first known him only as an oddity. The farmers who employed him as a surveyor soon discovered his rare accuracy and skill, his knowledge of their lands, of trees, of birds, of Indian remains, and the like, which enabled him to tell every farmer more than he knew before of his own farm. So that he began to feel as if Mr. Thoreau had better rights in his land than he. They felt, too, the superiority of character which addressed all men with a native authority.

Indian relics abound in Concord, arrowheads, stone chisels, pestles, and fragments of pottery; and, on the river bank, large heaps of clamshells and ashes mark spots which the savages frequented. These, and every circumstance touching the Indian, were important in his eyes. His visits to Maine were chiefly for love of the Indian. He had the satisfaction of seeing the manufacture of the bark-canoe, as well as of trying his hand in its management on the rapids. He was inquisitive about the making of the stone arrowhead, and, in his last days, charged a youth setting out for the Rocky Mountains, to find an Indian who could tell him that: "It was well worth a visit to California, to learn it." Occasionally, a small party of Penobscot Indians would visit Concord, and pitch their tents for a few weeks in summer on the river bank. He failed not to make acquaintance with the best of them, though he well knew that asking questions of Indians is like catechizing beavers and rabbits. In his last visit to Maine, he had great satisfaction from Joseph Polis, an intelligent Indian of Oldtown, who was his guide for some weeks.

He was equally interested in every natural fact. The depth of his perception found likeness of law throughout nature, and, I know not any genius who so swiftly inferred universal law from the single fact. He was no pedant of a department. His eye was open to beauty, and his ear to music. He found these, not in rare conditions, but wheresoever he went. He thought the best of music was in single strains; and he found poetic suggestion in the humming of the telegraph wire.

His poetry might be bad or good; he no doubt wanted a lyric facility, and technical skill; but he had the source of poetry in his spiritual perception. He was a good reader and critic, and his judgment on poetry was to the ground of it. He could not be deceived as to the presence or absence of the poetic element in any composition, and his thirst for this made him negligent and perhaps scornful of superficial graces. He would pass by many delicate rhythms, but he would have detected every live stanza or line in a volume, and knew very well where to find an equal poetic charm in prose. He was so enamoured of the spiritual beauty, that he held all actual written poems in very light esteem in the comparison. He admired Æschylus and Pindar, but when some one was commending them, he said, that, "Æschylus and the Greeks, in describing Apollo and Orpheus, had given no song, or no good one. They ought not to have moved trees, but to have chaunted to the gods such a hymn as would have sung all their old ideas out of their heads, and new ones in." His own verses are often rude and defective. The gold does not yet run pure, is drossy and crude. The thyme and marjoram are not yet honey. But if he want lyric fineness, and technical merits, if he have not the poetic temperament, he never lacks the causal thought, showing that his genius was better than his talent. He knew the worth of the Imagination for the uplifting and consolation of human life, and liked to throw every thought into a symbol. The fact you tell is of no value, but only the impression. For this reason his presence was poetic, always piqued the curiosity to know more deeply the secrets of his mind. He had many reserves,—an unwillingness to exhibit to profane eyes what was still sacred in his own, and knew well how to throw a poetic veil over his experience. All readers of "Walden" will remember his mythical record of his disappointments:—

"I long ago lost a hound, a bay horse, and a turtle-dove, and am still
on their trail. Many are the travellers I have spoken concerning them,
describing their tracks, and what calls they answered to. I have met one
or two who had heard the hound, and the tramp of the horse, and even
seen the dove disappear behind a cloud, and they seemed as anxious to
recover them as if they had lost them themselves."

His riddles were worth the reading, and I confide that, if at any time I
do not understand the expression, it is yet just. Such was the wealth of
his truth, that it was not worth his while to use words in vain.

His poem entitled "Sympathy" reveals the tenderness under that
triple steel of stoicism, and the intellectual subtlety it could animate.
His classic poem on "Smoke" suggests Simonides, but is better than
any poem of Simonides. His biography is in his verses. His habitual
thought makes all his poetry a hymn to the Cause of causes, the spirit
which vivifies and controls his own.

"I hearing get, who had but ears,
And sight, who had but eyes before;
I moments live, who lived but years,
And truth discern, who knew but learning's lore."

And still more in these religious lines:—

"Now chiefly is my natal hour,
And only now my prime of life;
I will not doubt the love untold,
Which not my worth or want hath bought,
Which wooed me young, and wooes me old,
And to this evening hath me brought."

Whilst he used in his writings a certain petulance of remark in reference to churches or churchmen, he was a person of a rare, tender, and
absolute religion, a person incapable of any profanation, by act or by
thought. Of course, the same isolation which belonged to his original
thinking and living detached him from the social religious forms. This
is neither to be censured nor regretted. Aristotle long ago explained
it, when he said, "One who surpasses his fellow citizens in virtue, is no

longer a part of the city. Their law is not for him, since he is a law to himself."

Thoreau was sincerity itself, and might fortify the convictions of prophets in the ethical laws, by his holy living. It was an affirmative experience which refused to be set aside. A truth-speaker he, capable of the most deep and strict conversation; a physician to the wounds of any soul; a friend knowing not only the secret of friendship, but almost worshipped by those few persons who resorted to him as their confessor and prophet, and knew the deep value of his mind and great heart. He thought that without religion or devotion of some kind, nothing great was ever accomplished: and he thought that the bigoted sectarian had better bear this in mind.

His virtues of course sometimes ran into extremes. It was easy to trace to the inexorable demand on all for exact truth that austerity which made this willing hermit more solitary even than he wished. Himself of a perfect probity, he required not less of others. He had a disgust at crime, and no worldly success could cover it. He detected paltering as readily in dignified and prosperous persons as in beggars, and with equal scorn. Such dangerous frankness was in his dealing, that his admirers called him "that terrible Thoreau," as if he spoke, when silent, and was still present when he had departed. I think the severity of his ideal interfered to deprive him of a healthy sufficiency of human society.

The habit of a realist to find things the reverse of their appearance inclined him to put every statement in a paradox. A certain habit of antagonism defaced his earlier writings, a trick of rhetoric not quite outgrown in his later, of substituting for the obvious word and thought its diametrical opposite. He praised wild mountains and winter forests for their domestic air; in snow and ice, he would find sultriness; and commended the wilderness for resembling Rome and Paris. "It was so dry, that you might call it wet."

The tendency to magnify the moment, to read all the laws of nature in the one object or one combination under your eye, is of course comic to those who do not share the philosopher's perception of identity. To him there was no such thing as size. The pond was a small ocean; the Atlantic, a large Walden Pond. He referred every minute fact to cosmical laws. Though he meant to be just, he seemed haunted by a certain chronic assumption that the science of the day pretended completeness and he had just found out that the savans had neglected to discriminate a particular botanical variety, had failed to describe the seeds, or count the sepals. "That is to say," we replied, "the block-heads were not born in Concord, but who said they were? It was their unspeakable misfortune to be born in London, or Paris, or Rome; but, poor fellows, they did what they could, considering that they never saw Bateman Pond, or Nine-Acre-Corner, or Becky Stow's Swamp. Besides, what were you sent into the world for, but to add this obser-vation?"

Had his genius been only contemplative, he had been fitted to his life, but with his energy and practical ability he seemed born for great enterprise and for command: and I so much regret the loss of his rare powers of action, that I cannot help counting it a fault in him that he had no ambition. Wanting this, instead of engineering for all America, he was the captain of a huckleberry party. Pounding beans is good to the end of pounding empires one of these days, but if, at the end of years, it is still only beans!—

But these foibles, real or apparent, were fast vanishing in the inces-sant growth of a spirit so robust and wise, and which effaced its defects with new triumphs. His study of nature was a perpetual ornament to him, and inspired his friends with curiosity to see the world through his eyes, and to hear his adventures. They possessed every kind of interest. He had many elegances of his own, whilst he scoffed at conventional elegance. Thus he could not bear to hear the sound of his own steps, the grit of gravel; and therefore never willingly walked in the road, but in the grass, on mountains, and in woods. His senses were acute, and he remarked that by night every dwelling-house gives out bad air, like a slaughter-house. He liked the pure fragrance of melilot. He honored certain plants with special regard, and over all the pond-lily,—then the gentian, and the *Mikania scandens,* and "Life Everlasting," and a bass tree which he visited every year when it bloomed in the middle of July. He thought the scent a more oracular inquisition than the sight,—more oracular and trustworthy. The scent, of course, reveals what is concealed from the other senses. By it he detected earthiness.

He delighted in echoes, and said, they were almost the only kind of kindred voices that he heard. He loved nature so well, was so happy in her solitude, that he became very jealous of cities, and the sad work which their refinements and artifices made with man and his dwelling. The axe was always destroying his forest—"Thank God," he said, "they cannot cut down the clouds. All kinds of figures are drawn on the blue ground, with this fibrous white paint."

I subjoin a few sentences taken from his unpublished manuscripts not only as records of his thought and feeling, but for their power of description and literary excellence.

"Some circumstantial evidence is very strong, as when you find a trout in the milk."

"The chub is a soft fish, and tastes like boiled brown paper salted."

"The youth gets together his materials to build a bridge to the moon, or, perchance, a palace or temple on the earth, and, at length, the middle-aged man concludes to build a woodshed with them."

"The locust z-ing."

"Devil's-needles zig-zagging along the Nut-Meadow brook."

"Sugar is not so sweet to the palate, as sound to the healthy ear."

"I put on some hemlock boughs, and the rich salt crackling of their leaves was like mustard to the ear, the crackling of uncountable regiments. Dead trees love the fire."

"The blue-bird carries the sky on his back."

"The tanager flies through the green foliage, as if it would ignite the leaves."

"If I wish for a horse-hair for my compass-sight, I must go to the stable; but the hair-bird with her sharp eyes goes to the road."

"Immortal water, alive even to the superficies."

"Fire is the most tolerable third party."

"Nature made ferns for pure leaves, to show what she could do in that line."

"No tree has so fair a bole, and so handsome an instep as the beech."

"How did these beautiful rainbow tints get into the shell of the fresh-water clam, buried in the mud at the bottom of our dark river?"

"Hard are the times when the infant's shoes are second-foot."

"We are strictly confined to our men to whom we give liberty."

"Nothing is so much to be feared as fear. Atheism may comparatively be popular with God himself."

"Of what significance the things you can forget? A little thought is sexton to all the world."

"How can we expect a harvest of thought, who have not had a seed-time of character?"

"Only he can be trusted with gifts, who can present a face of bronze to expectations."

"I ask to be melted. You can only ask of the metals that they be tender to the fire that melts them. To nought else can they be tender."

There is a flower known to botanists, one of the same genus with our summer plant called "Life Everlasting," a *Gnaphalium* like that, which grows on the most inaccessible cliffs of the Tyrolese mountains, where the chamois dare hardly venture, and which the hunter, tempted by its beauty, and by his love, (for it is immensely valued by the Swiss maidens,) climbs the cliffs to gather, and is sometimes found dead at the foot, with the flower in his hand. It is called by botanists the *Gnaphalium leontopodium,* but by the Swiss, *Edelweisse,* which signifies, *Noble Purity.* Thoreau seemed to me living in the hope to gather this plant, which belonged to him of right. The scale on which his studies proceeded was so large as to require longevity, and we were the less prepared for his sudden disappearance. The country knows not yet, or in the least part, how great a son it has lost. It seems an injury that he should leave in the midst his broken task, which none else can finish,—a kind of indignity to so noble a soul, that it should depart out of nature before yet he has been really shown to his peers for what he is. But he, at least, is content. His soul was made for the noblest society; he had in a short life exhausted the capabilities of this world; wherever there is knowledge, wherever there is virtue, wherever there is beauty, he will find a home.

Suggestions for Further Reading

This highly selective bibliography includes scholarship that is directly engaged in analysis of the importance of natural science in Emerson's work.

Allen, Gay Wilson. "A New Look at Emerson and Science." *Literature and Ideas in America: Essays in Memory of Harry Hayden Clark.* Ed. Robert Falk. Athens: Ohio UP, 1975. 58–78.

Bosco, Ronald A. "'The Tendencies and Duties of Men of Thought' and 'The Transcendency of Physics': Ethics and Science in the Later Emerson." *Emerson at 200: Proceedings of the International Bicentennial Conference.* Rome: Aracne, 2004. 325–35.

Branch, Michael P. "Paths to *Nature*: Emerson's Early Natural History Lectures." *Emerson for the Twenty-First Century: Global Perspectives on an American Icon.* Ed. Barry Tharaud. Newark: U of Delaware P, 2010. 219–42.

———. "Ralph Waldo Emerson." *American Nature Writers.* Ed. John Elder. Vol. 1. New York: Scribner's, 1996. 287–307.

Brown, Lee Rust. *The Emerson Museum: Practical Romanticism and the Pursuit of the Whole.* Cambridge: Harvard UP, 1997.

Clark, Harry Hayden. "Emerson and Science." *Philological Quarterly* 10.3 (1931): 225–60.

Dant, Elizabeth A. "Composing the World: Emerson and the Cabinet of Natural History." *Nineteenth-Century Literature* 44.1 (1989): 18–44.

LaRosa, Ralph C. "Invention and Imitation in Emerson's Early Lectures." *American Literature* 44.1 (1972): 13–30.

Lopez, Michael. *Emerson and Power: Creative Antagonism in the Nineteenth Century.* De Kalb: Northern Illinois UP, 1996.

Neufeldt, Leonard N. "The Science of Power: Emerson's Views on Science and Technology in America." *Journal of the History of Ideas* 38.2 (1977): 329–44.

Noble, Mark. "Emerson's Atom and the Matter of Suffering." *Nineteenth-Century Literature* 64.1 (2009): 16–47.

Obuchowski, Peter A. "Emerson's Science: An Analysis." *Philological Quarterly* 54.3 (1975): 624–32.

Paul, Sherman. *Emerson's Angle of Vision: Man and Nature in American Experience*. Cambridge: Harvard UP, 1952.

Pelikan, Jaroslav. "Natural History Married to Human History: Ralph Waldo Emerson and the 'Two Cultures.'" *The Rights of Memory: Essays on History, Science, and American Culture*. Ed. Taylor Littleton. Tuscaloosa: U of Alabama P, 1986. 35–75.

Robinson, David M. *Apostle of Culture: Emerson as Preacher and Lecturer*. Philadelphia: U of Pennsylvania P, 1982.

———. "British Science, the London Lectures, and Emerson's Philosophical Reorientation." *Emerson for the Twenty-First Century: Global Perspectives on an American Icon*. Ed. Barry Tharaud. Newark: U of Delaware P, 2010. 285–300.

———. "Emerson's Natural Theology and the Paris Naturalists: Toward a Theory of Animated Nature." *Journal of the History of Ideas* 41.1 (1980): 69–88.

———. "Fields of Investigation: Emerson and Natural History." *American Literature and Science*. Ed. Robert J. Scholnick. Lexington: U of Kentucky P, 1992. 94–109.

Rossi, William. "Emerson, Nature, and Natural Science." *A Historical Guide to Ralph Waldo Emerson*. Ed. Joel Myerson. Oxford: Oxford UP, 2000. 101–50.

Strauch, Carl F. "Emerson's Sacred Science." *PMLA* 73.3 (1958): 237–50.

Von Frank, Albert. "The Composition of *Nature:* Writing and the Self in the Launching of a Career." *Biographies of Books: The Compositional History of Notable American Writings*. Ed. James Barbour and Tom Quirk. Columbia: U of Missouri P, 1996. 11–40.

Walls, Laura Dassow. *Emerson's Life in Science: The Culture of Truth*. Ithaca: Cornell UP, 2003.

———. "'Every Truth Tends to Become a Power': Emerson, Faraday, and the Minding of Matter." *Emerson for the Twenty-First Century: Global Perspectives on an American Icon*. Ed. Barry Tharaud. Newark: U of Delaware P, 2010. 301–17.

———. "'If Body Can Sing': Emerson and Victorian Science." *Emerson Bicentennial Essays*. Ed. Ronald A. Bosco and Joel Myerson. Boston: Massachusetts Historical Society, 2006. 334–66.

Wilson, Eric. "Emerson's *Nature,* Paralogy, and the Physics of the Sublime." *Mosaic: A Journal for the Interdisciplinary Study of Literature* 33.1 (2000): 39–58.

———. *Emerson's Sublime Science*. New York: St. Martin's, 1999.

Index

lect to Natural Science," xi, xvii, xx,
xxv, 208–9; *Representative Men,* xxii,
225; "Right Hand of Fellowship,"
xxixn2; "The Uses of Natural History," xi, xvi–xix, xxvii, 37, 58, 129,
185, 225–26
Euler, Leonhard, 100
evolution. *See* "Theory of Animated
Nature"

Faraday, Michael, xx, 127, 171, 176
farmers, 18, 65, 175, 186, 204–5, 217;
as connected to nature, 60, 86,
192–93. *See also* agriculture
fishermen, 92, 172, 222
Fontenelle, Bernard le Bovier de,
36, 63
Fourier, François Marie Charles, 61,
176, 211
Fresnel, Augustin Jean, 220
Fulton, Robert, 25

Galileo, 12–13, 29, 126
gardens, xiii, 4, 116, 168–70, 192, 196–
97. *See also* agriculture; Cabinet of
Natural History
genius, 13–14, 32–34, 88–89, 124–28,
136–41, 144, 172–73, 225–26; as
distinguished from talent, 129–30,
140–41, 144–45, 238; and language,
172–73, 177–79, 210–11, 217; Thoreau as, 233, 237–41
geology, xxvi, 91, 154, 176, 181, 201–2,
206, 211; as evidence of evolution,
27–28, 38–43, 121–22, 184
God: as creator, xiii, 4–5, 36, 84–85,
88–89, 104, 190; as supreme being,
100, 104; as universal mind, 127,
212; as universal power, 141, 147.
See also spirit
Goethe, Johann Wolfgang von, 58,

67–68, 93, 168, 178, 200, 218, 225;
quotations of, 29, 61, 120, 203; and
urpflanz concept, xxii, 114, 118

Haller, Albrecht von, 33
Harvard University, ix, xvi, 208,
225–26
Hatchett, Charles, 70
Herschel, William, 12, 141
hieroglyphics, 6, 67, 74, 205–6. *See
also* book of nature
history, 23–24, 68, 85, 107, 144, 173–
76, 183, 197; of science, 114–19,
125–28. *See also* geology
Homer, 80, 82, 140, 204, 209, 224
Hooke, Robert, 119
Huber, François, 31
humanity: as distanced from nature,
65, 154, 204–5; as having dominion
over nature, 50, 56–57, 110–11, 125,
206–7, 312
Humboldt, Alexander von, 29, 48, 54,
67, 126, 175–76
Hunter, John, 33, 69, 218

idealism, 95–103, 148, 164, 208–9
imagination, 58–59, 238; act of, 67,
173–74, 220–22; and analogy, 199,
205–6, 208–9, 211; defined as,
96–97
Indians, 11, 48, 53–54, 84–85, 153,
167, 186, 193–95, 203–4, 214; and
Thoreau, 228, 234–37. *See also*
Penobscot; Pequots
individualism, xiii, xvi, 90, 226–27. *See
also* self-reliance
infinite mind. *See* spirit
intellect, 10, 30–31, 110, 115, 145–46,
178–80, 209, 220; as corresponding to nature, 38–39, 82–86, 129,
132–33, 165–66, 170–74, 189–90,

intellect (*continued*)
211–12; cultural understanding of,
129–31; as dynamic, 223. *See also*
genius

Jardin des Plantes, xvii, xix, xxviii, 17,
19, 172. *See also* Cabinet of Natural
History
Johnson, Samuel, 198, 201
Jussieu, Antoine Laurent de, xviii–xix,
20, 211

Kalm, Peter, 188
Kepler, Johannes, 33, 126, 168, 173, 211

Lagrange, Joseph-Louis, 60–61
Lamarck, Jean-Baptiste, 115
landscape, xxv, 6, 80, 185, 205–6; and
delight, 53, 83, 97, 152–53, 199–
201; unity of, 75–77, 104–5, 135
language, xvii–xxv, 17, 210; as limited,
xxv, 62–63, 86–87, 94, 103, 132–35,
148–49, 159–64, 175–76, 199, 220;
nature as source of, 35–36, 83–89,
138–40, 165, 222, 232–33; as universal cipher, 66–67, 87, 133, 147,
155, 210–11. *See also* analogy
Laplace, Pierre-Simon de, 24, 36, 41,
60–61, 125–28, 141, 173
laws: of moral nature, 16, 41, 108, 165,
174, 240; of nature, 33–34, 56, 96,
155–56, 182, 240–41; —, correspondence between, xvi–xvii, 8, 34–36,
61, 68–69, 87–88, 91–93, 105,
112–13, 115–19, 122–26, 169–70,
184, 208–9, 211–16, 221–24
Leibnitz, Gottfried Wilhelm von, 88
Liber naturae. See book of nature
Liebig, Justus von, 220
Linnæus, Carolus, xviii–xix, 29, 68, 85,
126, 187–88, 198–200

literature, 63–64, 98, 112, 140, 153,
183, 220; as negative influence,
144–47. *See also* art; language;
poetry
lyceum, xi, xxvii, 17–18, 37, 58–59, 229
Lyell, Sir Charles, 176

magnetism, 56, 91, 116, 118–19, 127,
181; animal, 22, 109; electro-, 162,
176
mechanics, 89, 116, 134, 165; arts, 24,
78, 130–31, 219; laws of, 35–36, 170
men of thought. *See* genius; intellect
mesmerism, 154, 176, 181–82
metamorphosis. *See* "Theory of Animated Nature"
metaphor, 35, 87. *See also* analogy;
language; proverbs
Michelangelo. *See* Angelo, Michael
microscopes, 4, 66, 116–17, 120, 202,
213, 217, 234–36
Mitscherlich, Eilhardt, 41
moral laws. *See* laws, of moral nature

Napoleon Bonaparte, 68, 78, 125–26,
138, 173, 212, 218, 220
Native Americans. *See* Indians
naturalist: "best read," xiii, xxiv–xxix,
105; poetic, xxi–xxvi, 113, 164–65,
225–26. *See also* genius
natural laws. *See* laws, of nature
Natura naturans. See "Theory of Animated Nature"
Newton, Isaac, 68, 119, 126–28, 141,
167, 173, 224; and discovery of gravity, 12–14, 32, 114

order: of the mind, xii; of nature, xii,
xiv–xv, xviii, 2–3, 112–13, 124, 128,
134; of things, xxii, 41, 52, 74, 82,
99, 168; of the universe, 63, 128; of

the world, 7, 104, 120–21, 134. *See also* "Correspondence, Doctrine of"; design

ornithology, xxvi, 20, 23, 201–2

Ørsted, Hans Christian, 127

Owen, Richard, xx, 176

Penobscot, 237

Penrose, Francis, 200

Pequots, 193

perception, xxi–xxviii, 72, 153, 177–79; and delight, 18, 52–53, 69, 78–79, 201, 205, 218–19; improvement of, 58–59, 65, 69, 138–39, 185, 197; limited, 109, 126; Thoreau's acute, 225, 232–34, 236, 238. *See also* vision

Perkins, Jacob, 25

phrenology, 115, 154, 184, 224

physics, 100, 127; laws of, 87, 91

physiology, 32–33, 56, 68–70, 91, 105, 117–18, 125, 134, 143, 154

Pindar, 82, 140, 206, 238

Plato, 88, 99, 107, 155, 174, 190, 209, 220, 225; and analogy, 205–6, 210–14; and reminiscence, 169–71

Plotinus, 101, 214, 231

poet, the, xii, xxi–xxviii, 75, 131, 140–42, 158, 178–80, 202, 215; and language, 58–59, 67–69, 87, 97–100, 160–61, 164–65, 199, 210–11; the Orphic, xxiv–xxv, xxix, 107–8, 110; and perception of nature, 135, 146, 173–74, 196, 204–6, 232–33; and science, 125–28, 141, 153. *See also* Chaucer; Homer; naturalist, poetic; Pindar

poetry. *See* art; literature; poet

polarity, 56, 63, 66, 119, 208, 211–16

porosity, 66, 220

professor, qualifications of a, xxv–xxvi

proverbs, 11, 35–36, 87–88. *See also* "Correspondence, Doctrine of"; language

Pythagoras, 67, 88, 172, 197

reason, 48–50, 68–69, 76, 84–85, 89–91, 96–102, 108–9, 116, 123–25, 210. *See also* analogy; "Correspondence, Doctrine of"; relation

Réaumur, René A. F. de, 31

reformer. *See* social reform

relation, xxii–xxiii, 14, 42, 65, 73, 82–89, 105–17, 165, 206; between senses, 49; ray of, xvii–xxi, xxvii, 19–22, 60, 66–69, 76, 85, 210; as sympathy, 35, 171–73, 219; universal, 141, 184. *See also* analogy; "Correspondence, Doctrine of"; reason

religion, 174, 179; critique of, xiii–xvi, 37, 72–73, 101–2, 149–51, 162–63; and science, 8, 10–15, 92, 126, 210

Rousseau, Jean-Jacques, 185, 190

"savages." *See* Indians

Schelling, Friedrich Wilhelm Joseph von, 172–73

science: critique of, xxiii–xxiv, xxvii, 19, 58, 64, 105–9, 120, 125–26, 206, 241; heroes of, 24, 33–34, 68, 126; homology of, 117, 184, 210–12, 220–22; and language, 36, 68, 125–28; men of, 37, 123–24, 128; purpose of, 117

scientist. *See* naturalist

scripture, ix–x, xv, 6, 8, 10, 16, 89, 140

self-reliance, xxviii, 215. *See also* individualism

Shakespeare, William, 45, 80, 97, 224

social reform, 132–33, 142, 166, 217, 230

society, 18, 89, 216, 240; critique of, xx–xxiii, 23–24, 74–75, 144–46, 154, 160, 164, 175. *See also* city
Socrates, 82
Sophocles, 99
spirit, xxviii–xxix, 7, 75–77, 83–85, 88–89, 93–96, 102–5, 107–10, 119–22, 129, 139–40, 145–46, 174, 222–24, 239; as divine effort, 2, 167, 216; as infinite mind, xv, 15, 94; as supreme being, 100, 104; as universal mind, 127, 212; as universal power, 141, 147; as universal, 93, 103
spiritual laws. *See* laws, of moral nature
Steffens, Henrik, 210
sublime, the, 22, 47–50, 75, 97, 140; describing, 75–76, 132; and science, 33–34, 39, 224
supreme being. *See* spirit
Swedenborg, Emanuel, xvii, 67, 88, 109, 112, 115, 146, 171–73, 176, 205–6, 218
sympathy. *See* relation
system of nature. *See* design

talent. *See* genius
taxonomy. *See* classification
telescope, 13, 28–29, 55–56, 127, 201, 206
theology. *See* religion
"Theory of Animated Nature," 4, 69–71, 110, 114, 120–21, 129–30, 134–37, 154–55, 185, 216–20
Thoreau, Henry David, xxvi–xxvii, 185–86, 225–26

Transcendentalism, xvi, 72–73, 129, 225–26

understanding, 60–61, 89–90, 108–9, 181–82, 214–16. *See also* classification
Unitarianism, 1, 14; Emerson's resignation from ministry of, ix–xvi, 17. *See also* religion
unity of nature. *See* design
universal mind. *See* spirit
universal power. *See* spirit
universal spirit. *See* spirit
urpflanz. See under Goethe
useful arts. *See* mechanics

virtue, 81–82, 89, 94, 102–4, 137, 141–44, 160, 175, 243
vision, 66, 96–103, 109. *See also* perception

walking, xxv–xxvii, 65, 150, 185–204, 222; Thoreau and, 226–28, 231–35, 241
Watt, James, 25
Winckelmann, Johann Joachim, 200
wisdom, 75, 90, 94–95, 144–45, 175, 221, 232–33; as omnipresent, 109–10, 123, 163; as spirit, xv, 10, 14–16, 57
Wordsworth, William, 37, 190–91

zoology, 54, 90–91, 212, 218, 226; cabinets of, xviii, 116, 172